BRAZIL

HOW TO USE THIS GUIDE

The first section consists of useful general information—Facts at Your Fingertips—designed to help you plan your trip, as well as local facts, business hours, local holidays, time zones, and customs that will be of use while you are traveling.

Next are essays to help you with the background of the area that this Guide covers—the cultural scene, some historical insights, and so on.

Following these essays comes the detailed breakdown of the area, geographically. Each chapter begins with a description of the place or region, broadly describing its attraction for the visitor; this is followed by Practical Information to help you explore the area—detailed descriptions, addresses, directions, phone numbers, and so forth for hotels, restaurants, tours, museums, historical sites, and more.

Two vital ways into this book are the Table of Contents at the beginning and the Index at the end.

FODOR'S TRAVEL GUIDES

are compiled, researched, and edited by an international team of travel writers, field correspondents, and editors. The series, which now almost covers the globe, was founded by Eugene Fodor in 1936.

OFFICES
New York & London

FODOR'S BRAZIL:

Area Editor: EDWIN TAYLOR
Drawings: LASZLO ROTH and MICHAEL KAPLAN
Maps and City Plans: C.W. BACON, M.S.I.A., JOHN HUTCHINSON, DYNO
  LOWENSTEIN, LESLIE S. HAYWOOD

FODOR'S®
BRAZIL

All the following Guides are current (most of them also in
the Hodder and Stoughton British edition).

FODOR'S COUNTRY AND AREA TITLES:

AUSTRALIA. NEW ZEALAND AND SOUTH PACIFIC
AUSTRIA
BELGIUM AND LUXEMBOURG
BERMUDA
BRAZIL
CANADA
CANADA'S MARITIME PROVINCES
CARIBBEAN AND BAHAMAS
CENTRAL AMERICA
EASTERN EUROPE
EGYPT
EUROPE
FRANCE
GERMANY
GREAT BRITAIN
GREECE
HOLLAND
INDIA. NEPAL. AND SRI LANKA
IRELAND
ISRAEL
ITALY
JAPAN
JORDAN AND HOLY LAND
KOREA
MEXICO
NORTH AFRICA
PEOPLE'S REPUBLIC OF CHINA
PORTUGAL
SCANDINAVIA
SCOTLAND
SOUTH AMERICA
SOUTHEAST ASIA
SOVIET UNION
SPAIN
SWITZERLAND
TURKEY
YUGOSLAVIA

CITY GUIDES:

AMSTERDAM
BEIJING. GUANGZHOU. SHANGHAI
BOSTON
CHICAGO
DALLAS AND FORT WORTH
GREATER MIAMI
HONG KONG
HOUSTON
LISBON
LONDON
LOS ANGELES
MADRID
MEXICO CITY AND ACAPULCO
MUNICH
NEW ORLEANS
NEW YORK CITY
PARIS
ROME
SAN DIEGO
SAN FRANCISCO
STOCKHOLM. COPENHAGEN. OSLO. HELSINKI. AND REYKJAVIK
TOKYO
TORONTO
VIENNA
WASHINGTON. D.C.

FODOR'S BUDGET SERIES:

BUDGET BRITAIN
BUDGET CANADA
BUDGET CARIBBEAN
BUDGET EUROPE
BUDGET FRANCE
BUDGET GERMANY
BUDGET HAWAII
BUDGET ITALY
BUDGET JAPAN
BUDGET LONDON
BUDGET MEXICO
BUDGET SCANDINAVIA
BUDGET SPAIN
BUDGET TRAVEL IN AMERICA

USA GUIDES:

ALASKA
CALIFORNIA
CAPE COD
COLORADO
FAR WEST
FLORIDA
HAWAII
NEW ENGLAND
PACIFIC NORTH COAST
PENNSYLVANIA
SOUTH
TEXAS
USA (in one volume)

GOOD TIME TRAVEL GUIDES:

ACAPULCO
MONTREAL
OAHU
SAN FRANCISCO

CONTENTS

CONTENTS

SUPPLEMENTS

FACTS AT YOUR FINGERTIPS

FACTS AT YOUR FINGERTIPS

DEVALUATION, REVALUATION, INFLATION. With contin
in rates for currency, not to mention the value of the dollar and s
prices and ratios throughout this book are bound to change. So kee
mind, please. . . .

WHEN TO GO. Tropical rains are always intermittent
and allow time for outdoor activities. In most towns the
rain comes at a certain time during the day and thus
seldom interrupts activities because they are planned
around it.

There are festivals, special events, and sporting attractions year round.
Seasons below the Equator are the reverse of the north—summer, December
21 to March 20; winter from June 21 to September 20. Temperatures vary with
altitudes—warm along the coast, colder in the highlands.

AVERAGE TEMPERATURE CHART IN ° FAHRENHEIT

Rio de Janeiro

	Jan.	Feb.	Mar.	Apr.	May	Jun.	Jul.	Aug.	Sept.	Oct.	Nov.	Dec.
Max.	84	85	83	80	77	76	75	76	75	77	79	82
Min.	73	73	72	69	66	64	63	64	65	66	68	71

HOLIDAYS. The following legal holidays are observed in Brazil: January 1,
New Year's Day; January 20, founding of Rio; Carnival, always four days before
Ash Wednesday; Good Friday; April 21, Tiradentes; May 1, Labor Day; June
21, Corpus Christi; September 7, Independence Day; November 2, All Souls;
November 15, Proclamation of the Republic; December 25, Christmas Day.

CARNIVAL WEEK. Brazil starts Carnival on the weekend preceding Ash
Wednesday. A word of caution about "carnival-time" visits. Many returning
tourists have complained about minimal hotel services resulting in their rooms
being left uncleaned, the beds unmade for days, and late or no breakfasts. Gas
pumps and garage services often closed down. Be prepared for the otherwise
orderly system to break down during such holiday time.

WHAT WILL IT COST. A day and night in Rio is not
typical, of course, for all Brazil, but the prices there are
close to standard for large cities.

A breakdown of the average tourist's expenses in Rio
for a day and night (exchange rates *approx.*):

1st Class Hotel		
(one person sharing Double)	US$50.00	£29.41
Three Meals (including service)	40.00	23.52
Four Taxi Rides	10.00	3.39
Two Drinks (Pisco Sours)	4.00	2.35
City Sightseeing Tour	20.00	11.76

3

of American Cigarettes	1.60	.94
Total Cost	$125.60	£71.37

Credit Travel and Credit Cards. A number of organizations in the United States, Canada, and Britain make credit cards available that will enable you to sign for hotel and restaurant bills, car rentals, purchases, and so forth and pay the total at one time on a monthly bill, either pay as you go or in installments after you return home. This is particularly advantageous for business people traveling on an expense account or on business trips, where the cost is deductible for income tax since the bill provides a voucher for expenditures. In these days of currency exchange rate fluctuations, cards save you the trouble of converting, as you'll be billed in dollars back home at the current exchange rate on the date of billing. Such organizations are the *Diners Club, American Express Card, Carte Blanche, Eurocard, Access,* and *Barclaycard.*

Traveler's checks are the best way to safeguard travel funds. They are sold by various banks and companies in terms of American and Canadian dollars and pounds sterling. Almost universally accepted are those of *American Express,* whereas those issued by *Bank of America* and *Citibank* are also widely used.

Best known and easily exchanged British traveler's checks are those issued by *Thos. Cook & Son* and the "Big Four" banks: *Barclays, Lloyds, Midland,* and *National Westminster.*

Changing traveler's checks or cash is easiest at your hotel but will cost you more (and it will be even higher in shops and restaurants!), so change at banks if you can afford the extra time. Also try to have on hand enough local currency for arrival at the next port of call to get you through the unnerving procedures with porters, taxi drivers, bellhops, and others. You can buy small packets for this purpose at *Deak-Perera,* and similar agencies. At time of writing the exchange rate was 2,000 cruzeiros to the U.S. dollar.

 INDEPENDENT VERSUS PACKAGE TOURS. When it comes to choosing among an all-inclusive, fully escorted tour, a loose, plan-your-own-itinerary package tour, or totally independent travel, the factors to be considered are time, convenience, and cost.

Package tours are the easiest to arrange and are probably the most economical and efficient way to get an overview of the most famous sights. If you have only a limited amount of time, a well-constructed package tour will focus your travel time and minimize costs by arranging for all transportation, transfers wherever needed, well-versed tour guides, and generally commodious accommodations.

Package tour operators have the advantage of booking great numbers of people at what might be considered wholesale prices. In addition, as a client of a tour operator you can pretty well rest assured that all your reservations will be honored: Airline and hotel managers are reluctant to "bump" tour members for fear of alienating the operator, who virtually guarantees full flights and fully booked rooms for extended periods, as one tour group moves out and another moves in. (And if by chance your room isn't what you'd anticipated, voice your displeasure in a friendly manner at the tour operator's desk and/or to the concierge; even if a change isn't possible that day, the hotel will usually make every effort to improve your situation as soon as another room becomes available.)

A good travel agent can make all reservations in advance for "GIT" (Group Inclusive Travel plans, which are built around transportation and lodging only) and "FIT" (Foreign Independent Travel, as it is known in the U.K.) travelers. In Europe a fee is sometimes charged for these services; in the U.S. the fees—except the cost of any necessary long-distance telephone calls or other out-of-the-ordinary expenses—are almost always paid by the airlines, the hotels, and other businesses.

SOME TOUR OPERATORS SPECIALIZING IN BRAZIL
In the U.S.:

AAA EAST FLORIDA
4300 Biscayne Boulevard
Miami, Florida 33137

ABREU TOURS
60 East 42nd Street
New York, New York 10165

AMERICAN EXPRESS
Travel Division
American Express Plaza
New York, New York 10004

BRAZILIAN VACATION CENTER
55 West 46th Street
New York, New York 10036

HOTUR
20 East 53rd Street
New York, New York 10022

IPANEMA TOURS
9911 West Pico Boulevard
Los Angeles, California 90035

LADATCO TOURS
2220 Coral Way
Miami, Florida 33145

MARNELLA TOURS
574 Walt Whitman Road
Melville, New York 11747

PORTUGUESE TOURS
321 Rahway Avenue
Elizabeth, New Jersey 07202

R.N. TOURS INC.
666 Old Country Road
Garden City, New York 11530

UNIQUE ADVENTURES
703 Market Street
San Francisco, California 94103

**WRIGHTWAY TOURS
INTERNATIONAL**
16030 Ventura Boulevard, Suite 201
Encino, California 91436

Special-Interest Tours. In the past few years several special-interest tours have been organized to visit Brazil. Your travel agent will have information on camera tours, horticultural tours, agricultural tours, and many others. Amazon River cruises and hunting tours and special package tours to Carnival in Rio are all available.

Amazon Explorers, Professional Bldg., Rte. 9, Parlin, N.J. 08859, specializes in tours to the Amazon Basin.

American Express (see the white pages of your telephone directory for your local AE office, or book through your local travel agent). The "Rio Express" runs eight days and includes air fare. The cost ranges from $696 to $929, depending on the time of year. They also offer a variety of South American tours with extended stops in Brazil.

Wright Way Tours, 16030 Ventura Blvd., Encino, California 91436, has a 12 day "El Barsileiro" excursion through Brazil with stops in Sao Paulo, Brasilia, Manaus, Salvador and Iquassu Falls. Land expenses are $799. Departures from Los Angeles, Miami and New York are available.

From Great Britain, *Bales Tours Ltd.,* Bales House, Barrington Rd., Dorking, Surrey RH4 3EJ, offers 15- and 24-day escorted tours covering Brazil, Colombia, Ecuador, Peru, Bolivia, and Argentina.

Plan-As-You-Go Travel. Wandering in Brazil on a plan-as-you-go basis can be the most rewarding way of all, or it can be a disaster, depending on the individual. To do it successfully you need a knowledge of Portuguese, some experience in foreign travel, an open schedule, and a good deal of willingness to take things and people as they are.

Brazil is still a virgin land for tourism, and the traveler's information booths, translators, and guides are not everywhere as they now are in Europe and other popular travel destinations.

To the stranger there is no friendlier country than Brazil. Nevertheless, the novice international traveler is advised to make some definite plans and reservations before leaving.

In-Between. A formula that provides experienced planning and guidance, avoids the sterility of standardized international hotels and airports, and gets you much closer to the real life of the countries you visit is touring by motorcoach and either staying in small hotels or camping out. This kind of travel is not only more colorful, but it is also obviously less expensive.

Official Tourist Information Offices. Because tourism is a relative newcomer to South America, few official or government travel information offices have been established abroad. Brazil, however, is represented by the Brazilian Tourism Authority, Embratur, suite 1336, 60 E. 42nd St. New York, N.Y. 10165.

STUDENT AND EDUCATIONAL TRAVEL. An increasing number of foreign students are being admitted to colleges and universities in South America—both as full-time students and at summer sessions. The two central sources for all basic information on study abroad are *The Council on International Educational Exchange,* 205 East 42nd St., New York, N.Y. 10017 and *The Institute of International Education,* 809 United Nations Plaza, New York, N.Y. 10017. CIIE publishes a *Student Guide to Latin America;* and *IIE's Handbook on International Study in the American Republics* contains a full listing of universities, university-level specialized schools, and schools of the arts, together with the fields that they cover and the degrees that they offer. Two other *IIE* publications that may be helpful are *Summer Study Abroad* and *U.S. College-Sponsored Programs Abroad: Academic Year.*

HOW TO GET THERE. *By Air.* The fact that international air travel is in a state of flux cannot be overemphasized. Furthermore, the political situation in South America tends to be unstable, which can affect air schedules even in countries not directly involved in a given problem. In addition, the mid-1982 bankruptcy of Braniff and the subsequent redistribution of its South American routes to other airlines will undoubtedly have repercussions for some years to come. Complicating the situation even more, the former distinction between charter and supplemental carriers and regularly scheduled airlines is now blurred: some self-proclaimed "charter" tour packagers are block-booking seats on major airlines at reduced prices, and major airlines are offering special charterlike prices in order to boost travel on certain routes. Regardless of formal status, *all* flights must meet the same U.S. government standards for aircraft maintenance and safety, crew qualifications, and reliability. Thus, though there will be minor variations in meals and service frills, you will be just as safe on a charter flight as on the most expensive scheduled flight (and flying to Brazil on standard flights is indeed expensive).

In general, the cheapest fares are going to be those available on charters or through package tour operators. Unfortunately, there are no standby fares to Brazil. Package and charter bookings will definitely save you money on the routes they cover, but they lock you into their schedules and itineraries.

The next best category of fares is known as APEX and Super-APEX, both of which are available on flights from most major U.S. and Canadian cities. Basic requirements change from airline to airline but generally include twenty-one day (or so), round-trip, advance booking and a minimum stay. Certain changes are allowed on standard APEX bookings, usually for a service charge; Super-APEX is slightly cheaper, but no alterations can be made and there may be additional restrictions.

There are a host of other fare categories ranging from full-fare economy (generally used by business travelers) right up to first class. All these fares and the restrictions that govern them are changed from time to time, depending on the time of year (peak, low, or "shoulder" periods), how heavy competition is at any given moment, and how well traveled a particular route is. The advantage of an independent booking at a full economy rate is that you may be able to add in additional stopovers at little or no extra charge. Here again, the rules vary and change frequently. Similarly, you are more likely to be able to change your reservations as you go when flying regularly scheduled major airlines. If you are going by other than a charter or a package tour, it is best to consult with a travel agent about routing and price.

As mentioned, the redistribution of Braniff's routes will have an impact for some time to come (Braniff having been one of the major carriers to South America), as other carriers try to build profitable service. The majority of flights terminate in Rio, though the national *Varig Airlines* also services São Paulo, Manaus, Brasilia, and other destinations, primarily from Miami and New York. Among the airlines serving Brazil from Europe are *Varig, Aerolineas Argentinas, Air France, British Caledonian, Iberia, Lufthansa, Pan Am, SAS, Swissair,* and *TAP. Pan Am, Varig,* and *South African Airways* fly to Rio from points in the Pacific and Africa.

An unusually lucid and systematic survey of the whole situation, with candid appraisals of the advantages and the disadvantages of the various alternatives is *How to Fly for Less, A Consumer's Guide to Low Cost Air Charters and Other Travel Bargains,* by Jens Jurgen, published by Travel Information Bureau, 44 County Line Road, Farmingdale, N.Y. 11735. In addition to a detailed discussion of the ins and outs of the charter flight business, the book contains listings of charter flight programs by destination and a directory of charter and tour operators. Good for initial "comparison shopping" are the travel sections of most major Sunday newspapers, which are invariably overflowing with enticing charter tour and package tour offerings.

Sometimes changes are not within your control. Airlines, like hotels, almost always overbook (assuming that business is good) and are then forced to "bump" passengers, that is, refuse passage, because the plane is full, despite the fact that you have a confirmed, "guaranteed" reservation in hand. The best way to avoid this situation is to arrive at the airport several hours ahead of departure time in order to be assigned a seat as soon as possible. (Some carriers assign seats to frequent travelers when they make their reservations; have your travel agent check to see if this is possible.)

The chances are that the airline will make every effort to get you onto another flight as soon as possible because the carrier is subject to a fine if it fails to get you to your destination (for reasons other than mechanical or weather problems) within four hours of your originally planned arrival time. In some instances, you may be entitled to compensation for the delay, although the regulations for international carriers are not as strict as for domestic (U.S.) lines.

In the event that you are bumped against your wishes (sometimes the airlines ask for volunteers and even offer such inducements as cash or a certain amount of credit toward a future trip), the airline will almost always offer to cable its office in the city where you are headed and have its personnel phone anyone who might be meeting you at the airport to tell them of your delay. In our experience, such calls are rarely made, and we recommend that you insist on making your own telephone call at the airline's expense. Airline personnel will put up strong resistance but will usually give in if you are persistent. You should also demand a copy of the CAB's printed regulations covering the situation, plus any other forms that you need. For full information, write to the Office of Consumer Affairs, Civil Aeronautics Board, Washington, D.C. 20428, for a copy of the free pamphlet, *Air Traveler's Fly-Rights*.

Note: Children from two to twelve usually fly at half the adult full fare. A child under two not sitting alone in a seat is charged 10 percent of full fare when the child is accompanied by an adult passenger. You will be charged full fare for a second infant unless there is a second adult passenger traveling with you.

 BY SEA. A great many steamship companies offer various kinds of service between world ports and the South American continent, although passenger service has been steadily diminishing throughout the world with the expansion of containerization. Alcoa Steamship Co., for example, formerly an important carrier of tourists to the southern continent, now has no passenger service whatever. However, more cruises call at South American ports than before. What you get on a cruise is a very pleasant vacation in a floating luxury hotel, plus overviews of several countries by way of their major port cities only. Below we give a list of all the important cruise services available to South America, followed by sources of information on freighter travel.

From North America:

Cunard Line, 555 Fifth Ave. New York, N.Y. 10017

Epirotiki Lines, 551 Fifth Ave. New York, N.Y. 10017, operate a 12-day "Caribazon" tour through the Caribbean and South America. Brazilian ports include: Manus, Boca da Valarie, Santa Rem, Amazon, Belem. Prices range from $1,850 to $2,495.

Sun Lines, 1 Rockefeller Plaza, Ste. 315 New York, N.Y. 10020, offers two-Amazon river trips (14 and 16 days), as well as two Rio excursions (15 and 17 days). Both are out of Fort Lauderdale, Florida. Stops in Manus, Salvador, and Bahia highlight this cruise that operates during Rio's carnival week. Prices run from $2,910 to $6,460, air inclusive.

Freighter travel is a specialized field in itself that is too large to be covered in detail here but very rewarding if you have an open schedule.

A great number of banana boats, tramp steamers, and tankers also cross the Caribbean from Tampa, New Orleans, and Texas ports bound for South America. Their schedules and prices often depend on where their cargo takes them, and a good travel agent can track down the right ship for you. Freighter travel is adventurous, relaxing, and often very inexpensive—it's well worth investigating. The cost factor can be particularly attractive because what you get, if your schedule permits, is in fact a leisurely cruise at rates of around $30 to $100 a day, whereas by going on a cruise liner you will pay perhaps $150 to $200 or more a day for comparable accommodations because you are paying for a whole extra infrastructure of entertainment that you may neither need nor want and which is absent from the simpler, quieter life of a freighter. And what freighters may lack in the way of entertainment and refinement, they make up for by way of informality, relaxation and cost (though flying is almost always cheaper). For details, and to help you choose from the lines available, consult either of the following specialists: *Air Marine Travel Service*, 501 Madison Avenue, New York, N.Y. 10022, publisher of the *Trip Log Quick Reference Freighter Guide;* or *Pearl's Freighter Tips*, 175 Great Neck Road, Great Neck, N.Y. 11201.

A final note: the "air-sea" cruises that are so popular in other parts of the world are beginning to catch on for South America too. These are package tours that take you to South America by ship and you return by plane—or vice versa—and they are easily arranged. Under present agreements, the price works out to half the round-trip air fare plus the one-way steamship fare less 10 percent.

In addition to the American lines listed above, many Scandinavian and several other foreign lines offer service from the U.S.A. and Canada to South America. These lines usually begin the voyage in their own countries, stop at a U.S. port, and continue to South America.

From Europe:

Ships of many nations connect European and South American ports by offering a great variety of services: *Delta Cruises*, Mundy Travel Ltd., River House, 119/121 Minories, London E.C.3, for example, makes regular South American crossings, calling at over 20 ports. Individual air/sea holidays, starting and stopping at your choice of ports, are available. *Princess Cruises*, P&O Cruises Ltd., Beaufort House, Saint Botolph St., London E.C.3, also offers a selection of cruises to South American ports.

Some other European passenger and cargo ships that serve this area are *Hamburg-South American Line* (German) and *Polish Ocean Line* (Poland).

SHIPBOARD TIPPING. A hard question to answer is "How much to tip?" Tipping is a personal matter. The amount depends on service received, length of trip, and type of accommodations. Those who serve are bedroom steward and waitress who have the most to do for you and should be tipped accordingly; stewards who may be called upon for breakfast in bed or for special service; deck steward and night steward if he serves you; wine steward if you order wines with meals; tips to bar steward as you are served or percentage of total bar bill at end of cruise; bellhop; tips for errands. Passengers usually tip on shipboard as they would in a first-class resort hotel under the American Plan (room and all meals).

BY CAR. Roadbuilding in Central and South America has progressed to the point that one can drive all the way from the United States to Brazil with just one short sea voyage. There is no road yet from Panama to Colombia, but several shipping lines transport cars and passengers from Panama to Buenaventura or Cartagena in Colombia or La Guaira in Venezuela. About 85 percent of the principal highways and main roads are good to excellent and hard surfaced. The rest with few exceptions are adequate dirt roads, open year round, but there are still too many rough and hazardous areas to make driving pleasurable. Good hotels exist along the entire route; with careful planning, a room with bath or shower can be had every night.

A reliable, fairly new car, preferably of a well-known make, for which spare parts are available in South America, is a must. Good repair facilities are available; gasoline and oil can be obtained everywhere, but high-test premium gasoline is hard to come by except in the capitals. Use tires with tubes, and take extra tubes along. Consult your automobile dealer about what spare parts to carry, and be sure to take a towing cable, hand pump, pressure gauge, and tube repair kit.

For border crossings, besides car registration and license, you'll need about 25 passport size photos and a *Carnet de Passages en Douane*. The AAA, 8111 Gatehouse Rd., Falls Church, Va. 22042, will issue one for $85, plus a $200 deposit, which is refundable when you surrender the Carnet Letter of credit. A letter stating that your car value is 150 percent more than its list value is needed from the bank to secure a Carnet. No Carnet is needed for a tourist vehicle to enter Brazil for up to 60 days. Formalities are completed at the border. Also required are Inter-American driving permits and Inter-American registration papers plus a country identification plaque on the automobile. You cannot sell your car in Brazil; plan to drive or ship it.

Buy insurance in the U.S. beforehand. If you have an accident, pay the judgments against you and collect the amount afterward. Never leave your car unguarded or unlocked—there are organized gangs in every major city, expert at breaking into and stealing cars.

Shipping cars. There are ample facilities for shipping automobiles from the U.S., but unless the owner is planning to reside in Brazil for some time, it is advisable to rent a car.

Best suggestion for travelers wanting to see Brazil by car is to rent automobiles in the various cities.

 PASSPORTS. Americans: Passports and visas—the latter available from the nearest Brazilian Consulate—are required for travel to or in Brazil. A tourist visa, valid for 90 days, is easily obtainable and free. A 2' X 3' passport photo, passport, and a round-trip ticket will secure your visa. Canadian and British citizens do not need visas.

Passports must be valid for at least six months from the intended date of arrival in Brazil. Adult passports are valid for 10 years, others for five years. When you receive your passport, write down its number, date and place of issue separately. If it is later lost or stolen, notify either the nearest American Consul or the Passport Office, Department of State, Washington D.C. 20524, as well as the local police.

If a resident alien, you need a Treasury Sailing Permit, Form 1040 C, certifying that federal taxes have been paid; if a non resident alien, Form 1040 NR; apply to your District Director of Internal Revenue for these. You will have to present various documents: (1) blue or green alien registration card; (2) passport; (3) travel tickets; (4) most recently filed Form 1040; (5) W-2 forms for the most recent full year; (6) most recent current payroll stubs or letter; (7) check to be sure this is all! To return to the U.S. you need a reentry permit if you plan to stay abroad more than one year. Apply for it in person at least six weeks before departure at the nearest office of the Immigration and Naturalization Service or by mail to the service, Washington, D.C.

Canadian citizens may obtain application passport forms at any post office; these are to be sent to the Central Passport Office, 125 Sussex Drive, Lester B. Pearson Building, Ottawa, Ontario. You may apply in person to the province in which you reside. However, a mailed application must be handled by the central office. A remittance of $20 Canadian, three photographs, and a birth certificate or certificate of Canadian citizenship (naturalization papers) are required. Canadian passports are valid for five years and are nonrenewable.

British citizens may apply for a passport at any U.K. passport office or British consulate, either by mail or in person. Two photographs, a birth certificate or proof of citizenship (naturalization papers), and £5.50 are required.

HEALTH CERTIFICATES. No vaccinations are required to enter Brazil unless coming from an infected area. However, the U.S. Public Health Service advises yellow fever inoculations for travelers to Brazil.

WHAT TO TAKE. (See the Brazil *Practical Information* section, later, for "What to Wear?" information.) (1) Electricity—Rio and Sao Paulo have both 110- and 220-volt AC, 60 cycles. Most hotels have converters for your convenience. (2) Bring your own shoe-shine equipment; except in the barber shops of large hotels, stands are hard to find. (3) Local druggists have preparations for local problems, but you might carry some antidiarrhea capsules. Most stomach upsets come from overindulgence—strong seasonings, shellfish, heavy wines, and so on. Try to eat lightly your first day or two in a new place. (4) When you buy drip-dry clothing, be sure to get dacron-cotton blends in preference to nylon, which can be very hot and damp in the tropics. (5) Finally, each passenger is allowed one piece of carry-on baggage small enough to fit under a seat. First-class passengers are allowed two pieces of checked luggage, though the sum of the length, width and breadth of either piece cannot total more than 62 inches. Economy fliers are also allowed two checked bags, though the combined dimensions of both taken together cannot exceed 106 inches, and neither alone can exceed 62. Once you are in South America, however, some domestic airlines still go by weight allowance in which first-class customers are allowed 30 kilos (66 lbs.) of baggage, and economy passengers 20 kilos (44 lbs.).

RENTAL CARS. Most major cities have local or international Rent-A-Car Services. Avis has extensive operations throughout the continent, and there are several good local car-rental services in various cities. Hertz is also well represented. Prices in Rio range from $12 a day for a small Volkswagen to $50 per day for a limousine. Add 5% tax.

MAIL AND TELEGRAPHIC SERVICES. Major hotels will hold mail for arriving guests. Another possibility is to have the mail forwarded to the local *American Express* office or agency. General Delivery in most of South America is not recommended for visitors. Telegraphic service is available everywhere. Many hotels have cable facilities.

ELECTRICAL CURRENT. Most of the top hotels have transformers for current and adapters for plugs for guests with foreign electric razors, slide projectors, and so on. Usually 110 or 120 volts, AC 60 cycle in Rio and São Paulo.

TOBACCO. Available in great variety everywhere. Brazil produces its own cigarettes and cigars—some excellent—some very poor. Quality tobacco products are always available everywhere but often at inflated prices. A pack of American cigarettes will usually cost approximately $1 (U.S.) in Brazil.

The best bet is to buy the tax-free cigarettes on your air flights. Most international flights offer American or English cigarettes for sale at considerable savings.

COSMETICS. No problem here. In fact, the ultra *chic* women of Rio and São Paulo usually introduce visitors to many of the latest beauty aids and cosmetics. In the world of fashion, the leading South American capitals are as smart as Paris, Rome, and New York.

DRY CLEANING AND LAUNDRY. Good service is available in the better hotels. Usually the best dry cleaning and laundry service in Brazil is done in the private plants of such leading hotels as those of the Intercontinental chain. Prices run from expensive to outrageous for dry cleaning, but in all fairness, it's extremely expensive to maintain these pioneer cleaning plants.

READING MATTER AND NEWS. English-language newspapers and magazines are for sale in all leading cities. With timely jet schedules to South America, there is little delay in receiving airmail editions of New York and Miami newspapers. International editions of news magazines are on sale in all leading hotels.

Two daily English-language newspapers, the *Brazil Herald* and the *Latin American Daily Post,* are published in Rio. They are indispensable to the visitor (and resident).

DRINKING WATER AND MILK. The best general rule is to drink bottled water in Brazil. Many of the public water systems date almost to colonial times and are not 100 percent safe. Be sure to ask for bottled water (it is usually in your hotel room when you arrive). There are several excellent mineral waters bottled in South America that make drinking bottled water a pleasure rather than a hardship.

Pasteurized milk is available in almost every major city. The one rule to remember is to have the bottle opened at your table.

CLOSING HOURS. Opening and closing hours naturally vary from city to city. The best rule to follow is to remember that many shops close for the customary two- or three-hour Latin luncheon. Plan your shopping between 10:00 A.M. and noon and 3:00 P.M. and 6:00 P.M. and you'll find stores open. In the larger cities many of the big department stores are now staying open during the lunch hours. Rio stores open 8:00 A.M.-6:30 P.M. Sat. 8:30 A.M.-1:00 P.M.

FACTS AT YOUR FINGERTIPS 13

 PHOTOGRAPHER'S HINTS. The best advice is to carry sufficient color film. Several of the smaller countries still do not stock fresh color film in all sizes, and to avoid disappointment, carry more color film than you plan to use (you'll end up using it all in highly photogenic Brazil). Film is very expensive. Black and white film (usually fresh) is usually available in large cities. A good filter for bright sunlight, as well as mailing containers for sending color film home, if you plan to be gone more than three months, is a must on your photo checklist. Airmail your film home—don't use surface mail—it's painfully slow between South and North America.

X-rays. When you fly, remember that in spite of official claims to the contrary, airport security x-ray machines do in fact damage your photographic films in about 17 percent of the cases. Have film inspected separately, or pack it in specially lined protective bags available in photo supply stores. One such is Film-A-Shield, available from Sima Products, 4001 W. Devon Ave., Chicago, Ill. 60646, $8.95 postpaid.

A final hint—a small tip, before you shoot, to those whom you use as models, insures a smooth relationship.

 MEDICAL TREATMENT. In Brazil there is no shortage of competent, trained, English-speaking doctors. The International Association for Medical Assistance for Travelers (IAMAT), 736 Center St., Lewiston, N.Y. 14092, has participating doctors in every South American country. All speak English. The rates are standardized at $20 office call, $30 house or hotel call, and $35 for night or holiday calls. They will send, on request, a booklet listing these physicians, which you can carry on your trip. The booklet takes from 6 to 8 weeks delivery time, so order it well in advance of your trip.

British residents may rely on Europe Assistance, 252 High St., Croydon CRO 1NF, which operates an on-the-spot medical assistance service throughout the world. Three weeks coverage in Brazil costs £9.20.

Pharmaceuticals pose no problem for the visitor. All major cities have excellent drugstores and many offer "round the clock" service.

 USEFUL ADDRESSES. The *Organization of American States,* 1889 F St., N.W., Washington, D.C., 20006, issues several inexpensive booklets on Brazil. The *U.S. Government Printing Office,* Washington, D.C., sells maps of South American countries. The *Chamber of Commerce of Latin America in the U.S.A.,* 1 World Trade Center, Rm. 3549, New York, N.Y. 10048, has business information.

Also, the *London Chamber of Commerce,* Latin American Section, 69 Cannon St., E.C.4.

The *Hispanic Council,* Canning House, 2 Belgrave Square, London, S.W.1, issues *British Bulletin of Publications on Latin America.*

Miles into Kilometers

Miles	Kms.	Miles	Kms.	Miles	Kms.
1	1.6093	10	16.09	100	161.
2	3.22	20	32.19	200	322.
3	4.83	30	48.28	300	483.
4	6.44	40	64.37	400	644.
5	8.05	50	80.5	500	805.

6	9.66	60	96.6	600	966.
7	11.27	70	112.7	700	1127.
8	12.87	80	128.7	800	1287.
9	14.48	90	144.8	900	1448.
				1000	1609.3

For Tire Pressure

Kilograms into Pounds

Kgs.	Pounds	Kgs.	Pounds
1	2.2046	40	88.18
2	4.4	50	110.23
3	6.6	60	132.28
4	8.8	70	154.32
5	11.0	80	176.37
6	13.2	90	198.42
7	15.43	100	220.46
8	17.64	200	440.92
9	19.84	300	661.39
10	22.05	400	881.85
20	44.09	500	1102.31
30	66.14	1000	2204.62

Pounds into Kilograms

Pounds	Kgs.	Pounds	Kgs.
1	0.45359	40	18.14
2	0.907	50	22.68
3	1.36	60	27.22
4	1.81	70	31.75
5	2.27	80	36.29
6	2.72	90	40.82
7	3.18	100	45.36
8	3.63	200	90.72
9	4.08	300	136.08
10	4.54	400	181.44
20	9.07	500	226.8
30	13.61	1000	453.59

Conversion Tables for Motor Fuels and Oils
Liters into Quarts and Gallons

1 U.S. gallon equals 0.8327 Imperial (British) gallon or 3.78 liters.
To arrive at British gallons equivalent for liters, multiply U.S. figures by 0.83.

Liters	Qts. (U.S.)	Liters	Gals. (U.S.)	Liters	Gals. (U.S.)
1	1.0567	1	0.2641	40	10.57
2	2.11	2	0.53	50	13.21
3	3.17	3	0.79	60	15.85
4	4.23	4	1.06	70	18.49
5	5.28	5	1.32	80	21.13
6	6.34	6	1.59	90	23.78
7	7.40	7	1.85	100	26.42
8	8.45	8	2.11	200	52.84
9	9.51	9	2.38	300	79.25
10	10.57	10	2.64	400	105.67
		20	5.28	500	132.09
		30	7.93	1000	264.18

Quarts and Gallons into Liters

1 Imperial (British) gallon equals 1.2 U.S. gallons or 4.5 liters.
Add 20% to liters in table to arrive at equivalents in British gallons.

Qts. (U.S.)	Liters	Gals. (U.S.)	Liters	Gals. (U.S.)	Liters
1	0.9463	1	3.7853	40	151.41
2	1.89	2	7.57	50	189.27
3	2.84	3	11.36	60	227.12
4	3.79	4	15.14	70	265.
5	4.73	5	18.93	80	302.8
6	5.68	6	22.71	90	340.7
7	6.62	7	26.50	100	378.5
8	7.57	8	30.28	200	757.1
9	8.52	9	34.07	300	1135.6
10	9.5	10	37.85	400	1514.1

20	75.71	500	1892.7
30	113.56	1000	3785.3

CUSTOMS—RETURNING HOME U.S. residents who are out of the U.S.A. at least 48 hours and have claimed no exemption during the previous 30 days are entitled to bring in duty-free up to $400 worth of bona fide gifts or items for their own personal use. Do not think that *already used* will exempt an item. If you buy clothing abroad and wear it during your travels it will nonetheless be dutiable when you reenter the U.S.

The $400 duty free allowance is based on the full fair *retail* value of the goods (previously, the customs' estimation was on the wholesale value). You must now list the items purchased and *they must accompany you when you return.* So keep all receipts handy with the detailed list, and pack the goods together in one case. The $50 mailed gift-scheme (see below) is also based on the retail value. Every member of a family is entitled to this same exemption, regardless of age, and their exemptions can be pooled. Infants and children get the same exemptions as adults, except for alcoholic beverages and tobacco. Beyond the first $400 worth of goods, inspectors now assess a flat 10% duty on the next $1,000 worth; above $1,400 duties vary according to the kind of merchandise.

One quart of alcoholic beverages up to 100 cigars (non-Cuban!) may be included in the exemption if you are 21 years of age or older. There is no limitation on the number of cigarettes you bring in for your personal use, regardless of age. Alcoholic beverages in excess of one quart are subject to customs duty and internal revenue tax. Approximate rates are (1/5 gallon); brandy or liquor, $2-$3; champagne 90¢; wine 15¢. The importation must not be in violation of the laws of the state of arrival. Furthermore, your tobacco and alcohol may be reported to the authorities in your own home state, to be taxed by them.

Only one bottle of certain perfumes that are trademarked in the United States (Lanvin, Chanel, etc.) may be brought in unless you can completely obliterate the trademark on the bottle, or get written permission from the manufacturer to bring more. Other perfumes are limited by weight or value.

Foreign visitors to the U.S. (nonresidents), and U.S. military personnel returning from duty abroad should inquire separately about regulations and exemptions pertaining to them.

You do not have to pay duty on art objects or antiques, provided they are over 100 years old.

Gifts which cost less than $50 may be mailed to friends or relatives at home, but not more than one per day (of receipt) to any one addressee. Mark the package: Unsolicited Gift—value less than $50. These gifts must not include perfumes costing more than $1, tobacco or liquor; however, they do not count as part of your $400 exemption.

Do not bring home foreign meats, fruits, plants, soil, or other agricultural items when you return to the United States. To do so will delay you at the port of entry. It is illegal to bring in foreign agricultural items without permission, because they can spread destructive plant or animal pests and diseases. For more information, read the pamphlet "Customs Hints", or write to: "Quarantines", Department of Agriculture, Federal Center Bldg., Hyatsville, Maryland 20782, and ask for Program Aid No. 1083, entitled "Traveler's Tips on Bringing Food, Plant and Animal Products into the United States."

Procedures for customs and immigration have been greatly simplified recently. Customs declaration forms are distributed on your plane or ship before you arrive. If your purchases are worth no more than $400 you fill out only the identification portions of the form and make an oral declaration when you pass the inspector. If you have over $400 worth you must make a written declaration. Under the Citizens Bypass Program, American citizens can show their passports to the customs inspector and eliminate the separate inspection by an immigration officer.

British residents. except those under the age of 17 years, may import duty-free from *any* country the following: 200 cigarettes or 100 cigarillos or 50 cigars or 250 grams of tobacco; 1 liter of alcoholic drink over 22% volume (i.e. whiskey and other hard liquor), *or* 2 liters of alcoholic drink under 22% vol. plus 2 liters of still table wine. Also 50 grams of perfume, ¼ liter of toilet water and £28 worth of other normally dutiable goods (this last to include not more than 50 liters of beer).

Canadian residents: In addition to personal effects, the following articles may be brought in duty free by people 16 or older: a maximum of 50 cigars, 200 cigarettes, 2 pounds of tobacco, and 1.1 liters of wine or liquor, provided these are declared to customs on arrival. The total exemption is $300, and solicited gift mailings can be up to $25 in value. Canadian customs regulations are strictly enforced; it is recommended that you check what your allowances are and make sure you have kept receipts for whatever you have bought abroad. For complete details, ask for the Canadian Customs brochure, "I Declare."

BRAZIL

Colossus of the Continent

by
DAVID ST. CLAIR and **GUY LYON PLAYFAIR**

(David St. Clair is a former Rio-based writer and art critic and former correspondent for Time *and* Life *magazines. He is also the author of* Macumba in Brazil *and* The Mighty, Mighty Amazon. *Music, architecture and the cinematic arts are presented by Guy Lyon Playfair, a British-born journalist and amateur musician, who lived many years in Brazil and has written extensively on all aspects of Brazilian life.)*

"Seja bemvindo," or Welcome to Brazil.

If there is one word to sum up this amazing country it is "diversity." It is so big and covers so many square miles through all sorts of vegetation that there is nothing that is "typically" Brazilian. The tourist coming here will find everything he expected, and lots more he never dreamed existed. He will be enchanted with the natural beauties (both scenic and human), delighted with the friendship and smiles of the people, shocked at the poverty and ignorance, exhausted during the pagan Carnival madness, and touched by the Catholic piety. He will relax on the beaches, have a nervous breakdown driving in the traffic, gain weight by eating the rich food, and lose it by dancing a wild samba until dawn. He will be delighted with the "tomorrow is another day" attitude, exasperated if his airplane is hours late. He can wear heavy sweaters and eat beefsteak with the gauchos of the south, and the very next day be sweating in a pair of bathing trunks and eating alligator steak in the Amazon. He can take pictures of himself in front of colonial slave blocks in Bahia or in front of a 33-story all-glass air-conditioned office building in Rio. He can spend a week and go away satisfied that he has seen Brazil. He can live here for years and still not know the country.

Diversity is everywhere. The people are a mixture of Portuguese settlers, indigenous Indians, and imported Africans. To this have been added peoples from Italy, Germany, Poland, England, and even from faraway Japan. The language also has been touched by this diversity. In the south a pair of men's socks are called "capim." In the north they are called "meias."

Diversity manifests itself even in religion. The Vatican likes to call Brazil "the largest Catholic nation on earth," but a large percentage of Brazilians attend macumba or candomblé services regularly, pray to gods that are mixtures of Christian and African and wear both a cross and a voodoo charm for good luck. The diversity also can be seen in the larger cities with modern office and apartment buildings planted right beside sprawling favela slums of wooden shacks and tin can thatched roofs.

The tourist with a little bit of time can taste this magnificent diversity for himself. Spend a day or two in Bahia sampling the 17th-century Portuguese and African atmosphere, take a plane to Rio and savor its uniquely Brazilian charm. Then go to São Paulo where you dine in the very best international restaurants and live it up in air-conditioned hotels amidst the bustle of business as usual. Grab a plane headed west and have the pilot put you down amidst the primitive stone-age Indians of the Xingú river basin. You will have visited the equivalent of several different countries and spanned centuries, yet you will have been in Brazil all the time.

A Glance at Brazil's History

Brazil was discovered in 1500, just eight years after America. How Columbus missed this giant of the Western Hemisphere and touched down upon little San Salvador remains one of the mysteries of that era. Spain was badly in need of new territories and when they put all their money on Columbus they made a mistake, for Portugal was also in need and backed a sea captain named Pedro Alvares Cabral. The Portuguese king was in a landgrab race for the new colonies with the Spanish rulers, and both of them wanted as much as they could get in the shortest amount of time. There were great things coming out of India that could be sold to fill the royal coffers, later to be converted into ships and arms and manpower to dash across the seas again and grab more land.

When Cabral sighted Brazil he thought that he was seeing India, but upon landing and finding none of the expected Maharajas or a road clearly marked "Cathay," he reasoned that he had discovered some-place new. He thought it was an island and sent out a search party to walk around once and come back again. What Cabral had stumbled upon was, of course, not an island, but the biggest hunk of land to be claimed in the entire New World.

The Tupi natives were friendly, much to everyone's surprise and pleasure; and after celebrating Mass, Cabral left a few men to watch his new country and then hurried back to Portugal.

The Portuguese referred to the new colony as "The Island of Santa Cruz" (Holy Cross); later when their error was discovered they called the new colony "Land of Santa Cruz." But with the coming of mer-chant ships from the mother country and the vast exporting of a hard wood called "brazil," the people of Portugal began to refer to the place as "The Land of Brazil." From there it was an easy step to calling it simply Brazil.

The Portuguese Move In

The Portuguese were not harsh masters. They made friends with the Indians, and though they looked for golden temples and lost cities, they didn't start slaughtering right and left when they failed to find any. They were more interested in trade, and the long coastal lands of their new-found colony were richer agriculturally than anything the Spanish had been able to claim.

Farmers arrived from Portugal to set up huge sugar and spice farms. They plowed from the present-day city of Olinda down almost to Rio. The land was rich, the nights cool, and there was lots of elbow room. But workers were scarce, and imitating their Spanish enemies, they set out to enslave the local Indians.

The Indians would have none of it and ran deeper into the jungle rather than submit. The delicate Tupis were not accustomed to toiling long, hot afternoons in cane or cotton fields and died off rapidly. So slaves from the bulge of west Africa were brought in. Swooping down along the Guinea coast and as far south as Angola, Portuguese slave traders attacked villages, killed off the weak, and shackled the strong. The trip to Brazil was long and rough and many died on the way, but those that managed to survive the voyage were brave, hardy, and resourceful.

Soon great wealth was flowing to Lisbon, and the Royal coffers were expanding from the raw materials the Portuguese traded with the rest of Europe. So envious were the other land-hungry nations of the era that the Dutch, French, and Spanish all tried to encroach on Portugal's claim. Much of her new wealth was spent in keeping the intruders at bay.

While riches were being reaped from the soil in the northeast, other riches were being dug up in the mountains to the south. No sooner had the present site of Rio de Janeiro been put on the map than thousands of fortune hunters poured through it on the way to the mines of Minas Gerais. Here were what seemed like entire mountains of amethysts, aquamarines, and diamonds waiting to be scooped up. A procession of miners and trouble-makers took over an area many times bigger than

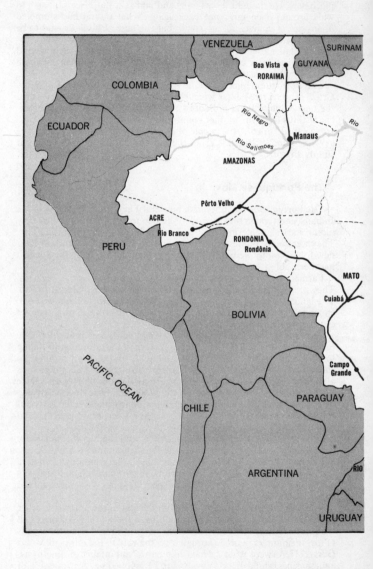

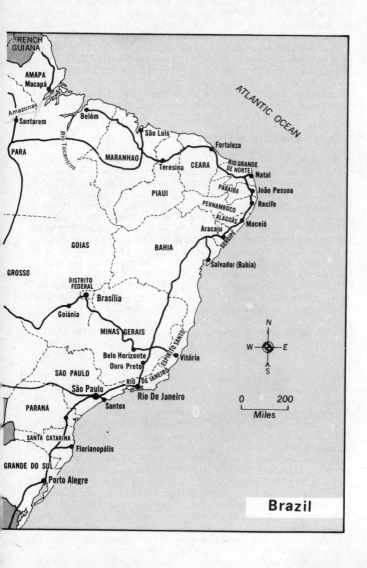

Brazil

Alaska, and along with their thirst for gems brought with them a taste for the better things in life. Wealth made them remember how the nobility had lived back home, and as soon as a miner had enough to live, he wanted to live well. By the boat loads from Portugal came carpenters, stonemasons, sculptors, and painters to build churches, palaces, and cities in the Brazilian wilderness. Up went such architectural treasures as Ouro Preto and Diamantina. There were gas lights and golden horse-drawn coaches in the streets and gem-studded and silver ornaments in the churches. Lace came from Europe to adorn milord's cuffs, and actors and musicians brave enough to make the trip from Portugal had diamonds tossed to them after their performances.

The Flag Bearers of Empire

Other men were busy too. A hardy group of adventurous, bloodthirsty crusaders banded together near what is now São Paulo and set out to find more diamond mines and more riches. Carrying the flag of the new colony, these "Bandeirantes" (Flag Bearers) pushed out in all directions, claiming each new step for Portugal. There had been a treaty of Tordesillas signed between Portugal and Spain in the year 1494. It was the idea of Pope Alexander VI, who wanted as little blood spilled in the New World as possible. Both sides agreed to the dividing of the southern continent in a straight line from what is now Belem on the Amazon River to a little east of Porto Alegre. Everything to the west belonged to Spain, everything to the east to Portugal.

Fortunately for modern Brazil the Bandeirantes knew nothing of this treaty, or else didn't have a compass. For they spread out over thousands of miles, planting their banner on the banks of the Amazon to the north, Paraná to the south, and on the Paraguayan and Bolivian frontiers to the west. Spaniards, so busy with wars with the Indians, hadn't any idea what was going on in the heart of their lands. When they finally woke up it was too late, for the Brazilians had claimed it all.

Brazil was ruled by Portugal for many years; then when Napoleon captured Portugal, the royal family fled to the new colony. It was like a shot in the arm for the New World. At once the exiled royal family opened the ports of Brazil to trade with some European nations, especially with Napoleon's enemy, England. Then when the French were defeated, the king, Dom João VI, went back to Portugal and left his young son Pedro I to govern. But Pedro had ideas of his own and did away with a number of reforms his father had set up. He proclaimed Brazil's independence on Sept. 7, 1822. As a new nation, Brazil had a long way to go and a lot to learn; but the royal family lived well in a series of palaces filled with silver chandeliers and brocaded chairs. So unsure was the nation and so ineptly governed, that after a series of costly wars with Argentina and Uruguay, Dom Pedro I stepped aside in favor of his son Pedro II, who was only five years old. A series of regents then came into power that managed so badly parliament finally decreed Dom Pedro II "of age" when he was just 14.

Then came almost half a century of peaceful and fruitful ruling on the part of the Western Hemisphere's only Emperor (if you don't count the short reign of Maximilian in Mexico), who mingled with his subjects, made a trip to the United States, and declared that he would rather have been a school teacher than an emperor. Under his constant vigilance the nation prospered, trade agreements were signed, an attempt by Argentina to take control was put down, and slaves were freed. But a democratic movement was brewing in the military, and in spite of progress and prosperity the army took over and banished Pedro and his royal family back to Portugal. On November 15, 1889, the Republic was born.

Thankful for the Nighttime

From here on, Brazilian history grows dull with the parade of easily forgettable presidents and minor revolutionaries. There were all sorts of problems that needed to be solved, and very few able men around to solve them. Brazil stuck mostly to what the U.S. was doing politically, while staying close to France for its cultural instruction. Politicians made a number of efforts to gain power at the expense of the nation but the proud giant, in spite of them, kept growing.

Brazil has had very few actual internal wars and has never had a real, bloody revolution à la Spanish-American style. There have been some skirmishes among the gauchos in the south, and once in 1932 the state of São Paulo took on the rest of the nation. It lost.

Getulio Vargas was a strongman who took over in a military coup in 1930. The country was horrified, but soon liked the idea of having one man in charge and did very little except grumble against him. When he was deposed by another military coup in 1945 he sat out his exile on his home ranch in Rio Grande do Sul and prepared for the elections. In 1951 he was elected—legally this time—president of the Republic and right beside him rode his protegé João "Jango" Goulart, later to govern the nation. Vargas tried to be more democratic this second time around and supported labor unions and the like, but still that old obstacle, the Latin military, was against him. After a long period of interoffice fights and counter charges, the tired old man put a pistol to his heart and pulled the trigger.

After him came President Café Filho, and then the dynamic spendthrift Juscelino Kubitschek. Kubitschek built Brasilia from a dream into a multimillion dollar reality and put industry and commerce on a fast pace to compete with the rest of the world.

His immediate successor was Janio Quadros, a thin man with a thick moustache who insisted that everything be done exactly his way. He wrote little notes that became law, and tried to squeeze the growing giant of a nation into a special form that he never quite defined. Under some pressure, he suddenly resigned one day in August 1961 and threw the nation as close to a civil war as it has ever come.

The successor to Quadros was leftist-leaning, rabble-rousing Jango Goulart, the old pupil and confidant of Dictator Vargas. The military wanted little of Jango and his friends, and above all did not want the plans and mass platitudes of Vargas back again. In a dramatic ten days, the military kept Jango—on his way home from a trip to Red China when Quadros resigned—out of the capital and virtually a prisoner in his home state of Rio Grande do Sul. Congress hastily voted in a Parliamentary system, drastically curtailing the President's powers, and Jango finally took office, managing to persuade the people to vote the old presidential system back the following year.

Under Goulart the country seethed with strikes and instability. Prices soared to an all-time high and red-tinged politicians were appointed to key positions all over the nation. Goulart himself became swayed by ambitious leftists and many Brazilians feared for their country as never before. Then on March 31, 1964, Goulart was overthrown by the military. As before, the revolt was virtually bloodless, and while Goulart and his family fled into exile in Uruguay, where he died in 1977, the army clamped down and installed one of their own men, General Humberto de Alencar Castello Branco, as president. Again, Brazil had a military government, but this one was different. The Army seized Brazil by the scruff of its neck and shook it—hard. Sweeping reforms paid dividends as inflation began to drop, exports to rise, and overall growth to move out of the red where Jango had left it to a steady 10 percent within 5 years. Hundreds of old-time politicians lost their political rights, and two new parties replaced the countless former ones. In 1967, Castello Branco handed over the presidency to Marshal Costa e Silva, who closed Congress and made things difficult for dissident students and labor leaders. Upon his death in 1969 he was replaced by General Emilio Garrastazu Médici, who continued the Army's reform policy, strengthened the economy, waged war on illiteracy, and initiated bold development plans for the Northeast and Amazon regions.

Médici was succeeded in 1975 by retired General Ernesto Geisel, son of German immigrants and Brazil's first Protestant president. Geisel, who was previously head of the state petroleum enterprise, Petrobrás, maintained most of the policies that brought about Brazil's "economic miracle" and at the same time tried to bring more political liberty and an equitable distribution of wealth. But the petroleum crisis caused problems, and the country's growth slowed from 9.2 percent in 1976 to about 6 percent in 1977 as his government took anti-inflationary measures. Inflation, however, soared again in 1980, hitting 110 percent. This sudden upward surge forced the Brazilian government to take strong anti-inflationary measures in 1981, which, together with the general economic recession in the western world, produced the country's first negative growth since World War II. In 1983 growth was 3.9 percent negative. Trade problems forced a devaluation of the cruzeiro by 30 percent in February, 1983—over 200 percent inflation.

The current president of Brazil, João Figueiredo, a former army general chosen by the military to succeed Geisel, has vowed to return the nation to democracy. Since taking office in 1979, Figueiredo has taken the country a long way toward realizing that goal. Press censorship has ended, political prisoners have been released, and exiles living abroad have been able to return without facing arrest or harassment. General elections for all offices except president were held in November, 1982.

The present political climate of Brazil is one of hope for the future as the military steps down from 20 years of uninterrupted rule to turn the reins of government over to a civilian president. The country will have a truly democratic government in 1985.

Brazil Up to Date

When you stop and remember that most Brazilians in the cities have an education that goes only to the eighth grade and that many in the interior who have but three or four years of schooling are considered "educated," you will marvel that anything has been done to improve the country at all. Ill-housed and ill-fed people cannot be depended upon to worry about anything but themselves. Give these people jobs and a sense of dignity and they will start to be concerned with their problems.

In spite of these problems, Brazil is making giant strides into the industrialized world. Already its economy ranks as the eighth largest in the free world, its gross national product is twice that of Mexico, and Brazilian exports sell so well abroad that they now bring an annual positive trade balance to the country.

Brazil has shown more gains in manufacturing, exports, agricultural, and educational improvements than any other nation in Latin America. Although the desire to put everything off until tomorrow and go to the beach today is always strong, there are many men who are doing things for their country.

The population of São Paulo is now over 10 million and Rio around 8 million inhabitants. Industrially speaking, São Paulo is now the heartbeat of Latin America economy. It has few unemployed, and an intelligent system of social services and public improvements. Across the nation highways are being cut through jungles and over mountains. Twenty-five years ago the road between the two cities was unpaved and impassable during the rainy season. Today there is a double-lane toll freeway, partly financed by U.S. aid. But although highway construction has been a top priority of all post-1964 governments, there are still only about 50,000 miles of paved highway in the whole country, little more than the U.S. had in 1840.

For its manufacturing, Brazil needs power and lots of it. In the past few years the country has been building huge plants in the Paraná River area to service São Paulo, one in the interior of Minas Gerais and two others in the northeast. The mighty Itaipu project, being built in partnership with Paraguay, was inaugurated in 1982 and is the largest hydroelectric power plant in the world. Brazil also has its first nuclear power plant operating near Angra dos Reis between São Paulo and Rio. Two more plants are under construction. With this energy, Brazil manufactures enough plastics, textiles, automobiles, toys, canned foods, cement, and chemicals to satisfy the home consumer without importing. But some wheat, rubber, petroleum, paper, and machinery for both light and heavy industry must be imported. Economists predict, however, a likelihood of the country becoming self-sufficient in food and many other critical resources in the near future. Brazil hopes enough oil will be discovered offshore to bring self-sufficiency in that area too, and for the first time in decades the national oil monopoly Petrobrás has invited private foreign companies back to search for oil.

With respect to health, the government has been busy with the eradication of malaria, and today the mosquito is a problem only in the remote regions and not in the cities. Efforts have been concentrated in Belem and Manaus to stamp out the dreaded Chagas disease that comes from the bite of little beetles. The Butantan Snake Farm in Sao Paulo has been doing great work with venoms from snakes, spiders, and scorpions making antidotes for the bites and supplying them free of charge to doctors and interior clinics. Hospitals are being built all over the nation, but the problem of persuading doctors and nurses to leave the big cities to staff them remains. Almost every town has a free clinic that is open day and night for anyone who needs attention; they do everything from setting broken legs to delivering babies.

Many efforts have been made in recent years to update the country's education system on all levels, starting with a nationwide literacy campaign and ending with university reforms. Secondary education has been restructured to stress the practical arts and sciences more heavily than preparation for university; previously, the system turned out a huge surplus of poets and politicians, but too few plumbers, scientists, and computer programmers.

Brazilians are eager to learn. Private courses proliferate everywhere. Under the government-sponsored Rondon Project students are visiting remote areas of Brazil and finding out what makes their country tick—or what failed to make it tick in the past.

Geographically Speaking

People get set ideas of Brazil's geography either from seeing too many picture postcards or remembering too many Hollywood films. Actually a great part of this enormous nation consists of hilly uplands, plateaus, and low mountains. There is a vast plain that stretches far into the Amazon region and another that spreads out through the Mato Grosso and into Bolivia and Paraguay. The Brazilian highlands that meld politically to become the Guiana highlands are some of the oldest geological formations anywhere on earth. These hills are granite and other tough stones that are heavily veined with gold, diamonds, and a variety of semiprecious stones. The Serra do Espinhaço (Spiny Mountains) that run from northern Minas Gerais to Bahia also contain iron ore, gold, and manganese. Here the highest mountain in central Brazil can be found, old Pico da Bandeira (Flag Top), which stands 9,482 feet. Another recently discovered peak in the state of Amazonas is even higher—Neblina (Haze) reaching 9,889 feet. One of the world's largest lava plateaus is to be found in the south of Brazil; termed the Paraná plateau; it is covered with dark, purple-colored soil that is excellent for raising coffee. Along the coast rich deposits of oil have been found.

The eastern side of the Brazilian highland descends abruptly into the sea and has been given the name "The Great Escarpment." There is no coastal plain but a sloping series of steppes that continues far out into the water. All along this there is a series of small rivers and sandy beaches. Wide expanses of white sand reach from way above Recife down past the Uruguayan border. Some beautiful, unspoiled beaches can be found in the far north and the far south. The sands in the states of Paraná and Santa Catarina, for example, are solid and pure. The lack of tourists and year-round dwellers keeps them that way. This combination of sand and escarpment has given Brazil some of the finest natural harbors in the world. Rio is perhaps the best known, but the harbors at Santos, Bahia, Recife, São Luiz, Vitória, and Ilhéus have contributed greatly to the wealth of the nation.

All That Water

Brazil's rivers are some of the longest and deepest in the world. For scientific study, they've been broken into the three major systems that drain the country's highlands. The first, in the north, is the mighty, almost unbelievable Amazon River, fed by the waters that pour down through jagged peaks, lush jungles, and rich plateaus. Its tributaries sound and look exotic and offer the visitor who is not afraid of discomfort some of the most unforgettable experiences in Latin America. There the great Tocantins and the Araguaia flow. There are the mysterious and unexplored Xingú, the rubber-laden Tapajós and the Madeira. To the far west runs the impressive, and almost unknown, Rio Negro.

The second river system gathers the waters from southwestern Minas Gerais and empties them into the placid yet treacherous Paraná. The water on the western slope of the São Paulo Escarpment flows until it reaches the sea by joining the Rio de la Plata near Buenos Aires.

The almost legendary São Francisco, the largest river wholly within Brazil, is the third system. Beginning in the plateau near Brasilia it flows northward for over a thousand miles until it pours into the sea between the states of Sergipe and Alagoas. Navigable and studded with power plants, the São Francisco has been the main artery to the heart of Brazil for generations.

Visitors come here expecting to suffer from the heat, and when they don't it is always a pleasant surprise. The Amazon area usually hovers around 80 degrees Fahrenheit, but the humidity-filled atmosphere makes it seem higher. In January of 1963 the thermometer recorded the hottest day in Rio's weather history: 104 degrees in the shade. And this was exactly the same time that the United States was freezing with temperatures of 25 to 30 degrees below zero. Rio usually has a soft warm 73 degrees all year round. The seasons are just the reverse of what they are in the United States and Europe. The cold days in Rio (average temperature 65) come in June and July; the hot days from January to March. In the south of the country a yearly frost is common, and in some parts of Santa Catarina and Rio Grande do Sul snowfalls have been recorded.

Rains should give the tourist nothing to worry about. They come up quickly and go away just as fast. In the Amazon it rains every afternoon for an hour or so from January to June. In the northeast it seldom rains, but when it does it really pours. In Rio a brisk, two-hour downpour is more likely in the months from December to April (but not *every* day so don't plan your trip around the rains) than the rest of the year.

The vegetation in Brazil is of many sorts. In the Amazon Basin and those places along the coast where the rainfall is very heavy, there is a tropical rain forest where broadleafed trees and shrubs grow to gigantic proportions and as many as 3,000 different species of trees have been catalogued within a single square mile. Through these tall shady trees very little sunlight manages to filter down, and consequently the ground is rich in decaying foliage and industrious bugs and small animals. In the northeast, lack of rain has produced a parched desert of hundreds of square miles, where cattle and humans die together in their search for water. In the south huge stands of pine trees grow wild and are used in the manufacture of paper. There are open prairies that start in São Paulo state and run down into Argentina to form the Brazilian pampas. In the northeast rain forests stand the huge Jacaranda trees and the very wood that gave the nation its name, the Brazil tree. The Jacaranda is a hard, beautifully grained dark wood almost like mahogany. Most of the fine colonial furniture that one sees in the antique shops was made from this wood. Durable yet attractive, it is one of the most sought-after materials in use today.

King Coffee

That a country as big as Brazil used to be a "one crop" country was always amazing to outsiders. They looked at the hunk of land that dominates the Latin American map and tried to imagine the entire United States living from an economy of tomatoes or cucumbers. Yet Brazil, with its great size and population, has managed to do just that until recently. Economic history has been a succession of various agricultural "kings."

First there was sugar. It was the earliest crop established on the new lands. The Portuguese crown eagerly awaited the money that sugar gave to the Royal coffers. The climate along the coast, from far below Bahia to way above Recife, was perfect for its growth. It was hot and muggy with abundant rainfall. It added to the nation's prosperity, population, and culture. Then other empire builders like Great Britain and France began to plant and sell sugar on the world market. The Brazilians had to lower their prices and improve their quality to meet the competition. But the English-speaking and the French-speaking peoples preferred their own sugar, put high tariffs on the Brazilian product and almost drove it completely out of competition.

Fortunately rubber was just coming into its own in the Amazon. There were all sorts of uses for rubber in the United States and in Europe. Once it had been discovered that rubber could be vulcanized for longer lasting and more efficient service, there was almost no industry that didn't want and need Brazil's crop. The town of Manaus grew to international importance. Jenny Lind came to sing there. Men lit their cigars with ten dollar bills and housewives sent their laundry to be washed and ironed in England. Supporting all this luxury were thousands of Indian, black, and white day laborers, working deep in the malarial jungles under slavelike conditions. The rubber trees grew wild and had to be worked where they were found. Planting them produced no rubber at all. Then an Englishman visited the interior and smuggled out a few hundred rubber seeds which he took to Indonesia and cultivated. There the trees flourished, and in seven years Indonesia

was competing with Brazil. The Brazilians, proud and overly sure of themselves, refused to lower their prices to meet the new competition. Buyers flocked to Indonesia and almost overnight Brazil was driven out of the rubber market.

The next crop to rise to importance was coffee, first in the State of Rio de Janeiro, then in São Paulo. Coffee had become an important cash crop in southern Brazil, and with rubber out of the way, all energy was devoted to increasing coffee production. São Paulo had the ideal climate of chilly weather followed by warm and rainy days. There was fertile land that was more European in makeup than in Bahia or other places. There was also the added advantage of Italian and German immigrants who wanted to be farmers and raise a cash crop. With everything working smoothly, coffee soon became the most important national product and Brazil depended heavily on it.

Coffee actually built the gigantic industrial city of São Paulo. With the money the growers got from the exports and the taxes the state got from the growers, new industries were started and new ideas tried. There were even many small industries that sprang from the by-products of coffee. The protein in coffee is used to modify certain oils and tars. The carbohydrates are used in the making of cellulose, dyestuffs, and plastics. The coffee bean oil is used in dozens of varied industries. While production has increased elsewhere, particularly in Africa, Brazil remains the world's biggest coffee grower. Surpluses have disappeared, due in part to controls imposed by the International Coffee Agreement.

THE BRAZILIAN WAY OF LIFE

What Is A Brazilian?

The people of Brazil are a symphony in colors. There are few other nations on earth where such a wide spread of skin tones from whitest white to yellow to tan to deepest black are all grouped under one nationality.

Brazil has long been praised for its alleged lack of discrimination and overt racial prejudice. A "black revolution" like that in the United States is unlikely to occur in Brazil. But the surface calm is deceptive. There are few, if any, black or mulatto diplomats, judges or ranking government officials, very few physicians, dentists, college professors, lawyers, or ranking officers in the armed services. In the latter case, a large proportion of enlisted men are black or mulatto but they are commanded by whites.

This mixture that makes Brazil and Brazilians began way back in the colonial days when the first Portuguese sailors were left to manage the new land. They were sailors and they were men, and like all sailors and men they felt the need of feminine companionship. They took to calling on the local belles in the nearby Indian villages, and when the Portuguese ships came back to the new land for them, there was a whole crop of babies at the dock.

Some of these babies were looked upon as heirs of their white fathers and, under this more paternalistic system of African slavery than that

30

practiced in the U.S., were often freed with their mothers and allowed to learn and practice a trade. The father knew that the mother would stay on and work for him and that she needed a place to rear the child. Making her free just made her more attached to her benefactor, and she raised the child teaching him to respect and be grateful for the "patron" that gave him his birthright.

In the old plantation houses it was quite common for a man to have both a white wife and a colored one, both sets of children growing up free and equal in the eyes of the father. There were times when the mulatto son turned out to be the smarter and more gifted, and might even be allowed to inherit a share of the plantation on his father's death.

This mixture of white and black and Indian today forms the base of what is simply called the "Brazilian race." There is no hesitancy on the part of some Brazilians to declare that they have black ancestry.

In spite of the many thousands of African slaves imported over the years, it's very difficult to find a pure black. Today open liaisons between white women and blacks or mulattoes are rare and still meet with considerable social disapproval.

There is no discernible feeling of unity among Brazilian blacks or between blacks and mulattoes similar to the organizations of Afro-Americans that brought about the far-reaching social reforms in the U.S. over the past 20 years.

Indians and Immigrants

It is easier to find a pure Indian. In the center of Mato Grosso and in the Amazonian states, tribes still roam along the watersheds and the deep jungles exactly as they did thousands of years ago. Very little is known of their origins. They seem to have none of the ability that the Indians of Peru or Mexico had in pottery or painting but bear remarkable resemblance to the tall proud Polynesians. Theories abound as to their origin, many people having the idea that they drifted over the Andes from Peru about the same time that other Peruvian Indians were taking boats for the South Seas. Others say they were always in the heart of the jungle and have been flushed out because of the scientific light of the 20th century. Still others hold them as remnants of the original peoples from the lost continent of Atlantis. Whoever they are, and wherever they came from, they make up one of the most interesting segments of the Brazilian population.

Unfortunately, the Brazilian Indian has suffered largely the same fate as has his U.S. and Canadian cousin in being pushed back constantly and falling ready victim to European avarice and disease.

Immigrants also make up a large percentage of Brazil's populace. And once they have become established they are considered Brazilian and no longer as "foreigners." Of all countries, Portugal still sends the most immigrants per year. There are a great number of Italians (especially in the industrial São Paulo area) and many Germans and Poles in the rich agricultural south. A current and very important group of immigrants to Brazil are the Japanese. Many of them came before World War II, and a great many more followed. Because of special treaties signed between Brazil and Japan, they were given land, special farming equipment, and special considerations. What they have managed to do with the land, especially in the Amazon area where they've filled local markets with fruits and vegetables hitherto unknown, is truly impressive. Two Japanese-Brazilians have served as cabinet ministers, and in large measure it is the baseball-loving Japanese immigrants who are responsible for the São Paulo ball team reaching championship level.

All of these races and nationalities have managed to get mixed together in Brazil's melting pot, and there is a beneficial national trait of "live and let live" that is commendable.

Of Differences and Samba

Brazilians are a relatively good-natured people and, unlike some of their neighbors, would rather sing than cry, rather dance than fight. To a Carioca from Rio, everything is a wonderful joke and nothing is really too serious to laugh about. It's even better when a song can be made up about it.

Brazilians are Brazilians and want visitors and the rest of the world to remember that. They are not "Latin Americans" (a term they intensely dislike), they do not speak Spanish (although they understand it), and their capital city is not Buenos Aires (though some tourists seem to think it is).

Many differences stem from the fact that it was the Portuguese and not the Spanish who discovered and civilized the land, and the fact that the African influence is stronger in Brazil than in any other South American country. They try so hard to be apart from the rest of the nations on the big leaf that is South America, that sometimes the effect is exaggerated. Their main cultural iron curtain is their language. They are proud that they speak Portuguese and are not at all upset that the rest of the world has yet to master it. They polish their language, write excellent novels and poetry in it, and never bemoan the fact that outside of Brazil, Portugal, Angola, Mozambique, Guinea-Bissau, and Goa none of it can be understood without a translator.

Brazilians don't like revolutions, wars, and fast deaths. They've never had a bloody uprising, don't get overly concerned about politics, and rather than stage bloody riots over food shortages are content to stand patiently in line and wait their turn. But Brazil's military prowess must not be disdained. She was the only South American republic to send an army to Europe in World War II to fight in Italy on the Allied side.

The Church of the Spirits

Brazil is officially a Roman Catholic country. The Holy See in the Vatican likes to boast that it is the "largest Catholic country in the world," and at first glance it may appear to be, for there are beautiful churches and cathedrals ranging from the colonial to the baroque and modern all over the nation. The church owns huge parcels of choice lands in Rio and São Paulo; and in interior towns long-robed fathers and nuns can be seen everywhere. When a president takes the oath of office there is always a priest and a Bible close at hand. Children study catechism, are baptized with the names of saints, and attend Catholic schools. Everybody wears a religious medal or two. Taxi and bus drivers have prints of St. Christopher prominently placed, and in June the two biggest winter celebrations are reserved for St. John and St. Peter. To the tourist, overcome with the gold and gems of Bahia's São Francisco church or the impressive concrete modernism of the cathedral designed by Oscar Niemeyer in Brasilia, Catholicism and allegiance to Rome seem to be everywhere. Actually, much of this is on the surface. The real church for masses of Brazilians is the church of the spirits.

The Portuguese brought their religion all ready made to the new colony and planted it right along with the rows of cotton and sugar cane. The Indians had their own gods whom they worshipped and, even when driven into slavery, refused to relinquish. When the African blacks were beaten and chained aboard stinking slave ships bound for the new world, they may have been forced to leave their families and their possessions behind, but they brought along their gods. And what an impressive array they were.

Foremost among them was Iemanjá who was the goddess of the rivers and water. There was also Oxalá who was the god of procreation and harvest. Exú was a wicked spirit who could cause mischief or death. There were others of lesser rank, but all powerful, like Ogun, Oxôssi, Xangó, and Yansan. They arrived in Brazil together with the slaves who, when things were going badly, turned to the gods of their homeland.

The Catholic Church was naturally against this, threatened excommunication to the whites who did not control their slaves' religious outbreaks, and threatened corporal punishment to the slaves themselves if they continued to believe in their old gods. The slaves, most of whom came from the very best and aristocratic native tribes, were smart enough to realize they couldn't fight the priests but would have to compromise. So they took on all the ritual of Rome but didn't take their old gods from the high places.

Many times all they did was give the African god a new Christian name. Thus Iemanjá became the Virgin Mary and was queen of the heavens as well as queen of the seas. Oxalá, already most powerful in Africa, became the most powerful in Rome, Jesus Christ. Exú, full of evil to begin with, became Satan. Ogun became St. Anthony, Obaluayê became St. Francis, Yansan, St. Barbara, and Oxôssi was turned into St. George. On their altars, along with the sacred white feathers, the magical beads, and the bowls of cooked rice and cornmeal, were placed plaster statues of the Virgin, Christ, and gleaming crosses. The Roman Church was content to let matters lie, hoping for an eventual dying off of African tradition over the years and a strengthening of Christian beliefs—which hasn't been the case.

Bahia is still the stronghold of the voodoo religion, which they prefer to call "Candomblé." Rio holds second place with its powerful "Macumba" and Recife is third with its spiritist doctrine called "Xangô." Visitors to all three places—as well as almost any small town across the nation—can witness a voodoo ceremony. All it takes is an arrangement with someone who knows the right time and place, and the patience and good manners to sit through the ceremony once you get there.

Rites on the Beach

There is no stranger or more pagan sight in all Latin America than that which takes place on the sands of Copacabana Beach each New Year's Eve. Travelers who have seen things all over the world still stare at this with fascination and disbelief. For under the warm, tropical sky with the tall modern apartment buildings for a background, literally thousands of voodoo worshippers meet to pay homage to Iemanjá, the goddess of the sea.

The end of the old year is a time for thanksgiving and the beginning of a new year is the time to ask for the things that will make you happy for the next twelve months. From all over the city stream the faithful, determined to start the new year off right. They are of all ages, both sexes, and all colors and economic brackets. Armed with fresh flowers, candles, and cachaça (sugar cane alcohol), they invade the beach around ten P.M. and get ready for the stroke of midnight. Some draw mystic signs in the sand. Others lay out a white tablecloth loaded with the gifts that a proud, beautiful woman would like to receive. There are combs, mirrors, lipsticks, hair ribbons, perfumes, and wines. Around this offering they set a chain of lit candles and chant and sing over it. Some of them bring bouquets of flowers with notes asking for special favors tucked in among the blossoms. Even whole spiritist temples show up in full force, with their white costumes, drummers, and altars. They rope off a section of the beach, light candles, and begin to dance. Others bring a live chicken or goat that will be sacrificed to the goddess.

By 11:20 P.M. the six-kilometer-long beach is a mass of white-dressed bodies and flickering candles. From a distance it looks as if it has been invaded by millions of fireflies. Amid the worshippers, the curious and the tourist may freely wander, if he is careful not to step on an offering or to offend the goddess in any way.

At exactly midnight, fireworks, sirens, and bells can be heard from all parts of Copacabana, Ipanema, and Leblon beaches. Now the festivity reaches its maximum. Shrieking, sobbing, and singing, the mass of humanity rushes into the water carrying the flowers and gifts for the goddess. Others stay patiently on the shore waiting for the third wave after the stroke of midnight to come up and claim their offering. Be it hypnotic suggestion or whatever, the waves suddenly seem to grow in size and come slapping onto the sand with a new fury. Once the water has carried the gift into the sea, the giver relaxes and goes home, for this means that the goddess was satisfied with what he gave and has promised to grant his wishes. If the ocean should throw the offerings back, this is considered an ill omen.

Many are the aristocratic white Carioca women who decline to attend the festivities but, nevertheless, excuse themselves to place bare feet in water on the stroke of midnight!

Legends and Folklore

In a country like Brazil that is composed of so many different ethnic groups, whose history is filled with pirates, African slaves, Indians, gold and rubber fever, and strange primitive religions, there is bound to be a rich supply of legends and folklore. The tales of ghosts, witches, special cures, and magic words stretch from the cattle country of the south to the reptile and piranha country of the Amazon.

Most popular is a little fellow named Saci-Pereré. He is a small black who wears a red nightcap and hops around on one leg. He is typically Brazilian in his sense of humor, his ability to get himself into and out of trouble, and his habit of playing jokes on unsuspecting stuffed shirts. Normally found in the forest, he has come with modern times to the city as well and stirs up problems while continuing to smoke his long-stemmed pipe. He can make food burn in the pots, frighten cattle, and startle lonely travelers on dark roads. Sometimes he makes himself seen, but most of the time he is invisible. Brazilian children, in order to escape the blame of a bad deed, tell their parents that "Saci did it."

If you go treasure hunting in Brazil and your soul is not clean, the only thing you'll find for your efforts will be lumps of coal. And pregnant women should be careful of an Amazonian demon called Caruara who shoots arrows into their backs and makes them suffer until the baby is born.

There's another more dangerous creature roaming the Amazon forests called the Capelobo. It has the body of a human but is covered with long, silken hair. In place of a face it has an anteater's head, and when it comes across a man wandering in the jungle it grabs him, crushes him with an embrace, and sucks the victim's brains out. The whites in the area say it is the spirit of an Indian. The Indians claim it is the spirit of a white.

November 2nd is a religious day, consecrated by the Catholic Church, corresponding to Memorial Day. A devout Brazilian would not hunt or fish on this day but would visit the cemetery, buy flowers, light candles, and pray that all the spirits that are set free just for that day won't harm him. He must also stay out of places where a man was killed or where someone died, for the first place the spirit returns is to the scene of his death. Should it have been a murder the spirit will strike down the first living person he sees there to avenge himself. Needless to say the cemeteries in the backlands (as well as in the cities) are crowded on that day.

The Figa

The one folklore item that every visitor notices almost immediately upon arrival in Brazil is the *figa*. It is a hand, usually the left hand, with the thumb sticking up between the first and second fingers that have formed a fist. It is probably one of the oldest amulets against the evil eye in the Western Hemisphere. It symbolizes fertility, passion, and good luck, wards off envy and jealousy, and keeps wicked spirits at bay. They are made of almost anything from wood or plastic to turtle shell and even gold, silver, and precious stones. They also come in sizes so small that they can be hidden behind a gold cross on a necklace or as big as a real human fist. Because it does so much good, you can't just go out and buy one for yourself. Someone has to buy it and give it to you as a present. Many tourists buy them for their traveling companions, and the companion turns around and buys one for the first purchaser. If you have no one to buy one for you and you want to wear one, go ahead. It won't bring you bad luck, but it won't bring you good luck either. Another important thing: if you lose your figa, do your utmost to find it; because while it's not on your person all the bad luck that it has warded off will come crashing down on you.

The Brazilians are great holiday lovers. They use any excuse to take off a day from work, close the banks, stop the wheels of industry, and just stay home doing nothing. They take full advantage of every religious holiday and celebrate all the civic ones as well, both state and federal. All in all they have 10 days set aside as official holidays. (Americans working in the Embassy or Consulates get another nine because they celebrate their country's holidays as well!) Christmas is celebrated in large family gatherings, where dining room tables overflow with holiday delicacies. Homes are decorated with nativity scenes, Christmas trees, and gifts are given out on Christmas Eve.

Good Friday is celebrated all over Brazil with masses and candle-lit parades through the streets. Usually the most prized figure of Christ is taken out and put in the center of a procession, draped in black. While a chorus of the faithful (in some interior towns it is the entire population) follow behind chanting funeral dirges, the image is carried up one street and down the other and later returned to the church. When Easter morning dawns, it is just like any other old Sunday. There are no special celebrations, no Easter finery, but families do gather for luncheon.

Dia de São João

One of the most popular days of the year is June 23rd, the feast day of São João (St. John). Everywhere his birthday is celebrated, both in the cities and the interior towns. He is considered one of the nicest saints in the heavenly collection and enjoys good music and a good drink just like his earthly believers do. Because he sleeps all day, the Brazilians make huge bonfires at night and send up fireworks to explode in the sky. This will wake him up and he will come down (in spirit) and join in the fun. Streets are roped off and people dress in backlands clothes. A mock marriage is performed, complete with drunken priests and an irate father holding a shotgun to the groom's back. Single women leave a pan of water outdoors the night before and on St. John's day will see the face of their husband-to-be reflected in it. Also if a spinster puts two needles in a pan of water the night before and wakes up to find them together on the saint's day that means marriage is not far off. Another way is to write the names of various possible husbands on pieces of paper, roll them up and drop them into a bottle filled with water. On St. John's day, the name that is unrolled will be the future husband.

The Flamboyant Fine Arts

Art in Brazil is as varied, far-flung and exotic as the country itself. There is nothing that can be labeled "Brazilian art," in just the same way that one can't say "Brazilian climate" or "Brazilian scenery." The distinct mountains, rivers, desert areas, and jungles have separated artistic endeavours into regional groupings as they have separated the people themselves. The lack of communications as well as the lack of an understanding, culture-conscious people has kept almost all art forms identified with regions rather than with the nation as a whole. Those artists (i.e., painters, sculptors, writers) who have managed to create some ripple on the national scene soon find that only a small percentage of the people are interested in what they have produced. These people tend to be the intellectuals, upper and café society of large cities, and critics of daily newspapers. An exception to this rule are the primitivists whose unpretentious, colorful, and spontaneous paintings of the common life of Brazil appeal to all tastes and have found wide acceptance outside of Brazil as well as with tourists visiting the country.

It's difficult to say who is the "best" Brazilian painter today. A number of artists have risen to the top fast, been declared "King" and then suddenly died. Perhaps the man most revered by the nation, and whose canvases now sell for small fortunes, was Candido Portinari. He was the first one to paint his way to international fame. Coming from a small coffee plantation in the interior of São Paulo, he experimented with Brazilian themes and colors and was never really satisfied with the results of his labors. Once he sent for 60 pounds of earth from different areas and mixed the black, purple, reddish, and yellow dirt with his paints. Because of this, his whites were more brilliant and his shadows had more depth, which served perfectly to portray the humble people he captured on his canvases. Being the first man to paint backlands scenes in addition to the glamour that the art world attached to his just being Brazilian, soon made Portinari world famous. He did such an expert job on the murals for the Brazilian Pavilion at the 1939 New York World's Fair that American art critics insisted that he send an exhibition to the United States of his other works. It toured 200 cities and encouraged the University of Chicago to publish a book on him. In 1962 Portinari died, the victim of slow lead poisoning from the very canvases he made live. The entire nation went into mourning. His old house in Brodosquy, where he was born, is now a national museum of his works.

Ranking slightly behind Portinari in terms of fame and international acceptance is the late Emilio di Cavalcanti. A born Bohemian, he came from a family of poets and generals, yet caroused in the underworld of Rio with prostitutes and professional thieves. He painted only what he felt like—usually seductive mulatto women—and scorned upper society. After he and a group of friends startled the Brazilian art world in 1922 with an exhibit of French impressionists and cubists he went to Paris and drank with Picasso, Ernst, and Chirico. On his bright canvases, everything he lived through is applied. In vivid tones of green, yellow and red, surrounded by thick black outlines, he painted full-blown black women or a smirking cat with all-knowing eyes.

Clay Into Art

Regional art is varied, interesting, and unfortunately breakable. The best things being done are the ceramic jugs, dishes, plates, statuettes, and nativity scenes from Bahia northward. Most of the village markets are full of earthenware products, made in the region for use right at home. People adapt themselves to their locale, and in areas where there was good rich clay, it was quickly molded into kitchen utensils. While not so elaborately painted as the Mexican ware nor with a tradition so far back as Peruvian pottery, Brazilian ceramics can definitely stand on their own merit. In the north most items are molded into pleasing shapes, be they animal, human or just spheres or cubes, and fired to a bright red color. Then they are hand painted with white floral and abstract designs.

Music

Brazil is one of the world's most musical countries, and talent flourishes in the tropical climate as exuberantly as the exotic creepers that grow two inches a day. Brazil is well known for having invented the samba and bossa nova, but just take a look at the list of "serious" musicians Brazil has also given the world in this century: composers Heitor Villa-Lobos, Claudio Santoro, Camargo Guarnieri, and Marlos Nobre; pianists Guiomar Novaes, Ophelia de Nascimento, Jacques Klein, Roberto Szidon, Joao Carlos Martins, and Nelson Freire; singers Bidu Sayao, Maura Moreira, Maria d'Apparecida, João Gibin, and Maria Lucia Godoy; guitarists Eduardo and Sergio Abreu; conductors Eleazar de Carvalho and Isaac Karabtschevsky; early music specialist Roberto de Regina and ballerina Marcia Haydée, to mention only a few.

The four musical centers of Brazil are Rio, São Paulo, Salvador, and Curitiba. Salvador has the best music school, where many rising young composers have learned their trade from a German-influenced faculty; Curitiba presents an annual music festival that puts anything similar in the rest of South America to shame, while both Rio and São Paulo offer a musical season that can match that of many a European capital in quality.

Rio's musical life, like the city itself, is essentially cosmopolitan, with fine musical performances. You never know whom you might discover for yourself at Rio's Teatro Municipal or Sala Cecilia Meireles (a rare example nowadays of a cinema's being converted into a concert hall). One advantage is that you can usually get a ticket if you show up half an hour before the concert, unless a major international star is appearing, in which case book a few days in advance.

There is also the popular music of Brazil which, in the form of bossa nova and samba, has reached out and embraced the entire world with its happy, vibrant rhythms. Brazilians are equally in love with their music and every city has dozens of bars and restaurants where drums and guitars blend into the hypnotic sounds of MPB (Brazilian popular music). For tourists wishing to buy records, there are plenty from which to choose. For pleasant bossa nova, try Vinicius de Moraes and Toquinho or Tom Jobim or João Gilberto. New names are Chico Buarque de Holanda, Milton Nascimento, and for something a bit more exotic, Ney Matagrosso. Top ballad singer is Roberto Carlos. Among female singers, Gal Costa currently is the reigning queen of Brazilian music. Other fine singers are Maria Bethania and Elis Regina. Record stores can be found along virtually any commercial district and in all shopping centers. If you see a record you like, ask to hear it first. Records, unfortunately, are also expensive in Brazil, running up to $10 for a popular LP. But nowhere else will you find the variety or quality of this exciting music.

Architecture

Brazilian architecture, though it has not fulfilled the bright promise of the thirties, has much to offer both the architectural student and the amateur photographer. The most striking modern building in Rio, the Palace of Culture, completed in 1945, is now protected as a national monument. When started, it was one of the most revolutionary buildings anywhere in the world, being one of the first to be built on *pilotis*— huge concrete pillars that leave almost all the ground level of the site free for patios, plants, and parking areas.

Le Corbusier, a long-time friend of Brazil, was largely responsible for the design, ably assisted by the brilliant Brazilian Lucio Costa, the man who planned Brasilia and the Barra de Tijuca suburb of Rio. Take a stroll among the pillars and gardens of the Ministry for a glimpse of what 20th-century city planning could be like if visionaries like Le Corbusier and Costa had their way. The block it occupies is an oasis of civilized urban delight in one of the world's most overcrowded and underplanned cities. (Students of population explosion may like to study the average Copacabana residential street, where the cars park on the sidewalks and the children play ball in the street, and draw their own conclusions.)

Equally delightful is a stroll around the Rio Museum of Modern Art, designed by the late Affonso Reidy, whose exuberant use of concrete is matched by his structural daring; the whole floor of the Museum's main wing is one single slab without divisions or central supports, and all around are the splendid gardens laid out by Roberto Burle Marx, one of the outstanding landscape gardeners of our time. A disastrous fire swept this building in 1978, but it is being restored. Its artistic holdings, however, can never be replaced and it will take years to find and acquire new ones.

From the air, São Paulo looks as if a child had flung all his bricks onto the floor at once, but from closer up you can see that some sort of order is at last being introduced into its chaotic sprawl.

For architects, though, Brasilia is the real thing. Despite its many problems, it is here to stay and is a truly great place to visit, wander around, and photograph. The air is fresh and unpolluted, the traffic

well organized by Brazilian standards, and many of its buildings, like
the new Foreign Ministry, are outstanding.

Contemporary Scene

The "hippie" generation of Rio and Sao Paulo offers an interesting
and colorful counterpoint for tourists. A hippie art fair is held on
Sunday in Rio at Ipanema's Praça General Osório, and in São Paulo
at Praça da República. Local paintings, sculptures, wood carvings,
leather goods, textiles, jewelry, etc. can often be purchased at bargain
prices.

Even more eye-catching are the young surfers on Ipanema beach and
around the Castelinho, where the smallest bikinis imaginable are worn
by virtually every Carioca girl. They are called "tangas" (from the
Indian word for loincloth) and in 1974 were launched in the English-
speaking world as "the string." In 1980, a "topless" movement also
began.

FUN-LOVING BRAZIL

Beaches, Carnival, and Food

Visitors to this country are always surprised to see how important the beach is to the Brazilians. Not just for those who live in the coastal cities, but even for those who live deep in the interior. Copacabana Beach or the fashionable "Arpoador" section of Ipanema Beach are focal points of life in Rio. From São Paulo, people go down the mountains to Santos to the beach. Gauchos in Porto Alegre fill the beaches during the summer months and the newcomers to Brasilia built their own beach.

Copacabana Beach has no private cabanas, no rest rooms, no place to change clothes. You either arrive in your suit at the beach or else you peel off your clothes right there with your bathing suit on underneath. There is no color line drawn, the rich lie on the none-too-clean sand with the poor, as fruit and soft drink sellers walk over them equally. As one upper-crust American tourist once put it: "It is probably the most democratic beach in the world."

Brazilians begin their beach life early. It is not at all unusual to see tiny babies in wicker baskets soaking up the sun alongside their bikini-clad mothers. When they get old enough to walk they are usually accompanied by a maid who hovers over them and many times gets her aproned uniform soaked when she has to dash into the water to pull them out. Once they are able to leave their maids they go to the beach with their friends. The boys learn to play soccer and to surf, while the girls have fashion shows with their dolls. Later on, these same children will do their homework on the beach, listen to rock music on the beach, meet a "steady" on the beach, show off their engagement rings on the beach, and when the cycle is completed bring their newly born babies to the beach.

Almost anything goes on there. Early in the morning you can see old men still trying to keep young by a sunrise dip or jogging. Muscle boys cavort there. Crooks steal there and politicians even used to campaign there.

Many business deals are closed there too. Often a weary executive won't want to go to all the trouble of putting on a white shirt and tie and will tell a client to meet him at the beach. The client also shows up in a pair of trunks rather than a dark suit and brings his briefcase. In spite of the sand, the fleas, and the noise of the shouting people, they manage to get their business done.

There are also many things to buy on the beach. A short list would include Coca-Cola, beer, ripe coconuts, skewered bits of filet mignon, salted peanuts, air-filled crackers, fresh oranges, candy-coated grapes, pineapple slices, bright-colored kites, melting ice cream, sunglasses, beach umbrellas, and ladies' bathing caps. The salesmen wander among the bathers and call attention to their wares by blowing on whistles, shouting, singing, beating a small drum or whirling a metal rachet that clatters loudly. Keep your eye on your belongings. There may be fast-working kids around, ready to snatch the unguarded purse or camera.

Another annoyance that Brazilians take for granted is the volleyball games that seem to spring up just as you have gotten comfortable and drowsy on the sand. From out of nowhere will appear eight to a dozen young men, their arms loaded down with poles, nets, rope and a leather ball. They plant the stakes, string up the net and mark off their boundaries in a matter of minutes. Many times the unsuspecting beachgoer, when he opens his eyes, will find himself in the middle of the playing field and must make a hasty retreat before the ball starts bouncing. Even those at the boundary lines aren't safe, for more often than not the ball comes sailing out into the crowd, hitting first an umbrella, then a stomach and finally a reposing face. Brazilians, with a disinclination for trouble, just pick up their towels and move elsewhere; it is the foreigners who get furious and threaten to take on both sides of the team at once. There have been laws passed that say a volleyball game cannot be played in certain sections of Copacabana Beach or started before 2 P.M., but they are frequently ignored.

At night the beach takes on a different character. Midnight swimming and fishing is allowed. And far out over the quiet sands, into the pitch blackness of the sea, the lights of a luxury ocean vessel can be seen flickering. When the weather turns sour and the beaches' undertow becomes dangerous, red flags of warning are posted to warn the foolhardy.

Carnival ! ! !

Then there is Carnival: that fast-moving, mad, unbelievable, music-filled, sleepless time when the entire nation rockets off into orbit and doesn't come back to earth for four days and five nights.

The official season is actually the Saturday night before and the days leading up to Ash Wednesday, but in practice the action starts Friday at 11 P.M. when the first "bailes" (balls) begin. Usually this period falls in February but can also come in March; however preparations are going on months before.

The visitor to Rio will start hearing the strains of Carnival in late December. At first it's nothing more than the gentle throb of drums from the hillside shanty towns, mingled with the ordinary sounds of the city at work. At night the drums get louder and voices are added, chanting a fast, spirited refrain. Soon the visitor notices little dark children parading through the streets, beating on old tamborines, tin cans, or the hoods of parked automobiles. Their naked feet dance in the dust of the streets and the sands of the beach. In front of the hotels they go through the motions of a fast Samba looking not only for tips and praise but also for a good time. Then, as the actual season draws closer, their parents and older brothers and sisters will parade through Copacabana in a cacophony of drums, whistles, triangles, and a weird, yelping instrument called the *cuica*. They will actually block the entire avenue, causing traffic to come to a halt while people hang out of their apartment windows and encourage them. The police do nothing to set the flow of cars in motion again, for usually they have left their posts and are dancing right in the midst of the revelers.

Stores that normally sell pens, books, and ink blotters suddenly deck their windows with coils of serpentine streamers and bags of confetti. Fabric shops, their wares spilling out onto the sidewalks, are crowded with men and women buying bright-colored silks and cottons. Other shops sell laces, stiff crinolines, masks, gold and silver chains, and decorated hats. Seamstresses double their prices and sew into the dawn, and all through the city runs an electrifying current of excitement. It affects not only the young but the oldsters as well, not only the Brazilians but the visitors.

Samba Schools Get Ready

This is a good time for the tourist to arrange for a visit to a Samba school, for they are at the peak of their practice sessions and admit anyone who is willing to pay a small admission and sit on a hard bench. The school usually belongs to a certain favela slum, and most of the dancers, nearly all blacks and mulattoes, live right there. They rehearse after work far into the night or on Saturdays and Sundays. Each Samba school also has a theme. And the rules of the Carnival commission insist that the theme be Brazilian.

Because they live in poverty throughout the year, they want to "act rich" during the throbbing night of glory; they pick a theme from the days of Brazilian colonial rule so that they can dress in fancy laces and expensive satins, wear powdered curled wigs and billowing hoop skirts. Their theme chosen, they then choose a specially written Samba to represent it and work out a complete dance routine to its rhythm. A Samba school can have as many as 3,000 people in it, each with his own job to do in the over-all pageant. Each school has a *bateria* or marching band of percussion instruments and drums, some of which number up to 300 men.

Such an organization costs money—in any country—and the members show great ingenuity in scraping up the needed funds. Costumes alone can cost as much as $1,500 apiece, which is a lot of money to anyone, especially for a man who earns but $80 a month. The top group of Samba schools parading Sunday night through Monday morning provides the greatest show of the entire Carnival. Because of traffic problems and subway construction, and most important the need for more bleacher space, the location has changed several times. In 1984, the Rio state government built a modernistic, concrete stadium to serve as permanent home to the samba school parade with top-quality facilities including a special section for foreign tourists that drew raves for being clean, orderly and comfortable, permitting the foreign visitors to enjoy at ease what is truly an incomparable event, easily the highlight of Carnival. Tickets for this section are sold only to foreign tourists through tour operators and travel agents, and in 1984 were going for $100. It is well worth the price.

The parades start around 8 P.M. (though scheduled for 6) and end at 10 or 11 the following morning, sometimes even later! Bleacher tickets are sold, at cheaper prices, for the other Carnival nights as well, to parades of "blocos," "frevos" and "great associations." If you don't get tickets, the *Daily Post* will tell you where the "secondary" Samba schools fighting to win a place in next year's top 12 will parade. You can watch these for nothing, and they are just as authentic.

The schools have their one night of glory as they vie with one another for the top prize offered by the Carnival commission. To win that top prize is just as important for them—and they practice just as hard—as the pennant is for any U.S. baseball team.

Days of Delirium

The city goes insane the weekend before Ash Wednesday. Samba is everywhere. Down from the hills stream the poor of Rio, gaudily bedecked in satins and tinsel, their faces powdered or smeared with paint. Out of swank apartment houses come the rich in their costumes costing many hundreds of dollars, laughing and embracing everyone they meet. Entire streets are blocked off from traffic, and Samba bands play 24 hours a day for anyone who wants to dance. And everybody does.

The Carnival Samba has no rigid routine of steps that one must follow. The feet move fast, the body shakes from the hips up and the arms are thrown overhead in complete abandon. The music penetrates to the very bones of the Brazilians, and they give themselves to it much as a canoe gives itself to a river's rapids. The tourist seeing this for the first time is aghast; but as his foot starts beating out the music, he discovers himself trying some of the steps he sees around him, and then he is carried by the crowd into the very midst of the laughing, sweating bodies. By this time all reserve is gone, and only hours later, when he has collapsed onto the moonlit beach, does he realize how far away from home he has really come. The next day, now bitten by the bug, he goes completely native.

Carnival is for everyone. The largely black poor have their street dancing and their parties in wooden-walled, tin-roofed shacks. The middle class give blow-outs in their apartments or visit a friend who has a home in the suburbs with a backyard to expand in. The rich have their parties at their sumptuous homes in the surrounding hills or go to one or all of the fancy dress balls.

These nearly all-white balls give the visitor a true and intimate picture of upper-class, movie-star-struck Brazilians at play. Crowded, hot, reeking with perfume and whisky, they are one never-ending confusion of noise, music, and bare flesh. Tickets should be purchased in advance from hotels or tourist agencies rather than taking a chance of buying them at the door. For those who don't wish to go to the expense of a fancy costume, black tie (frequently overlooked) is the rule. Business suits and ordinary dresses are not permitted at the better balls. Either you enjoy yourself in a loose costume or you swelter in European formality. Guests of honor are usually U.S. or European stars. Many costumes competing for prizes and notoriety are extravagant versions of legendary or imaginary fairy-tale "royalty" and represent investments of tens of thousands of dollars.

Carnival's Lavish Balls

One of the most exclusive Carnival balls is the "Hawaiian Night" at the Rio Yacht Club. It is held one week earlier beside the swimming pool under the tall palms—and the pool is where most of the sweating bodies end the night's festivities around dawn. Tickets here cost about $30 for members; for guests, prices are $20 for ladies and $40 for men.

Last year saw an infusion of new balls as Rio's top showmen competed with each other to turn out the biggest and most lavish carnival ball. The mammoth Canecão nightclub was again home to a series of four top balls. Individual tickets cost about $30—or for a mere $3,000 you can get a box for 20 persons. In 1984, a table for four cost $100.

The best of the new balls were held at Rio's spectacular new club, the Scala, which can handle nearly as many revelers as the Canecão, with its 6,000-person capacity.

Other leading balls last year included those of the Flamengo Club on Thursday, the Sugar Loaf Friday, the Hotel Nacional Monday, and the Monte Libano Tuesday. But every night there are dozens of less expensive balls at other clubs—all open to the public and equally crowded and frenzied.

When the dawn of Ash Wednesday finally comes to put an end to the revelry for another year, Rio looks as if it has been attacked by Roman hordes. Sleeping bodies lie everywhere. Drunks sit on curbstones holding their heads. Arabs wander dazedly down the center of the avenue accompanied by exhausted clowns, dishevelled Pierrettes, and stumbling African slaves. And while an army of street cleaners start sweeping up the tons of debris, somewhere a never-say-die Samba band can still be heard playing.

Some advice to the inexperienced attending Carnival balls and processions: Leave your inhibitions at home or at the hotel. Dress lightly. Be sure your shoes or slippers are comfortable. Leave papers (except Passport) and your "14 karat hardware" in the safe! Take along only as much money as you intend to spend and your credit card.

Food and Drink

In a few other South American countries the tourist may sample one or two plates in a restaurant and say that he has tasted the "national dishes." But just as Brazil is different from the rest of the continent in so many other ways, so is it different when it comes to food. It is good food and in most restaurants it is usually appetizing. What it is, though, is completely strange in comparison to what North Americans or Europeans are used to eating. Tourists who are finicky eaters probably won't like Brazilian food. But those who are ready to face anything that offers the challenge of a new gastronomical experience will have a field day here.

A word of history must be inserted if you are really to appreciate the local food. Like the plum pudding and roast beef of England, Brazil's food is also tied up in tradition and happenstance. The food of Bahia is as different from the food of Rio de Janeiro as the food of Rio Grande do Sul from that of the Amazon region. All of it has a reason. Most of it is simply delicious.

Bahian cookery to many people seems to be lots of little things clinging to one another in a rather oily sauce. In the early slave days the Africans were treated none too well as far as food was concerned. Their capturers had told their new masters that the African tribesmen knew nothing of steaks and chops and would eat almost anything. The master usually saved the scraps from the table or leftovers from the previous day to give to his slaves. Some slaves were allowed to fish, and others had permission to look for shrimp and clams. Consequently the black woman had to take advantage of every little scrap of food she could get her hands on. She remembered her cooking-pot training in Africa, put the bits together, added the milk of coconuts or the oil from the dendé palm, and fed her family. Over the years these catch-as-catch-can meals took on a regular form, recipes were worked out and names given. Today it is called Bahian food.

Some of the delicacies that are served nowhere else but in Brazil (and no place better than right in Bahia itself) are:

Vatapá, pieces of shrimp and fish, mixed with palm oil and coconut milk, pieces of bread, and served over white rice.

Sarapatel, with the liver and hearts of either a pig or a sheep; the Bahia women mix fresh blood of either animal, add tomatoes, peppers and onions and cook it all together.

Caruru, takes lots of fresh shrimp, bright green okra bulbs, onions, and red peppers to make it, and lots of courage to eat it.

In Rio Grande do Sul the *churrasco* is the big dish. It is pieces of beef skewered on to a metal sword and roasted outdoors over hot coals. This is served by sticking the sword point into the table and each diner cutting off a hunk with a sharp knife. There is a tomato and onion sauce to go over it if you wish. The gauchos of the interior will barbecue an entire steer this way. There is also a delicious dish called *galleto al primo canto,* which is a two-month-old rooster that has crowed for the first time. Cut into pieces, it is placed on a spit, basted with white wine and oil, and then served crispy and brown. Washed down with a bottle of red wine, this satisfies any diner's appetite.

Near the mouth of the Amazon a favorite dish is *pato no tucupi,* which is pieces of duck in a rich sauce that's loaded with a wild green herb that tingles in your stomach hours after eating. There's also a thick yellow soup called *tacaca,* laced with dried shrimp and garlic, served on street corners. Once your nose gets used to the strange smell, you'll enjoy this filling and nourishing bowl.

In the northeast, where refrigeration or even ice isn't found very often, leather-clad cowboys have been eating dried meat with beans or some green vegetable for generations. After killing the steer, the meat is heavily salted and hung over fence posts or on sticks out of the dogs' reach to dry in the sun. When the woman wants to make a meal, she lets the meat soak in water overnight and the next day it's ready for frying or boiling.

In Rio de Janeiro the favorite dish is *feijoada,* and no visitor to the city should go away without trying it, except in the hottest days of summer, when it is not normally served. It is thick stew made from black beans and garnished with such delicacies as chunks of beef, pork, sausages, chops, and sometimes pigs' ears and tails. This is put over white rice and garnished with a bright green boiled leaf called *couve* and slices of oranges. Originally a dish of the poor folk and those of the interior, *feijoada* has come into its own in Rio. The best day to eat it is Saturday because after one sitting you'll have no energy to do anything but sleep for the rest of the afternoon.

The Brazilians are not vegetable eaters. They live mainly on rice; potatoes are rarely served. They like olives (especially the big black ones from Portugal), radishes, and carrots for appetizers. Beans are another staple, as are squash, cabbage, and a strange, pale green thing called *xuxu.* Eggplant is served fried, broiled, baked, stuffed, and in cracker crumbs called *milanesa.* Unlike the rest of South America very little corn or corn products are used. Hearts of palm are inexpensive and used in salads, soups, and baked dishes. In the States a can of them is so dear that they are considered a delicacy. In Brazil *palmitos* are like any other vegetable, even though they have to chop down an entire palm tree to get at the white veined heart in the center.

On the drinking side of the ledger, let it go on record that the Brazilians like to. They manufacture almost every well-known alcoholic beverage and with the same ease drink all of them freely. Their beer is probably the best in the entire Western Hemisphere. Experienced world travelers and beer drinkers give first prize to Brazil all the time. There is no other nation that makes such highly alcoholic and highly palatable beer as Brazil. Draft beer, called *chopp,* is universally popular.

There is also a powerful clear liquid made from fermented cane alcohol called *cachaça*. It smells foul, and to the inexperienced palate it tastes foul. But mixed with the juice of a lemon or the orangish fruit, *maracujá*, it becomes a *batida*, used before meals to pep up the appetite and after meals to settle the stomach. A Rio *feijoada* should never be eaten without a *batida* beforehand. Because of its cheap price, *cachaça* is the whisky of the poor. When you see bartenders in the little coffee shops shake up a plain bottle and pour out a couple of fingers of some strange-looking liquid—and see the customer gulp it down and then spit on the floor—you'll know you are seeing *cachaça* being consumed. Because it is manufactured by over 2,000 independent little distilleries across the nation there is no uniform taste, and there are no special brands to recommend. The only sure way to find the one you like best is just to keep sampling. But be careful of your liver, your wind-pipe, and your stomach lining.

In the south of the country some of the best wines in Latin America are produced. While travelers rave about the wines of Chile and Argentina, few of them know about the wines of Brazil. There are all kinds, from mild rosé to deep burgundies to dry white wines that when chilled rival anything being bottled in the Hemisphere. And that includes the wines of the United States. They even make champagne in Brazil. A lucrative but little-known sidelight to the Brazilian wine industry is its exporting. Every year huge, unmarked wooden barrels of local wine are shipped to France and Italy where they are mixed with the best grapes of those lands. Rebottled and relabeled, the wines are exported all over the world as "genuine" French or Italian products. Brazilians know this and drink the homemade stuff with pleasure, letting the unsuspecting tourist pay three times as much for a bottle of the same wine dressed up in a French label.

PRACTICAL INFORMATION FOR BRAZIL

Because Brazil is a continent within a continent and is much too big to write about as a single entity, at least as far as practical information is concerned, we are not presenting all the facts and figures on Brazil in one *Practical Information* section. Most of the details you're looking for, such as listings of hotels and restaurants, will be found within separate subchapters for the major regions of the country. A few paragraphs on items of general interest are in order, however, and we'll lead off with them:

FACTS AND FIGURES. *Physical Features.* A giant country larger than the continental United States, Brazil includes the great Amazon basin at the equator, a vast subtropical central section, and the temperate mountain regions of the southern coast. It occupies over half of South America's land mass.

Climate. Rio is always pleasant with days and nights very much like summer in the midwestern U.S.A. São Paulo also has a mild climate. The vast Amazon rain forest and tropical section are hot and humid all year.

Population. 120,000,000. Rio 8,000,000. São Paulo 10,000,000.

Language. Portuguese (not, repeat *not,* Spanish!).

Archeological Attractions. Lagoa Santa, Sambaquis, Marajo.

SEASONAL EVENTS. *Carnival in Rio* is world's gayest. Costume balls, big club balls, gala street dances, lavish costumes, fireworks, and fun. Rio de Janeiro. Begins Friday night before Ash Wednesday, lasts four days. *Carnival in Salvador* (Bahia) rivals that of Rio and is less crowded with foreign tourists.

Other world-famous religious festivals in Bahia are those of the *Patron Lord of the Sailors* (Jan. 1–4) and *Our Savior of Bomfin,* which combines Catholic and African rites (Jan. 17–20).

Holy Week Celebrations throughout Brazil. Particularly notable in Ouro Preto, Minas Gerais State. March or April.

Biennial Art Exposition, São Paulo, brings together renowned international artists in Brazil's most important exposition. Odd-numbered years in September.

Grand Premio Brasil Horse Race. Rio de Janeiro. Aug.

Commemoration of Independence Day, Sept. 7. *Feira de Providencia* (3-day charity event), Rio, Sept. *International Piano Competition,* Sept. *Rio Circuit,* Santos-Rio Yacht Races, Oct-Nov. *Proclamation of Republic Day,* Nov. 15.

Macumba Ceremonies. Afro-Brazilian rites, exotic and unusual, often on sightseeing tours. All year. In Bahia they are called *Candomblé.*

HOW TO GET THERE. By air. From the U.S. to Rio and São Paulo there are smooth jet flights on six airlines: from New York, Miami, Los Angeles on *Avianca, Argentine Airlines, Pan American,* and *Varig;* from Dallas-Houston on *Pan American.* From Miami to Brasilia on *Pan American* and *Varig,* to Manaus and Belem on *Varig.*

From London to Rio and São Paulo: *British-Caledonian* (some flights stop in Recife), *Varig* (some stop in Bahia), and main European and South American airlines from other principal capitals on the Continent.

From South Africa: *South African Airways* and *Varig* have flights from Johannesburg and/or Cape Town.

From the Pacific, Australia, and New Zealand: *Qantas* through Tahiti to Acapulco and Mexico City, changing for South American destinations, or *LAN-Chile* from Fiji, Tahiti, or Easter Island through Santiago.

From the Orient: *Varig* or *Japan Air Lines* from Tokyo, or other airlines, changing for South America on the U.S. West Coast.

By sea. Passenger accommodation on freighters from the U.S. is offered by *Columbus Lines, Torm Lines Holland-America, Ivaran Lines, Moore-McCormack Lines,* one-way or round-trip cruises. *Lloyd Brasileiro, Brodin Line, Delta Line Cruises* call at Rio, Santos, and Paranagua. *Sunline Cruises* at: Rio, Vitoria, Salvador, and Recife. From Europe by: *Lamport and Holt Line Ltd.*

TEPSA buses connect with several countries and operate within Brazil.

TRAVEL DOCUMENTS. As of late 1978, Brazil began requiring tourist visas of all citizens of countries demanding visas of Brazilians. This includes the United States, but not Canada and Great Britain. To obtain one, at no charge, you must present your passport and one photo plus airline ticket or a letter from your travel agent at a Brazilian consulate in the region where you live. If you go in person it should take about two hours. Visitors do not need a smallpox certificate. Regulations change often, so check entry requirements just before departure.

CUSTOMS. Travelers from abroad may bring duty free to Brazil the following items: clothing; jewelry for personal use; personal books and magazines; articles for personal consumption, i.e., eatables, cosmetics, and domestic professional objects or souvenirs, excluding domestic electric appliances, to a total value of $100. Cigarettes and liquor for passengers arriving in Rio may be purchased at the duty-free shop while waiting for bags, before going through customs at the airport.

WHAT TO TAKE. Although not too many years ago men were required to wear coats and ties to take a streetcar or go to a movie in Rio, today informality is the keynote—fortunately, considering summer (December-March) temperatures occasionally reach a humid 40°C. (104°F.). Now one seldom sees a tie at Copacabana restaurants or nightclubs. Ironically, jackets and ties are needed in the daytime at some of the better downtown luncheon clubs where bankers and businessmen gather. A hat may be needed only on the beach or golf course.

Slacks and pantsuits are acceptable for ladies, and hats and gloves are never worn—not even to weddings. Shorts are rarely worn, but female beachwear is about the skimpiest you'll ever see. You will surely see the Brazilian "tanga" (the "string" originated in Rio). In wintertime (summer in the Northern hemisphere), there can be chilly days (in the lower 50s, F.), so a sweater or wrap is a necessity. As a general rule, dress in Rio as you would in Miami, but with seasons reversed.

In São Paulo, weather is cooler and dress is more formal. Sportswear is enough for a Brasilia sight-seeing trip of a day or two; if you stay longer or have diplomatic contacts, more formal clothing will be needed. But a man will rarely need a dinner jacket in Brazil—unless he wants to swelter at one of Rio's gala Carnival balls rather than wear a costume (a common, simple one consists of bright shirt, Hawaiian leis, captain's cap and shorts).

During winter (May to October), you will need warmer clothing in the South, whereas in Bahia, the North and Northeast, the climate is humid and tropical year-round. Sun glasses and a light raincoat or umbrella are good items to have along when visiting anyplace in Brazil. In some areas outside Rio and São Paulo, an insect repellent may be needed; "Off," "Autan," or "Super Repelex" sprays are all available locally.

CURRENCY. Inflation is still a problem, and the *cruzeiro* still is subject to fluctuations. Inflation used to work to the advantage of the tourist because it kept prices comparatively low by hard currency standards. Do not change too much of your hard currency at one time. The old *cruzeiro* was replaced by the *cruzeiro novo* in 1968, 1,000 of the former equaling *one* of the latter, though some old-timers still talk about "1,000 cruzeiros" when they mean "one cruzeiro." Foreign currency or Travelers Checks are changeable into cruzeiros at hotels, banks, and exchange shops marked "Câmbio." If you have an introduction to a "câmbio" shop, you may be taken into a back room and given the higher "parallel" (black) market rate. Many stores also take personal dollar checks at this rate. Official exchange rate at press time was approximately Cr$1,400–US$1, while the black-market rate was Cr$1,470–US$1.

TIPPING. At restaurants and nightclubs, when 10 or 15% is added to your bill, you usually add 5% more. In hotels, 10% is usually added to your bill as a service charge. However, you will find that porters, doormen, elevator operators, and chambermaids are accustomed to getting a small tip for their services, either at the time the service is performed, or when you check out. If a taxi driver helps with your luggage, a small tip of about 10% of the fare is expected. At the barber's or beauty parlor, a 10–20% tip is expected. Cinema and theater ushers do not expect tips. In general, tip washroom attendants, shoeshine boys, etc., about what you would tip at home. At airports, tip the last porter who puts your bags into the cab; they work on a "pool" system and all earnings go into a general kitty.

HOW TO GET AROUND. By air. There are four major commercial airlines *(Varig, Cruzeiro do Sul, Vasp,* and *Trans-Brasil),* which together fly over 3 billion passenger-miles a year. The airline companies take good care of their planes, have top flight mechanics, and first-class pilots, and crews who refuse to let a plane go up unless they are absolutely certain it is ready to fly. The service is nothing short of excellent and full course meals are the rule rather than the exception, followed always by a cup of the ever-present black coffee. Alcoholic beverages, however, are no longer served on domestic flights.

Their plane scheduling is fairly imaginative and is designed to meet both passenger needs and the competition. One of the most successful and most used of all the airline services is the popular "air bridge" between Rio and São Paulo. In 1959, the four air companies pooled their forces to set up a system to keep both passengers and planes constantly flowing between the two major cities. The traveler does not even need to buy a ticket or make a reservation in advance, he just shows up at the airport and gets aboard the next plane. During the rush hours there is a plane leaving every 30 minutes, and every hour on the hour up to 10:30 P.M. The air bridge has been a success since its inauguration, carrying more than 2,000 passengers a day. If you want to leave on a specific flight, make a reservation. The cost is about $40 one way.

So successful was the Rio-São Paulo bridge that in 1962 air bridges were inaugurated to Belo Horizonte and Brasilia. The flights are not so frequent, because the distances are greater, but the regular commuters who use it seem more than satisfied. Planes tend to fill up on weekends; book well in advance if you plan to fly anywhere on a Friday, especially to or from Manaus or Brasilia.

Even though the airlines make attempts to keep on schedule, exceptions can occur. Many people have spent nights in strange towns because their connecting flight left without them. In the interior, the wise passenger is at the airport at least half an hour before takeoff time, for many pilots anxious to get back to the cities spend only the bare minimum of time in the local fields.

By rail. Train service between Rio and São Paulo is comfortable. An overnight trip for two in private cabin costs about $22; there is a dining car, and your porter can even provide "room service." There is excellent regional service from São Paulo on the Paulista and Sorocabana lines and 24-hour service from São Paulo to Brasilia, and also from Rio to Belo Horizonte. Most service to other areas of Brazil is inferior to air travel. Travelers save both time and often considerable trouble by avoiding long rail journeys in Brazil.

By bus. With its growing highway network, Brazil can offer comfortable bus travel over most of the country, and even internationally. Unless you're in a tour group, however, you can't book straight through from, say, Montevideo to Rio. Instead, you buy a ticket from one principal city to the next—Montevideo to

Porto Alegre, then Florianópolis, Curitiba, São Paulo and Rio. But you'll need the hotel room and rest between each long leg anyway. On most-traveled routes, service is frequent and inexpensive. Between São Paulo and Rio (seven hours), for example, there is a bus every half hour all day long costing about $7, and night "sleeper" at $12.

WHAT WILL IT COST? In Brazil this comes down to a question of how comfortably you want to travel. It is possible to travel on an extremely low budget but this is only for those who want to rough it. First class travel is expensive due to the high costs of quality hotels and air travel. In between, unfortunately, there is very little to choose from as moderate hotels and restaurants outside of Rio de Janeiro and São Paulo tend to be of poor quality. In all areas of the country, though, you will find that top restaurants are significantly cheaper than their counterparts in the U.S. or Europe and for the most part the food is excellent. Bus travel is a fine alternative to the expensive air flights. Brazil has top quality regional bus companies with modern air-conditioned vehicles that crisscross the country on regular and on-time schedules. One warning though: keep aware of the distances. Brazil is larger than the continental United States. As for lodgings, if you are after a minimum of comfort and security you are better off avoiding anything not labeled first class.

Typical Expenses for Two

Room (first class, breakfast included)	$ 40
Lunch at inexpensive restaurant, incl. tip	$ 7
Dinner at moderate restaurant, incl. tip	$ 15
Sightseeing tour	$ 10
Evening drink	$ 2
	$ 74

THE LANGUAGE. A prime rule to remember for anyone visiting Brazil is that the national language is Portuguese and not Spanish. There is nothing that annoys a Brazilian more than to have a visitor make that mistake. They are extremely proud of their language and the literary and musical heritage that goes with it. It is not that Brazilians disdain the dominant language of their neighbors, it is just that they feel insulted that *norte americanos* are so ignorant of South American cultural differences.

Actually, Portuguese-speaking people readily understand Spanish, but Portuguese is not readily understood by Spanish-speaking people. Portuguese is a nasal and guttural language of Latin origin, heavily influenced by Arabic, and, like Spanish, has an extensive Arabic vocabulary.

Yet there exists a difference between the Portuguese of Brazil and the Portuguese of Portugal. It is a little like the differences between the English of the United States and the English of Great Britain.

But don't get discouraged right away. If you can speak Spanish you can get around in Brazil. You won't understand them but they will usually understand you. If you take the trouble to learn just a few Portuguese words to sprinkle in your conversation you will win your listeners over almost immediately. The statement that you read in many tourist folders, saying that everyone speaks English in Brazil and therefore you'll have no trouble, is pure fiction. Therefore a few minutes spent in brushing up on some Portuguese will pay big dividends.

Besides, it's a beautiful tongue, spoken by more people around the world than French.

The accents and other curlicues you find above or below the letters of many words actually make pronunciation easier. For instance the word for coffee is café. When you see this acute accent at the end of a word you accent that syllable and it becomes ca-FAY. That strange word for saint as in Saint Paul (São Paulo) is pronounced SOWN (as in "down"). When there is a *cedilla* under a "c" in a word like braço (meaning arm), you pronounce it like a soft "s" and it comes out bras-so. If the "c" doesn't have the *cedilla* you usually pronounce it hard like a "k," as in buscar (bus-kar). Also "q" in a word is pronounced like "k" and most "x's" have a shhh sound. Because of this you will run into many English words that have been twisted around by the Brazilians. The gasoline company Texaco comes out tay-SHA-ko. Other words borrowed from English that you may (or may not) recognize in Brazil are *lanche* (a quick lunch), *time* (a soccer team but pronounced tea-me), *football* (pronounced foot-tea-ball) and *cinema* (here it is sea-NAY-mah).

See Vocabularies at the end of the book for some useful words and phrases.

 SPORTS. *Soccer,* called "futebol" and pronounced fut-tea-ball, is as much a national heritage for Brazilians as wine is for the Frenchman and snow for the Eskimo.

The soccer the Brazilians play is a fast game, almost like a ballet, that begins when little boys take their first ball to the beach or into the middle of a vacant lot. You can see them bouncing the ball off their knees, giving a backward kick with a bare foot and sending it to a buddy who butts it with his head. In Brazil as well as the rest of the international playing world, only the goalkeeper is allowed to touch the ball with his hands.

If you like sports at all and are in Rio on a Sunday when two of the major Rio teams are playing each other, you should visit the huge Maracana soccer stadium. The four main Rio teams are Flamengo (Brazil's most popular team), Vasco (chiefly identified with the Portuguese colony in Rio), Fluminense (the high society team), and Botafogo (the least definable in personality). If you try to go, talk it all over ahead of time with someone at the hotel who can tell you how to get there, when to go, how to buy tickets, and so forth. Unlike baseball, U.S. or Canadian football, rugby, cricket, and the like, soccer is easy to understand even if you've never seen it before. But even if the game doesn't turn you on, the stadium is impressive, and the crowd itself is half the spectacle. Soccer crowds in the British Isles and northern Europe can be extremely surly; and in the Mediterranean and other Latin American countries (as well as most of Brazil), they can be dangerously passionate. But the Maracana crowd is unswervingly good natured, and the stadium is exceptionally safely constructed, so don't worry about stories you may have read about soccer disasters. For one of the big games between two of the major local teams, large numbers of the rooters bring huge homemade flags, featuring the team's colors in a variety of designs made up themselves, and they wave these flags when their team comes on the field or scores a goal. Another feature you are not likely to encounter at the World Series or the Super Bowl is that drums start beating in various parts of the stadium well before the game and maintain their tom-tom rhythm without a break right through to the end. All in all, the crowd is one of the most colorful and exciting spectacles in sport. If you go, try to buy the highest-priced reserved seats. If you want to be with "the people" in the "arquibancada," be advised that it is plain concrete bleachers, so be sure to buy foam rubber pads to sit on before you go into the stadium.

Capoeira and More. Another sport that is purely Brazilian, not to be found anywhere else in the world, is the Capoeira. It is a fight, a dance, and a bit of judo all rolled into one. In the early slave days there were constant fights between the blacks, and when the owner caught them at it he had both sides punished. The blacks considered this unfair and developed a smoke screen of music and song to cover up the actual fighting. When a pre-arranged battle was to be fought, the natives brought their "berimbau," a bow-shaped piece of wood with a metal wire running from one end to the other, where there was a painted gourd. Using an old copper coin the player would shake the bow, and while the seeds in the gourd rattled he would strike the taut string. The effect is like background music for a Hollywood monster film. There would be a chorus chanting a fast song and the two fighters would get in the center and slug it out, primarily with their feet. Whenever the master came into view the fighters would do an elaborate pantomime of slashing the air with their fists and kicking out so as to miss their opponent. Over the years this was refined into a sport that is practiced in Bahia and Recife today. Both cities have their champions and there are many *capoeira* houses where the tourist can go to watch these dances. In Salvador (Bahia), they may be seen on any Saturday morning around the Modelo Market. The idea is to swing and kick to the mood of the music but without either man touching the other. The back-bending all the way to the floor, the agile foot movements to stay clear of a gleaming knife, and the strange African music make it a sport that needs great dexterity to play but is fascinating to watch.

There is also a *mountain climbing* society in Rio as well as a *spelunking* society that are happy to welcome experienced tourists on their weekend outings. If your meat is climbing up the pitted side of Sugar Loaf or delving deep into a grotto in Minas Gerais, any tourist agency can make the necessary introductions.

Rio has recently become a *hang-glider's* paradise. Taking off from a mountain peak, the colorful kites circle sometimes for hours before landing at the end of Gavea beach, beyond the Inter-Continental and Nacional hotels.

Water-skiing and *underwater diving* are also practiced by sportsmen in clubs all along the coastline. Brazilians are a very club-conscious people, and almost everyone you meet will be a member of something and will be able to take you to his particular club and introduce you around. They love to show off visitors and most clubs can only be entered with a member. Once you are inside you'll find the friendship and generosity for which the Brazilians are famous.

Horse racing is also immensely popular. The Grande Premio Brasil held first Sunday in August highlights the racing season. *Golf* and *tennis* are available in all leading cities. There are two golf clubs in Rio, where you can play by invitation only. *Yachting* is extremely popular in Rio. And there is *surfing* on the beaches.

For those who like to *fish,* Brazil can be a surprising wonderland. Many tourists try for some marlin fishing off the coast of Rio, and others go to the magnificent Foz do Iguaçu to try their hand at dorado. In the Amazon River there are monstrous fish called Pirarucú that reach up to 280 pounds each. The nation's rivers and streams are filled with a variety of game fish. No license is needed and no limit set.

If you have a taste for bigger game, you're out of luck today, because the government recently outlawed the hunting of big-spotted jaguars, wild boar, fleet-footed jungle deer, moss-backed turtles, and dozens of other animals which were once considered fair play. But a camera safari into the Mato Grosso or Amazon jungles can still be an adventure. Most travel agencies can tailor a program to suit you.

RIO DE JANEIRO

Cidade Maravilhosa

Rio de Janeiro has been cited by many experienced travelers as the most beautiful city in the world, with a natural setting surpassing even Hong Kong and San Francisco. It has everything. There are long stretches of soft sandy beaches and lines of tall palm trees. There are mountains covered with deep green untouched jungle and birds, butterflies, and flowers in profusion. There are great fleecy clouds floating lazily over the ocean, which pushes in cool breezes and an occasional rain storm. There are warm days and cool nights and starlit skies and huge full moons.

What nature has given, the Brazilians have embellished with their own personalities. Along the black and white mosaic promenades walk some of the loveliest women in Latin America. The men, well built and tanned from hours on the beach, add their note of masculine grace. Colonial buildings vie for space with modern air-conditioned skyscrapers. There is music everywhere, from the honking of taxi and automobile horns, to the soft sing-song voices of the blacks from the *favela* hillside shacks. There is an excitement in the air, curiously mixed with the tropical languor of let's-do-it-tomorrow.

But Rio is more than just a beautiful setting. It is a city that boasts its own ballet company, magnificent opera house, and dozens of cultural centers. It is a mecca for artists and the enterprising businessman.

It also calls the international drifter, the expatriate, and the fortune hunter. And in very recent years, with the construction of many luxurious, new hotels, it is South America's tourist capital as well.

São Sebastião do Rio de Janeiro is 15 miles long and varies from 2 to 10 miles wide. Nestling between the tall blue-green mountains and the deep blue-green sea, the city offers a breathtaking sight, by day or night. During the day the sun plays on the sand and palm trees, and the white buildings with their red tile roofs serve more to ornament its natural beauty than to detract from it. At night the city wears strings of glowing lights, giving the impression that strands of diamonds have been lazily entwined around the buildings and the mountains by some benevolent giant.

The most obvious attraction for the visitor is the beach. Just the name Copacabana inspires romantic images, and rare is the tourist who doesn't arrive in Rio and immediately unpack his bathing suit. Rio has 16 different beaches, scattered from the international airport in the north to the other side of the mountains in the south. Most popular is the one at Copacabana. There are no bathing fees for any of the beaches. Oceanfront hotels provide cabanas, towels and soap. Waves at the beach come in hard and fast most of the time, so don't expect to do much swimming, just a lot of splashing. Also be prepared to confront lots of people on the weekends and keep an eye on anything valuable.

Assuming you've had enough sun and that you want to see some of the city itself, here is a good plan:

Take a taxi or a bus marked Urca (a 15-minute ride from Copacabana, but hold onto your purse or wallet) to the cable-car station at the foot of Sugar Loaf. It is advisable to get there early for there are usually many people who want to make the visit—especially during school holidays, January to March and June to August. Once you are borne upward you'll have the pleasant sensation of space all around you and a vivid panoramic display of Rio and her natural beauties below. The car makes a half-way stop on Urca mountain, where there is a pleasant restaurant and a small amphitheater that occasionally has shows or popular concerts. Starting in 1978, this peak also became the site for a spectacular pre-Carnival ball. You can either linger here or transfer to the next car to go to the top, where you have the city at your feet and can identify the other points of interest that you must see before you leave. It is best to visit Sugar Loaf *before* you visit the Corcovado Christ statue, or you will remember Sugar Loaf only as an anticlimax. A nice family way to sightsee is on a "Bateau Mouche," which cruises Guanabara Bay. You get a different view of Sugar Loaf and a glimpse of Jurubaiba Island.

There are taxis waiting at the platform where you will return and ask the driver to take you—slowly—to the Gloria Church (Igreja da Gloria). On the way down Avenida Pasteur you will pass the high-walled Yacht Club (admittance strictly to members only but you can peer over the chain-barred entrance-way) and the pink-painted colonial buildings belonging to the Brazilian University. Coming out in front of the new tunnel of Pasmado, you'll go along Botafogo beach and after going around a bend you'll be in the Flamengo beach district where a major face-lifting has taken place. Here they have built the largest

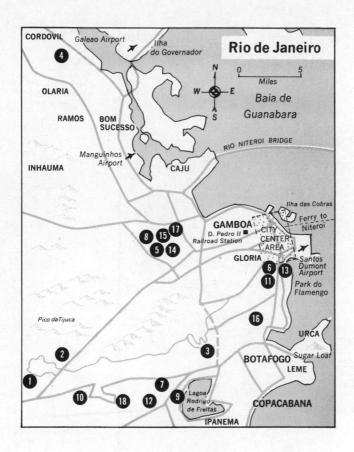

Rio de Janeiro

CORDOVIL · Galeao Airport · Ilha do Governador

OLARIA

RAMOS · BOM SUCESSO

Manguinhos Airport

INHAUMA · CAJU

Baia de Guanabara

RIO NITEROI BRIDGE

Ilha das Cobras · Ferry to Niteroi

GAMBOA · CITY CENTER AREA
D. Pedro II Railroad Station

GLORIA · Santos Dumont Airport

Park do Flamengo

Pico daTijuca

URCA · Sugar Loaf

BOTAFOGO · LEME

Lagoa Rodrigo de Freitas

COPACABANA

IPANEMA

Points of Interest

1) Alto da Boa Vista
2) Cascatinha
3) Corcovado
4) Church of Penha
5) Estadio do Maracana
6) Gloria Church
7) Botanical Garden
8) Zoological Garden
9) Joquey Club

10) Mesa do Imperador
11) Museum of the Republic
12) Museu do Cidade
13) Museum of Modern Art
14) Museu do Indio
15) National Museum
16) Palacio Guanabara
17) Quinta da Boa Vista
18) Vista Chinesa

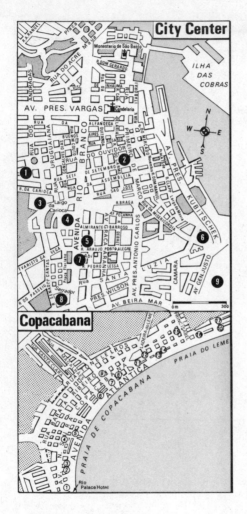

City Center

Copacabana

Points of Interest

1) Church of São Francisco
2) Cathedral
3) Convento de São Antonio
4) Municipal Theater
5) Museu de Belas Artes
6) Historical Museum
7) Biblioteca Nacional
8) Palacio Monroe
9) Santos Dumont Airport

Hotels

1) Riviera
2) Regente
3) Miramar
4) Savoy
5) Othon Palace
6) California
7) Olinda
8) Trocadero
9) Castro Alves
10) Continental Palace
11) Excelsior
12) Copacabana Palace
13) Lancaster
14) Ouro Verde
15) Plaza Copacabana
16) Meridien
17) Leme Palace

public park in Latin America on land reclaimed from the sea. Every ounce of earth was carted in by truck. The planting was done by master landscape gardener Roberto Burle Marx. Thanks to the Flamengo *aterro*, as it is called, you can now drive to and from Copacabana in a matter of minutes. The park is a delightful place for a late afternoon stroll. You can also explore it by tractor-drawn minitrain, and if you have small children with you, there is a fine playground, and a special space for model aircraft enthusiasts. Be sure to use the overpasses and underpasses to cross the main freeways; accidents are frequent on the *aterro* and just about everywhere else in Rio.

Favorite Church of the Imperial Family

The driver will turn off and climb a steep hill that is lined on both sides with houses harking back to the days of the Portuguese colonials and will let you off in front of the big wooden doors of the Gloria Church. Built in the 18th century, it was the favorite spot of the Imperial Family and contains many fine examples of art from both the Old and the New Worlds. The site of the church was once the hut of a hermit who, in 1671, with the help of two mysterious youths (angels), sculptured a beautiful statue of Our Lady of Glory. Seventeen years later, when the image had been accredited with miraculous powers, the hermit returned to Portugal, taking the image with him. But the ship sank into the ocean, and the statue washed ashore at Lagos, Portugal. In 1924 a copy was enshrined in its place in the Gloria Church. The Brazilians still want the original image returned. On August 15, the church is lighted up like a baroque birthday cake, and silhouetted against the dark sky and the palm trees it is one of the loveliest sights in Brazil.

Walk down the street you drove up and then along the Praça (park) Paris. Laid out by a French architect a good many years ago, it reminds many Parisians of home, with its marble statues, trimmed hedges, reflection pools, and water fountains. On the opposite side of the avenue you'll see the contrast in the ultramodern Monument to the Brazilian Dead of World War II. Brazil sent troops to fight in Italy and suffered heavy losses. Much of this area has recently been torn apart to make way for Rio's long overdue and highly controversial Metro. Despite a series of financial crises and floods, the final stations have now been completed, linking the downtown area with the edges of the north and south zones of the city.

Museums and Historic Sites

Have lunch in the area, perhaps in the rooftop restaurant of Mesbla, Rio's largest department store, right across the street from the Passeio Público, oldest public park in the city. Filled with tall shade trees, small lagoons and rustic bridges, it is a pleasant place to get in out of the sun. It also has its share of tramps and beggars and a large collection of alley cats.

Leave the park by the upper right-hand sidewalk and keep walking right over to Rio's main commercial heartline, Avenida Rio Branco.

Walk up Rio Branco Avenue and you will pass the National Library (worth a visit) and the Museum of Fine Arts (also worthwhile) on your right and the Municipal Theater on your left. If this theater looks familiar, it is because is an exact one-quarter scale copy of the Opera House in Paris. If you are here at lunchtime, drop in for an unforgettable meal at the Café do Teatro, downstairs in the opera building. Good cuisine mixes here with an incredible setting, reminiscent of a Cecil B. De Mille Biblical epic, complete with Egyptian pharaohs set in brightly colored mosaics. Two blocks farther down the Avenue on the left rises the 34-floor, air-conditioned, glass-paneled Edificio Avenida Central, Rio's first skyscraper.

If you walk through the arcades to the other side of this modern building and look across the street, you'll see the old Convent of Santo Antonio. Built between 1608 and 1619, it contains, aside from priceless colonial art objects, the tombs of Leopoldina, the first Empress of Brazil, and the Infante Dom Pedro de Bourbon. Beside the convent is the richest little church in Rio, the São Francisco da Penitência. Its interior is completely hand sculpted and covered in gold foil. It also has a remarkable altar and sacristy. The climb up the hill is worth it.

The former hill of Santo Antonio was removed, its earth used to form the Flamengo *aterro*. The site was transformed to a double avenue bordered by new buildings. These include the cone-shaped Metropolitan Cathedral—still unfinished—the aluminum-block headquarters building of Petrobrás (the government oil monopoly) and, across the avenue, the high-rise headquarters of the National Housing Bank. Behind this modern setting you will see the colonial arches built in 1723 to carry water down to the city.

Go back down Rio Branco, until you come to Rua Ouvidor. There are no automobiles permitted on this street and it buzzes like an overactive beehive. Don't be dismayed or taken in by the infected beggars or mothers with sickly children you see asking for alms in this area. Most of the sores are painted on and most of the children are rented out for the day. Of course there are some who are genuine, but the majority are not. The city has tried to clear the downtown streets of these pathetic cases, but they keep coming in from the interior faster than they can be sent out.

Five blocks from Ouvidor is the overly wide Avenida Presidente Vargas. Be careful crossing the street here, because Brazilian drivers are notorious for disobeying traffic lights. To your right is the back entrance of the squat, attractive Church of Candelaria. The front of the building once overlooked the waters of Guanabara Bay, but the view is now obstructed by buildings and elevated drives. The inside is vast, dark and relaxing after a walk in the sun.

Continuing downward on Rio Branco you will come to Praça Mauá and the beginning of miles of docks that have made the city such an important world trading center. Praça Mauá is peopled by all sorts, with heavy emphasis on foreign sailors. Now take a bus marked Copacabana and go back to your hotel and have a tall, cool drink. You've earned it today.

The Mother of Palm Trees

Another full day could start with an hour at the beach, a shower, and then a taxi ride to the Botanical Garden on Rua Jardim Botânico. Don't try to take a bus, or you'll get lost. The garden is one of the best in the world, say noted horticulturalists, and is carefully kept up. Covering an area of 567,000 square meters, there are over 135,000 plants and trees. There are 900 varieties of palm tree alone. Founded in 1808 by the prince regent Dom João, there stood near the entrance gate the famous *palma mater* transported from the West Indies and planted by the monarch. There is also a strikingly beautiful avenue of palms that is 740 meters long and contains 134 royal palms. Also be sure and see the bronze fountain dating back to 1820 and the mammoth Victoria Regia water lilies that measure 21 feet around. There is also a peaceful jungle atmosphere, lake and waterfall, a small greenhouse filled with flesh-eating Venus flytrap plants, and some rare trees from Indonesia, whose huge roots spread atop the ground like writhing cobras.

From there take another taxi to the Laranjeiras Palace, the residence of the President when he is in Rio. You probably won't be allowed past the guard, but the drive through the Guinle Park and past the luxurious private apartment houses that line it is worthwhile. Now still in your cab, take a quick look at Catete Palace on Rua Catete, Praia do Flamengo. Built of granite and rose-colored marble in 1862 by a wealthy coffee baron, it was purchased 32 years later by the federal government and used as the Foreign Office. Dictator Getulio Vargas, when he returned to power as duly elected President of the Republic, insisted on living rather than at the other palace where he had been tossed out. It was also at Catete that he killed himself in 1954. The palace, with its magnificent gardens, was converted into the Museum of the Republic when Brasilia was inaugurated.

Now you can have lunch downtown (perhaps at Le Tour revolving restaurant, which opened in 1977) and hop into another cab for a better look at the old aqueduct, over which little trolley cars cross on their way to the lovely residential area of Santa Tereza. You saw these arches from the other side yesterday, remember? Now, however, you will be standing in the newly renovated Lapa district. The parks and fountains inaugurated in 1975 are on a site that was once the center of Rio's bohemian nightlife and samba. Many of the surrounding buildings have escaped the march of progress; indeed, some have been protected as examples of Rio's architectural history. Look for the Automóvel Club, the Sala Cecilia Meireles music conservatory and the large white Convent of Santa Tereza, built in 1970 and now the home of a Carmelita order of nuns who have no contact with the outside world.

Now for a visit to one of the most charming corners of the city, the Largo do Boticário just off Rua Cosme Velho. Everyone will tell you it dates from colonial times, whereas in fact only one of its houses dates from earlier than the 1920s. Anyway, it is a pleasantly shady spot, one of its attractions being an English-owned antique store.

Now comes the treat, Corcovado. You can do one of two things. Continue in your taxi to the top of the mountain, which will give you a slow, unwinding, breathtaking view of all angles of the city, or go to Rua Cosme Velho 513 and take a tiny cogwheel train to the top. Trains leave every half hour and the ride is almost straight up through dense jungle. When you arrive you'll have to climb a number of stairs to get to the base of the statue. The statue is impressive up close and the view from the top simply indescribable. The statue, inaugurated in 1931, has a height of 120 feet and weighs 700 tons. The head alone weighs 30 tons; each arm weighs 30 tons and each hand 8 tons. The statue was designed by Frenchman Paul Landowski and paid for by contributions of the people of Rio.

The best time to visit the statue is in the late afternoon about one hour before sunset. The effect of the reddening sun against the buildings and the sea far below is stunning. Then wait patiently and one by one the lights of the town will start to come on, like fireflies awakening for the evening. Within half an hour the city will be dressed in sparkling diamonds and silhouetted against the dark shapes of Sugar Loaf and the blackening waters of the bay and ocean. Warning: the last trolley leaves at 7 P.M. and is always crowded. If you go up in a cab have him wait.

The third day's outing will give you time on the beach (be careful you don't get burned), then go to the Indian Museum, which opens at 11:30 every morning except Saturday and Sunday. Located in an old home at Rua das Palmeiras 55, it is a storehouse of Indian art work (feathers, ceramics, stone, and weaving), as well as a growing archive of films and recordings made of the indigenous people's way of life and music. Some of the guides are themselves full-blooded Indians, and there is always a possibility that you will see some visiting tribesman around the grounds.

Almost across the street is the Maracana soccer stadium, the biggest in the world. Built in 1950 for the World Championship Games, it can hold—and has held—as many as 200,000 people at one time. While the designers looked after the comfort of the spectators, they also considered the players, and there is a wide moat around the field to protect the poor athletes should they lose.

Within walking distance is the Quinta da Boa Vista Museum, a beautiful old pink and white building that used to be the Imperial Family's Rio palace, in a gemlike setting of landscaped parks, lakes and marble statues. The museum opens from noon to 4:00 P.M. every day except Monday and is filled with traces of Brazil's past, both historical and archeological. There are Indian funeral urns, reconstructed fossils, a fine collection of Amazon reptiles and insects, and one of the best collections of birds in the world. It is probably one of the best museums of its kind in Latin America.

Right beside the museum is the zoo. Open all day every day, it keeps most of its more important animals in unwalled natural settings. Be sure and note the colorful Amazon parrots as you go in (their squawking for attention will force you to notice them) and the hungry leer on the face of the jungle jaguar. Also don't miss the shaded jungle pool with the colorful red cranes and little white scavenger birds. The monkeys have an island of their own, as do the Amazon boa constrictors and the alligators. Take your camera along, and for a tip you can even get the guards to wrestle with a constrictor while you snap away. Somehow, it just doesn't feel like a zoo.

Now here you need another cab for a long ride out to the north zone to visit the Church of Penha just as the sun goes down. Perched high atop a mountain, and with 365 steps, it is a favorite place for repentant pilgrims to crawl on their knees. The inside is hung with crutches and silver charms representing parts of the body that were cured, thanks to the intervention of Our Lady of Penha. The view from the top is superb.

The Emperor's Picnic Table

On the fourth day, call another cab (fortunately they're not expensive in Rio) and make the voyage to the Tijuca Forest. On leaving Copacabana, you will pass through the neighborhoods of Ipanema and Leblon, climb higher to go around the Two Brothers mountain on Avenida Niemeyer, and go past the Gavea Golf Club and several new restaurants selling coconuts and fresh oysters at Sao Conrado. Have your driver stop at the Emperor's Table (Mesa do Imperador). Here is a mammoth concrete picnic table where the Emperor used to bring his royal court to dine. It has an unequaled view of the south zone of the city. Nearby is the Chinese View (Vista Chinesa), which also is impressive.

The forest itself was once part of a private estate belonging to the Baron de Taunay and is studded with exotic trees, thick jungle vines, and a delightful waterfall. Also be sure and see the tiny little Mayrink Chapel with an altar painting by Brazil's famed Candido Portinari. This chapel is very popular with Brazilians and, in spite of its cramped quarters, has seen many society marriages.

Other Views of Rio

If Brazil is a country of contrasts in its geography and its peoples, it's also a contrast in its economic levels. Though it has a large and rapidly growing middle class it is still a country of the very rich and the very poor.

At first glance the favela slum sections in Rio, nestling into the mountainsides in the south zone, seem to be pastel-painted, enchanted summer cottages with magnificent views of the ocean. Then on closer inspection you can see that there is no enchantment, just bleak despair and resignation.

The favelas themselves began back in the year 1897 when soldiers of the new Republic, having put down a revolt of the Monarchists in the state of Bahia, suddenly found themselves without a cause, without money and without a place to live. They had been encamped on a hill they named Favela because of the abundance of a wildflower with the same name. So when they arrived in Rio, they called their first settlement of shacks "favela" too. The soldiers assumed they had the right to any land that wasn't being used, and once their shacks were built there were few politicians willing to incur their wrath by driving them off.

The years from 1920 to 1940 saw the favelas grow alarmingly. Brazil was entering into world trade and needed more coffee, cocoa, and fruit to export. Workers deserted the cities for the farms, cultivating the land and shipping the produce to the coast. Then prices began to fall and with the fall the workers returned to the cities, along with other peasants who had lost their jobs. They took up residence in the favelas. When Dictator Getulio Vargas set the wheels of industry into motion, he made great promises to the Brazilian people. More flocked to the cities to work. From the north, truckloads of "nordestinos" converged upon Rio, anxious for the easy money but unlettered and untrained in mechanics. They found little work and much misery.

As Rio expanded her metropolitan area, cut through roads and erected new buildings, the poor were routed and tenements demolished. Land was plentiful in the far suburbs, but the working groups (maids, bus drivers, washerwomen) could not afford to live away from the centers of activity. Transportation was sporadic and expensive. The free schools and clinics were in town, not in the outlying suburbs. They were not truly free to move to the fresh air of the distant suburbs, for necessity bound them to the favelas.

The racial mixture of the favelas has been classified by the Census Department as 28 percent white, 36 percent black, 35 percent mulatto, and 1 percent oriental. These statistics point up the difference between Latin American, especially Brazilian, concepts of racial identity and the U.S. attitude. In the latter all mulattoes, regardless of black-white proportions or percentages of ancestry, are classified as "black." In Brazil, on the other hand, anyone *café au lait* or lighter in color is classified as "white," and anyone darker with a discernible trace of European ancestry is mulatto. Brazilian "blacks" are apparently of purely African descent.

Although some major favela eyesores have been entirely removed in the last few years, many still remain and nearly a fourth of Rio's population still lives in them.

The choice sites in any favela are at the bottom near the road and water supply. Many times there will be just one pump for hundreds of people, and those living at the top have to fill empty cans with water and carry them on their heads to their homes.

As would be expected under such conditions, normal sanitation practices are almost non-existent.

Work in Rio has been slow due to the large number of people to be rehabilitated. Welfare groups have been active in building better housing and in giving free lessons in mechanics, carpentry and the manual arts. A number of the poor of Rio have been moved into individual concrete houses, financed originally through the Alliance For Progress but now under projects financed domestically. Unfortunately, while these moves have solved some problems, they have created others. Many ex-favelados now live up to 25 miles out of town, making transportation a heavy expense, and although they are being encouraged to buy their new homes on the instalment plan, many cannot afford the low monthly payments and once again face eviction.

Unfortunately, these hillside slums have become breeding grounds for crime and in recent years Rio's crime rate has soared. Tourists can be prime targets for the legions of pickpockets and purse snatchers. While we do not wish to sound an undue alarm, it is always best to be cautious. Besides the *favela* area, other favorite hangouts for thieves in Rio are the beaches, the Santa Teresa trolley, the Maracana soccer stadium, and popular tourist attractions such as Sugarloaf Mountain and Corcovado (here be careful on the train to the top). When visiting any of these spots take only the essentials, no jewelry, as little cash as possible, no large bags, and hold on to your camera at all times. When on the beach watch out for overly friendly kids hanging around your blanket. They work in groups and while one distracts you another will be off with your valuables.

Exploring Around Rio

The main attraction for visitors in Petropolis, located in the mountains just north of Rio, after the elaborate Quitandinha (built as a hotel-casino, but now a private club), is the Imperial Museum, located in an ornate old palace once the summer home of the Emperor and his family. Dom Pedro II liked the climate and fresh air of the area so much that he ordered a residence built in 1845 and sent for German emigrants to found a city around it. The Germans liked the land as well as the monarch did, and their guttural language can still be heard in the streets today. The museum, open every day but Monday from noon to 5 P.M., contains clothes, jewels, and silver- and gold-plated items that the Imperial Family used. The rooms are as they were during the occupancy, and the Brazilian Imperial Crown with pearls and 44 diamonds is quite spectacular. Because the authorities do not want the inlaid wooden floors marred, you must put on a pair of soft cotton slippers over your own shoes. There is a cathedral nearby, begun by Pedro II, where the benevolent monarch and his wife, Dona Teresa Christina, now are entombed.

Teresópolis, an hour's drive from Petropolis past wooded hillsides and lovely homes and farms, belonged at one time to an Englishman named George March. In 1855 he sold his ranch to the government who cut it into lots and encouraged immigration. The town gets its name from the Empress Teresa, the same way Petropolis took its name from Dom Pedro. The most memorable thing about Teresópolis is the string of mountains it's on, the Serra dos Orgaos, which became a national park in 1939. Here is the 1,650-meter Finger of God pointing straight to Heaven, as well as the Finger of Our Lady, the Fish Mouth, and the Priest's Nose. Tallest of them all is The Rock of the Bell, which towers 2,263 meters above sea level. Alpinists climb these mountains every weekend, and if you're interested, ask your travel agent to put you in contact with a group.

Nova Friburgo, farther east in the same mountain range, came into being by command of the Imperial Family, but years before either Petropolis or Teresópolis (in 1818 to be exact). Most of the newcomers were either German or Swiss; the man responsible for laying out the city, with its parks and beautiful homes, was the Count of Nova Friburgo. The three main squares are symphonies in marble, eucalyptus, and bamboo. Be sure and visit the park of Sao Clemente with its pools and wide shaded paths.

On the coast north of Rio, Cabo Frio has wide white sandy beaches, long enough and hard enough to drive on. It is studded with architectural relics from the colonial days, including forts, a 17th-century Franciscan convent, and an ancient cemetery. All places are open to the public and tourists can wander around undisturbed to their hearts content. If you like water-skiing or fishing, make friends with someone from Rio who has a boat, or else convince a salty old fisherman that he should rent you his. You might also visit the little fishing village of Barra de Sao Joao and watch the men working with their long woven nets. The thatched roof cottages are mixed with modern summer homes of Cariocas who have discovered it as a weekend spot. Seven miles south on the beach is the fishing village of Arraial do Cabo. Here scores of Japanese fishermen live and bring in giant whales during the cold months from June to September.

Paquetá Island is the most beautiful in all Guanabara Bay. There, without benefit of automobiles or trucks and forced to use an antiquated ferry boat to come and go, live some 6,000 Brazilians who wouldn't live anywhere else. When you visit it, you'll understand why. There is a calmness that is most inviting, after the hectic madness of Rio. There are soft sandy beaches and some interesting rock formations along the coast. Territory of the Tamóio Indians, it was later taken as a private vacation spot by the king, Dom Joao VI, who arrived in Brazil in 1808. The cannon that was fired as a salute to the monarch each time he arrived is still there near the boat docks. Here you can rent a bicycle and go all around the island.

PRACTICAL INFORMATION FOR RIO

 WHEN TO GO. Almost any time is a good time to visit Rio, for the climate is not that variable and there is something interesting going on almost all the time. The hottest months of the year are January to March when the temperature has risen to a sweltering 104 degrees in the shade. But these months are also the months with the most rain, and even though the rain's cooling effects lessen as the water evaporates, the sudden showers do give pleasant respites. The beaches are heavily populated during these months, and the sun can be unbearably hot for fair-skinned tourists after 10 A.M. The coolest months of the years are July and August, when there is occasionally a gray cast to everything and the ocean comes crashing up over the sidewalks and fills the main avenue with sand. At this time Brazilians stay away from the beaches in droves, wear heavy Italian sweaters, and complain of the cold. Visitors from more northern climates find the air comfortable and many even prefer it to the blistering heat of January.

Of course the big event in the Rio calendar is Carnival, that impossible spectacle of madness that takes place from Friday night to the morning of Ash Wednesday. Carnival can be as early as the first week in February or as late as

March. These are the hot months, remember, so come prepared to sweat while you Samba. Make reservations well in advance.

The cultural year begins in April, with stars of international magnitude drawing capacity audiences during concert seasons for performance after performance. This is also the beginning for the artists and the galleries and hardly a week goes by without an important new showing of Brazilian painting or sculpture. Movie houses show many European art films, but remember that the movies are in their original language with Portuguese subtitles.

 HOW TO GET THERE. In this modern age almost everybody is in a hurry, and most tourists choose jet planes to make their arrival into Rio. The first terminal of the new International Airport of Rio opened in 1977. It is the most modern in South America and one of the most practical in the world, with only a few steps from curbside to check-in. The drive from Governor's Island, where the airport is located, to downtown Rio doesn't take more than a good half-hour's traveling. To go by bus to the downtown Santos Dumont domestic airport costs about 70 cents. There are, luckily, two taxi services—Transcopass and Cootramo—which charge you a flat fee, depending upon destination. This is paid at a counter just as you leave customs before starting the trip. There are also radio cabs, which charge significantly more than regular cabs. If you take a regular taxi, be prepared to argue the price beforehand. If you don't settle on a price in advance, be ready to pay more and even to be insulted if you don't give in easily. This is not meant to frighten you away from coming into Rio, but only to prepare you for what can happen.

If you have taken a ship you may either dock in Rio itself, or else in the city of Santos. The Customs shed is inside the Touring Club in the heart of downtown Rio, and taxi drivers and porters there are a little more honest than at the airport. If you arrive in Santos, you will have to go through Customs, then take a bus or a taxi to São Paulo (1 hour and 15 minutes), then take another bus (6 hours) or a plane (one hour) to Rio.

 HOTELS. Construction of fine, new international hotels and the ASTA (American Society of Travel Agents) convention in Rio in October 1975 have had marked effects on the city's hotel business. Older hotels have been remodeled or redecorated, and increased competition has made for improved service in nearly all. But even with five big hotels opening more than 2,300 deluxe rooms on the beaches, choice space is still scarce during Carnival, Gran Prix week, or when large conventions are taking place. So it is wise to book well in advance.

With the exception of the top hotels, rates in dollars have fallen drastically due to inflation and the devaluation of the cruzeiro. *Deluxe:* single $75–$120, double $80–$130; *first class:* single $30–$50, double $35–$55; *moderate:* single $15–$30, double $20–$35; *inexpensive:* single $7–$15, double $10–$20. Nearly all hotels are European plan, but most serve an ample Continental breakfast at no additional cost. Rates are quoted in U.S. dollars.

VIDIGAL-SÃO CONRADO (GÁVEA)

Deluxe

Inter-Continental Rio. Praia da Gávea 222. Opened its 500 air-conditioned rooms overlooking the beach and golf course in October 1974. Among its many attractions are a rotisserie, brasserie, snack bar, one of Rio's smartest cocktail lounges, lighted tennis courts, highly original discotheque, swimming pool with underwater bar stools and convention rooms. Convenient parking. $90 single; $100 double. 399–2200.

Nacional-Rio. Av. Niemeyer 769, also on Gavea beach. First to be built in the area, this tower has 520 wedge-shaped rooms, as well as 25 luxury suites and one floor of presidential suites. Three restaurants serve Brazilian and international specialties, and the nightclub usually features a Brazilian Samba floorshow. Across from lobby is Rio's biggest hotel convention center, theater, shops, heliport. Recent decline in quality. $55 single; $70 double. 399–1000.

Rio-Sheraton. Av. Neimeyer 121. The only hotel that can claim a near-private beach, with no street to cross to bathe in the Atlantic surf; in addition, it has its own fresh-water pools and two lighted tennis courts. Rio's first luxury-class hotel, 617 rooms, three restaurants, featuring Brazilian and international cuisine, a popular nightclub for dancing plus exciting Samba shows, outdoor amphitheater, health club, tennis courts, shops. $100 single, $105 double. 274–1122.

COPACABANA

Deluxe

Meridien-Rio. Av. Atlântica 1020. A late 1975 inauguration, this one near the beginning of Copacabana; its 36 floors make it the tallest building on the beach. It counts 552 rooms, including two presidential suites, 130 more in the luxury class and 29 cabanas. Panoramic rooftop restaurant and rotisserie serving international and French cuisine, pool, bars, nightclub, sauna, shops, beauty parlor. $100 single; $110 double. 275–9922.

Rio Othon Palace. Av. Atlântica 3264. Opened in 1976, this hotel soars 30 stories above the center of famed Copacabana Beach and combines traditional Brazilian charm with the latest advances in hostelry. Largest in the beach area, it has 606 air-conditioned rooms, two presidential suites and a variety of other luxury suites. Rooftop bar and pool with panoramic view, international restaurants, bars, nightclub, banquet facilities for up to 700, shopping gallery, beauty parlor. $90 single; $95 double. 255–8812.

Rio Palace. Av. Atlântica 4240. Most luxurious of all Brazilian-owned hotels. The 416-room facility is at the end of Copacabana Beach in a multi-story shopping complex. Numerous bars, restaurants, nightclubs, meeting rooms, and auditoriums. Two pools. $115 single, $130 double. 521–3232.

First Class

California. Av. Atlântica 2616. Modern rooms, bar, restaurant. 257–1900.

Copacabana Palace. Av. Atlantica 1702. A Rio landmark, recently renovated, with 400 rooms, 2 restaurants, 24-hour service, a sidewalk cafe with view to the beach on one side and pool on the other, theater. 257–1818.

Leme Palace. A posh establishment at Av. Atlântica 656 in the Copacabana Beach area known as Leme. 194 rooms, good restaurant and sidewalk bar, cozy rooftop bar. Entirely air conditioned. *H. Stern* store. 257–8080.

Luxor. Av. Atlântica 2552. Terrace restaurant. 257–1940.

Ouro Verde. Av. Atlântica 1456. One of 8 hotels in the world that retain the "discreet charm of the small hotels," according to *Fortune* magazine, this 66-room Swiss-owned and -managed jewel enjoys international prestige. Exquisite decor, all-round comfort, and courteous service. 542–1887.

Savoy Othon. Av. Nossa Senhora de Copacabana 995. 160 rooms. Fine restaurant and bars. 257–8052.

Moderate

Acapulco. Rua Gustavo Sampaio 854. 120 modern rooms, with a view of the back side of the Merídien across the street. 275–0022.

Apa. Rua República de Peru 305. Near Copacabana beach. 255–8112.

Biarritz. Rua Aires Saldanha 54. Near Copacabana beach. 255–6552.

Canada. Av. Copacabana 667. Near Copacabana beach. 257–1864.

Castro Alves. Av. Copacabana 552. Near Copacabana beach. 257–1800.

Debret. Av. Atlântica 3564. Air conditioned, ocean view. 521–3332.

Excelsior. Av. Atlântica 1800. 220 rooms, fine restaurant and bar with ocean view. Rates include one meal in addition to Continental breakfast. 257–1950.

Lancaster. Av. Atlântica 1470. Family atmosphere. 541–1887.

Luxor Continental. Rua Gustavo Sampaio 320 (Leme). 275–5252.

Miramar. Av. Atlântica 3668. Restaurant, rooftop bar, marvelous view. Reasonable. 247–6070.

Olinda. Av. Atlântica 2230. 257–1890.

Regente. Av. Atlântica 3716. Reasonable, recently renovated. 287–4212.

Rio Copa. Av. Princesa Isabel 370. 110 air-conditioned rooms in new hotel on busy street leading to the beach. 275–6644.

Trocadero. Av. Atlântica 2064. Fine Brazilian restaurant, *Moenda*. 257–1834.

Inexpensive

Martinique. Rua Sá Ferreira 30. Near Copacabana beach. 521–4552.

Plaza Copacabana. Av. Princesa Isabel 263. Near Copacabana beach. 257–7722.

Toledo. Rua Domingos Ferreira 71. Near Copacabana beach. 257–1990.

IPANEMA

Deluxe

Caesar Park. Av. Vieira Souto 460. 242 all air-conditioned rooms with TV and refrigerator. Two excellent restaurants, bar, beauty salon, barber shop, sauna, pool. Private security guards patrol beach on foot and with binoculars from hotel roof to protect guests and other bathers from "beach rats" out to relieve them of their valuables. $90 single; $100 double. 287–3122.

First Class

Everest-Rio. Rua Prudente de Morais 1117. 22-story hotel has 176 rooms and everything to make guests comfortable. Near beaches. 287–8282.

Praia Ipanema. Av. Vieira Souto 706. Near beaches. 239–9932.

Sol Ipanema. Av. Vieira Souto 320. Restaurant, bar, beauty parlor, sun deck, and children's pool on roof. Near beaches. 227–0060.

Moderate

Arpoador Inn. Rua Francisco Otaviano 177. At the beginning of the beach. Casually elegant, with 50 air-conditioned rooms and restaurant. 247–6090.

Carlton. Rua Joao Lira 68. Quiet surroundings. 259–1932.

LEBLON

First Class

Marina Rio. Ave. Delfim Moreira 696. On the beach beyond Ipanema. Modern new hotel with 100 air-conditioned rooms, bar, restaurant. 239–8844.

Marina Palace. Ave. Delfim Moreira 630. Brand new beach hotel, Rio's newest with 165 rooms. 259–5212.

DOWNTOWN

First Class

Gloria. Praia do Russel 632. In Flamengo not far from the city's center. 730 deluxe and first-class rooms. Fine colonial-style restaurant, bars, pool, terrace with view. Convention center. Overlooking Flamengo Beach. 245–8010.

Moderate

Aeroporto. Av. Beira Mar 280. Near city airport. 262–8922.

Ambassador. Rua Senador Dantas 25. 297–7181.

Ambassador Santos Dumont. Rua Santa Luzia 651. In the Clube de Aeronáutica building downtown. 240–1222.

Center. Rua Teófilo Otoni 82, downtown. Opened late 1975. Air conditioned, with refrigerator-bar in each room. 233–0662.

Flamengo Palace. Praia do Flamengo 6. 60 rooms, opened in 1975. 205–1552.

Florida. Rua Ferreira Viana 75. 245–8160.

Grande Hotel OK. Rua Senador Dantas 24. 292–4114.

Novo Mundo. Praia do Flamengo 20. Restaurant, bar. *H. Stern* store. 225–7366.

Regina. Rua Ferreira Viana 29. 225–7280.

Sao Francisco. Rua Visconde de Inhauma 93. Air conditioned, restaurant. 233–8122.

Apartment Hotels are also available with maid service. The top residential hotels are: *Apart Hotel,* Rua Barata Ribeiro 370; 256–2633. *Rio Flat Service,* Rua Alm. Guilhem 332 (Leblon); 274–7222. *Apart Hotel Barramares,* Av. Sernambetiba 3300 (on the beach in the Barra da Tijuca); 399–5656.

Inexpensive

Argentina. Rua Cruz Lima 30. 225–7233.

Empire. Rua da Gloria 46. Fine restaurant on top floor with magnificent view of the bay. 221–3937.

Guanabara Palace. Av. Presidente Vargas 392. In banking district. Restaurant, bar. 253–8622.

Paissandu. Rua Paissandu 23. 225–7270.

 HOW TO GET AROUND. At the airport, vouchers are issued at set prices for taxis, depending on your final destination. Inside Rio, taxis are the best way to travel. Your hotel can arrange with *Avis, National,* or *Hertz* to rent a Brazilian-made Volkswagen beetle for about $27 a day plus mileage. Most require an international driver's license and credit cards. Rio taxis have meters that start at around 25 cents US. as we go to press. Between 11 P.M. and 7 A.M. the number 2 on or above the meter indicates the higher night fare. This fare is also charged for driving you up steep hills, such as to the Corcovado, although some Rio taxi drivers refuse to climb hills.

In general, tourists in Rio should avoid city buses when alternatives such as taxis or comfortable air-conditioned buses are available. In particular, the 553 bus should be avoided like the plague. The Santa Teresa Trolley should be used with extra caution due to pickpockets and purse snatchers.

You get onto a bus at the rear and leave at the front, paying the conductor as you go through the turnstile. Buses only stop if you pull the cord by the side windows. Most bus fares start around Cr$175 (10 cents US.) and it is wise to have change ready. They won't change anything over Cr$1,000, and often they have no change at all. So keep plenty of coins handy for bus fares. New air-conditioned buses, called "frescoes" (big fresh ones), go to most sections of the city, for a fare of about 40 cents US.

If you want to take a tram ride, go to the station just off *Largo de Carioca,* take the tram marked *Dois Irmãos* and enjoy, for about 10 cents US., a breezy, rattling tour of the hillside Santa Teresa suburb, where many foreigners live. At the end of the line, you can take a bus on to *Silvestre,* have a snack, and come back the same way. But watch out for jewelry and camera snatchers and pickpockets.

For intercity travel from Rio, avoid trains, except to São Paulo, Brasilia, or Belo Horizonte. By air, flights leave daily to most major cities. Some internal flights leave from the international airport, and so details should be checked carefully.

For a glimpse of the real Brazil in comfort, take an intercity bus trip. Deluxe coaches are now available on a few main routes, and bus travel in general within Brazil is fast, reliable and cheap. Book well in advance, however, and check your reservation. The main bus station, known as the *Rodoviaria,* is five minutes from Praça Mauá by taxi.

A hydrofoil goes across the bay to Niteroi (40 cents), or drive across the impressive new bridge, paying a toll of 70 cents each way. There are ferries to Paqueta and other islands. You can also take a boat tour of Guanabara Bay, with lunch included.

USEFUL ADDRESSES. *American Consulate,* Presidente Wilson 147. *British Consulate,* Praia do Flamengo 284. *Canadian Consulate,* Av. Presidente Wilson 165. *Guanabara Tourist Office,* Rua Real Grandeza 293. *Automobile Club of Brazil,* Rua do Passeio 90. *Lions Club,* Rua Senador Dantas 74. *Rotary Club,* Av. Nilo Peçanha 26, 12th floor. *American Chamber of Commerce,* Praça Pio X 15, 5th floor. *The Union Church,* Rua dos Otis 63 in Gávea, interdenominational, English-language services. *Our Lady of Mercy Chapel,* Rua Visconde de Caravelas 48 in Botafogo, is the *American Catholic Church. Anglican Church,* Rua Real Grandeza 99. *Synagogue,* Rua Tenente Possolo 8. *Latin America Daily Post,* daily English newspaper, Rua do Rezende 65. *Sightseeing excursions:* Use, Av. Rio Branco 9; Breda, Av. Rio Branco 257. *American Society and the American Club,* Av. Rio Branco 123. *Touring Club of Brazil,* Praça Mauá, downtown. *Avis,* Rua Bolivar 17-A. *American Rent-a Car,* Rua Laranjeiras 147B. *Hertz,* Praia do Flamengo 244. *National,* Av. Copacabana 291-A.

MEDICAL SERVICES Since the closing of the Strangers' Hospital in 1967, English-speaking doctors can be contacted by calling the U.S. Consulate-General at 292-7117.

WHAT TO SEE? Rio is divided into zones of north, central, and south. The city is not so big that the area can't be covered in a nonstop two-hour taxi ride if traffic is light, but there are so many things to see that one day is not nearly enough; and one week is more like it. The north zone is the poorer area, with the lower economic classes and small individual homes. Away from the breezes of the ocean it can also be sticky hot. But it does have interesting and important spots to visit like the Church of Penha; the Museu Nacional, in the former Imperial Palace, Quinta da Boa Vista (Tues.–Sun., noon–4:30);

Maracaná (world's biggest soccer stadium); the Zoo; and the Indian Museum, Rua das Palmeiras 55 (Mon.-Fri., 10 A.M.–4:30 P.M.).

The central part of the city is the commercial area, with bustling Avenida Rio Branco and the overly wide Avenida Presidente Vargas. Here are all of the banks, important department stores, and office buildings. Here also is the Museum of Modern Art, Av. Infante dom Henrique, in reconstruction following a fire, but still with a fine restaurant and cafeteria, daily film showings, and a lovely garden; the badly-in-need-of-reform Museum of Fine Arts (Belas Artes), Av. Rio Branco 199 (Tues.-Sun., noon-6 P.M.); the National History Museum, Praça Marechal Ancora (Tues.-Fri., 11 A.M.–5 P.M., Sat.-Sun., 1:45–5 P.M.); the classic Municipal Theater; all the old Congress and Supreme Court buildings from when Rio was the nation's capital; and an area with movie houses called Cinelandia. Radiating from the center is the Roman-styled aqueduct built by the colonial Portuguese, a piece of the Old World remaining intact called Largo de Boticario, and the world-famed Corcovado mountain with the mammoth Christ statue.

Other museums in this area: Museum of Geology and Mineralogy, Av. Pasteur 404, Brazilian gems and semiprecious stones; Museum of Geography, Av. Calogeras 6-B (Mon.-Fri., 11 A.M.–5:30 P.M.), landscapes, maps; Museum of Pictures and Sound, Pca. Marechal Ancora (Tues.-Sun.); Museum of the Mentally Disturbed, Hospital D. Pedro II, Engenho de Dentro, over 50,000 works of art by the mentally disturbed; Museum of Sacred Arts, Praça Nossa Senhora da Gloria, a fine collection in one of Rio's most beautiful colonial churches; Museum of the Republic, Rua do Catete 153, the former Presidential Palace (Tues.-Fri., 9 A.M.–6 P.M., weekends 2 P.M.–6 P.M.); Museum of Villa-Lobos, Rua da Imprensa 16, memorabilia of the famous composer.

The south of Rio is the more chic, more expensive, more comfortable place to live. Here are the best hotels, restaurants, and beaches. Here is Copacabana and its sister neighborhoods, Ipanema and Leblon. A little farther are Avenida Niemeyer and São Conrado beach, where most of the newest and best hotels are located. Here also is the beautiful Lagoa (lagoon) Rodrigo de Freitas, the traditional Jockey Club, the calm and well-kept Botanical Gardens, Presidents' and governors' palaces, and, rising from the bay's blue water, Sugar Loaf.

Out of town via private car or taxi you have the junglelike Tijuca forest with its Emperor's Table, Chinese View and impressive waterfall.

 ART GALLERIES. Rio is very art conscious and supports a number of very good galleries. Prices are high, but the following are a few of many considered reputable, with high quality national or foreign works:

Bonino, Rua Barata Ribeiro 578 in Copacabana, has a great selection. *Petite Galerie,* Rua Barão da Torre 220 in Ipanema, leans toward the younger generation's more inventive newcomers. Others: *Atelier,* Rua General Dionísio 63, Botafogo; *Barcinski,* Av. Ataulfo de Paiva 23, Leblon; *Bolsa de Arte,* Praça General Osório 530, Ipanema; *Domus,* Rua Joana Angélica 184, Ipanema; *Escada,* Av. General San Martin 1219, Leblon; *Europa,* Av. Atlântica 3056, Copacabana; *Grafitti,* Rua Maria Quiteria 85, Ipanema; *Irlandini,* Rua Teixeira de Melo 31, Ipanema; *Loggia,* Rua Barata Ribeiro 334-A, Copacabana; *Mini-Galery,* Rua Garcia D'Avila 58, Ipanema; *Casablanca* and *Trevo,* in the Gávea Shopping Center, Rua Marquês de São Vicente 52; *21,* Rua Forme de Amoeda 76, Ipanema; *Vernissage,* Rua Maria Quiteria 42, Ipanema; *Marie Augusta,* Rua Real Grandeza 358, Mare 32. You're apt to see other attractive shops strolling in any part of Rio.

SPORTS. *Yachting* is a major sport in Rio and there are two yacht clubs in the Botafogo area that lies halfway between Copacabana and the center of town. Most exclusive and interesting is the Rio Yacht Club. Clubs are open to members only and gate crashing is not easy.

Tennis is popular. See the manager of the Rio Country Club or the Caiçaras in Ipanema or the Paissandu Club in Leblon for special permission to play. Only hotels with courts are the Inter-Continental Sheraton and Nacional.

Surfing is popular at Copacabana Beach, Ipanema's Arpoador Beach, and at Praia dos Bandeirantes. The sea is rough and dangerous.

Golf hasn't really caught on in Brazil as yet, but the two clubs that exist for it are stunning, beautifully trimmed places in the hills of Gávea. The Gávea Golf Club has many American and English members and a number of foreign firms keep memberships for their executives. The tourist can visit the club and admire the majestic scenery without being accompanied by a club member, but to play you must be invited. The Itanhanga Golf Club is nearby.

Ocean fishing goes on year-round, and if you don't know someone who has a boat you can always rent one. There are marlin as well as other ocean gamefish awaiting either your hook and sinker or your spear. No license is needed and the fish are so big you won't have to throw any of them back.

Horse racing events are held Thursday nights and weekend afternoons at the Jockey Club. An impressive place with excellent grass and dirt tracks, it runs the best horses in the nation for your pleasure. Betting is not only permitted, but encouraged, and when you do win (with the inflation as it is) you may need a basket to carry away your money. The first Sunday in August is reserved for the Grande Premio Brazil, which draws the finest bluebloods from all over Latin America. It is also an occasion for ladies to wear elaborate hats and gowns, and for the top brass, from the President on down, to show up glittering in medals.

Soccer rules supreme in Brazil, and will remain so for years to come. The best players in the world (this is no exaggeration) are on hand to delight the visiting soccer fan. Rio's top clubs have top players and any game that has teams like Vasco, Flamengo, Botafogo, or Fluminense can be counted on for plenty of excitement.

SHOPPING. Brazil is considered a "developing country" under the GSP customs exemption plan (explained above in *Facts at Your Fingertips*), so many of the things you buy here may be able to enter the U.S. wholly duty free. Get the latest list from the U.S. Customs Service before you go.

Top gem seller is *H. Stern,* who in the last 30 years has built an international organization with branches all around the world, including New York and St. Thomas (V.I.). Their headquarters are on Rua Garcia D'Avila 113, tel. 259–7442, with branches at Galeão International Airport, downtown Santos Dumont domestic airport, the Touring Club (landing pier), Sheraton, Inter-Continental, Meridien, Othon Palace Gloria, Nacional, Leme Palace, Copacabana, Marina, and all other principal hotels. They and other leading jewelers offer a one-year refund guarantee and worldwide service. Stern's has the largest selection in town at reasonable prices, from the low-priced to the extremely expensive. They also let you see their artists at work in the lapidary and jewelry workshops of their headquarters.

Stern's also has stores in these other principal Brazilian cities: São Paulo—Praça da República 242, Hotel Brasilton, Hotel São Paulo Hilton, Shopping Center Iguatemi, Shopping Center Ibirapuera; Brasilia—Hotel Nacional; Salvador—Hotel Othon Palace, Hotel Meridien, International Airport; Manaus—

Hotel Tropical, International Airport; Foz do Iguaçú—Hotel das Cataratas, International Airport.

For over thirty years the *Amsterdam-Sauer* Company has been a pioneer in lapidary art and the leading Brazilian specialist in emeralds. The owner, Jules Roger Sauer, is a well-known gemologist who has reactivated some old mines and opened a series of new ones. His company today has its own mining, cutting, designing, and jewelry divisions, as well as shops. Their headquarters are at Rua Mexico 41, downtown. Showcases at the hotels: Leme Palace, Savoy, Ouro Verde, California, Trocadero, Olinda, Lancaster.

Roditi, whose slogan is "The fastest growing jeweler in town," has branches in New York and Geneva. His main showroom is downtown at Av. Rio Branco 39, fifteenth floor. Shops are at Av. Rio Branco 133, Av. Atlântica 1702 (Copacabana Palace), Av. Atlântica 994 (next to Hotel Meridien), Av. Atlântica 2364, Rua Xavier da Silveira 22-A (Rio Othon Palace), and Av. Niemeyer 769 (Hotel Nacional Rio).

Maximino, a traditional jeweler and gemologist, has his head office with a magnificent gem museum downtown at Av. Rio Branco 25, and two branches at Copacabana: Rua Santa Clara 27 and Rua Figuereido Magelhaes 131. A couple of small but outstanding traditional jewelers, all with many years' experience, are *Joelharia Schupp* on Rua Gonçalves Dias 49, which has no branches but owns mines, and *Franz Flohr* on Rua Miguel Couto 23. The late Franz founded the shop back in 1936; his two sons, Gunther, a stonecutter, and Werner, a designer, are the present owners.

Ernani and Walter's ad says "No luxury store," meaning that his prices are highly competitive. His shop is at Praca Olavo Bilac 28, second floor, near the Flower Market. A number of small jewelers are to be found in this neighborhood, such as *Gregory and Sheehan.*

Burle Marx, whose head office is downtown at Pça Mahatma Gandhi 2, sells only at Rua Rodolfo Dantas 6 (next to Copacabana Palace). His specialties are unusually shaped semiprecious stones in one-of-a-kind settings. His necklace and bracelet designs have won prizes. The government often purchases jewelry from him as gifts for visiting dignitaries—the French premier's wife and the Empress of Japan, for example.

A relatively new addition to Rio's gem scene is *Mayer* at Av. Copacabana 291-E, just next to the theater of the Copacabana Palace Hotel. For collector specimens try *Edwin* at Rua Xavier da Silva 19-A behind the Othon Palace Hotel in Copacabana.

The best way to acquire souvenirs is to windowshop around your hotel on Copacabana, where there are numerous shops, such as *Casa de Folclore, Macumba Souvenir,* and *Liane,* that carry Indian artifacts, butterfly trays, wooden statuettes, stuffed snakes, silverware, etc. *Joe and Jack Band,* Rua Barata Ribeiro 157a, heads Rio's exclusive antique stores, offering European and Brazilian items and specializing in silverware, furniture, and fine Brazilian gems and jewels. *Freddy's,* at Av. Copacabana 331-B or Av. Atlântica 1896-B, offers 18-karat gold rings with any color gem setting for a little over $50.

For articles made of alligator skin, look for the specialty shop, *Souvenir do Brasil,* on Av. Rio Branco 25. For beautiful leather handbags visit *Rozwadowski,* Av. Rainha Elizabeth 152, suite 101. *Copacabana Presentes,* Av. Copacabana 331-A, specializes in leather and *crocodile items,* stones, skins, rugs, handbags, and belts. *Copacabana Couros e Ariesanatos,* nearby at Rua Fernando Mendes 45, also features *crocodile goods* and has exclusive designs for handmade bags and belts. Brazilian artistic wood carvings and native paintings by *Batista and Mady* are excellent souvenirs; visit their studio on Rua Pacheco Leão 1270 in Ipanema where an appointment may be made to see their works.

RESTAURANTS. Typical Brazilian food is varied, unusual and delicious, but one of the biggest troubles for the tourist is trying to get some of it. Almost all the good restaurants in Rio serve international-type food only and shy away from the home product. The Brazilian wants to eat something different from everyday fare when going out to dine. Try at least one *feijoada, vatapá,* or the mouthwatering *muqueca de peixe.*

The price classifications of the following restaurants are based on the cost of an average three-course dinner for one person for food alone; beverages, tax and tip would be extra. In Brazil a 10 percent service charge is included with the meal and an additional 5 percent tip should be left. Also the bread and appetizers plate placed on the table before you order is charged to your bill, running about $1.00 to $1.50. Price categories: *Deluxe,* over $20; *expensive,* $10–$20; *moderate,* $5–$10; *inexpensive,* less than $5.

TYPICAL BRAZILIAN DISHES

AlbaMar. *Moderate.* At the former Mercado Municipal. Try deviled crabs, fish chowder or fish filet in black butter. It's downtown and crowded at lunchtime, they close at 9:30 P.M. Nice view of Guanabara Bay.

The Brazilian "barbecue" restaurant is called *churrascaria.* The tab for 2 will run about $20.

Top honors go to the *Gaucha* on Rua Laranjeiras 114, off Largo do Machado. With an open patio is the *Jardim* at 225 Rua República de Peru in Copacabana; *Copacabana,* Av. Copacabana 1144, clean and modern; *Parque Recreio,* Rua Marques Abrantes 96 in Botafogo; *Rincao Gaucho,* Rua Marques de Valença 83; *Carretta,* in Ipanema, Rua Visconde de Pirajá 451 (Austro-Hungarian dishes, too); *Leme,* near Copacabana Palace, on Rua Rodolfo Dantas 16; *Majorica,* Rua Senador Vergueiro 11/15; *Roda Viva,* Av. Pasteur 520, at the funicular station to Pao de Açucar; try the *churrasco mixto,* pieces of beef and pork, or a *lombo de porco* (pork roast), filet mignon or T-bone. *Chamego do Papai,* downtown at Av. Erasmo Braga 64, in front of the "Palace of Justice," where lawyers and judges go for barbecued baby beef specialties. All *inexpensive.*

Chalé. Rua da Matriz 54. A converted colonial home, decorated with Brazilian antiques. *Moderate.*

Maria Thereza Weiss, Rua Visconde Silva 152 in Botafogo. Another colonial home and atmosphere. Noted for its exquisite sweets and desserts. *Expensive.*

Moenda. At the Trocadero Hotel, Av. Atlântica 2064. Nice atmosphere. Seafood specialties. *Moderate.*

Sinhá. Rua Constante Ramos 140. *Moderate.*

SEAFOOD

If fish is what you crave, then have lunch or an early dinner (they close at 8:30 P.M.) downtown at *Cabaça Grande,* Rua Ouvidor 12. Try the *muqueca* or a filet of white fish in shrimp sauce. *Moderate.* It's crowded at lunch time and no reservations are taken over the phone. (P.S. Don't be shocked by the rundown neighborhood it's in.) *Príncipe Legítimo das Peixadas,* Av. Atlântica 974, Leme. *Moderate.*

Also good are *Real,* downtown at Rua Pharoux 3 and at Av. Atlântica 514A; *Ilha dos Pescadores,* Estrada da Barra da Tijuca 793; and *Ancora,* Av. Sernambetiba 18151, all *moderate.*

CHINESE

China Town, Av. N.S. de Copacabana 435, *Oriento,* Rua Bolivar 64, both *inexpensive. Chon Kou,* Av. Atlântica 3880, *moderate. Great China,* Rua Siqueira Campos 12. *New Mandarin,* Rua Carlos Gois 344. Both *inexpensive.*

FRENCH

When it comes to French cuisine, Rio more than holds it own, beginning with the city's two best restaurants, *Le Pre Catalan, deluxe,* in the Rio Palace Hotel and *Saint Honore, expensive,* atop the Meridien Hotel, with a spectacular view to accompany the gourmet food. Leading the price list is *Maxim's,* newly inaugurated atop the Rio Sul Tower behind the shopping center of the same name.

Other excellent French restaurants are *Monseigneur, expensive,* in the Hotel Intercontinental; *Rive Gauche, expensive,* Av. Epitacio Pessoa 1484; *Florentino, moderate,* Rua Gen. San Martin 1227; *Le Relais, moderate,* Rua General Venancio Flores 365, in Leblon. *Le Bec Fin, deluxe,* Av. Copacabana 178A. *Hotel Ouro Verde, expensive,* Av. Atlântica 1456.

GERMAN

Lucas, moderate, Av. Atlântica 3744, pig's knuckles and sauerkraut in the tropics, with Brazil's own beer. *Alpino, moderate,* Av. Epitácio Pessoa 40. *Suppentopf, inexpensive,* Av. Princesa Isabel 350.

INTERNATIONAL

For international dishes, try *Antonio, moderate,* Av. Bartolomeu Mitre 297C, Leblon. *Lord Jim's Pub, inexpensive,* Rua Paul Redfern 63, Ipanema for delicious fish and chips. *Sarau, expensive,* restaurant of the Sheraton Hotel, Espace 47, Rua Farme de Amoedo 47, Ipanema. *The Fox, moderate,* Rua dos Jangadeiros 14, Ipanema, for excellent view as well as good food. *Rio's, expensive,* along the seashore in the Parque de Flamengo, Flamengo Park. *Castelo da Lagoa, moderate,* Av. Epitacio Pessoa 1560; international cuisine on Rio's sleepy lagoon. *Ponto do Encontro, moderate,* Rua Barato Ribeiro 750-B. *Nino's, moderate,* Rua Domingos Ferreira 242-A.

A new landmark opened in downtown Rio in 1978: *La Tour, expensive,* South America's first revolving restaurant, at the top of the 34-story Aeronautical Club building at Rua Santa Luzia 121, half a block from the American Consulate General. Spectacular view of the entire city. Open for lunch and dinner. Expensive.

Nearby, with a more stationary view of the bay from atop the French Consulate, is the *Avis, moderate,* at Av. Presidente Antonio Carlos 58, with Portuguese and international dishes; smart, sophisticated and expensive, but worth it.

In the same neighborhood, is the traditional *Vendome, moderate,* at Av. Franklin Roosevelt 194-A.

ITALIAN

Good are *LaFiorentina* and *Sorrento,* both located on the beach on Av. Atlântica Leme. Try the pizza and green lasagna. Also *Pappagallo,* Av. Prado Junior 237, Copacabana. *Enotria,* Rua Constante Ramos 115, Copacabana.

Tarantella, Av. Sernambetiba 850, Barra da Tijuca. *La Mole,* Rua Dias Ferreira 147, Leblon. *Pizza Nostra,* Rua Humberto de Campos 699, Leblon. *Giardino,* Rua Gomes Carneiro 132. All *moderate.*

PORTUGUESE

A Desgarrada, Rua Barao da Torre 667 in Ipanema is open for lunch and dinner, the latter with a lively show with Portuguese singing. Also good are *Casarao 99,* Rua Pompeu Loureiro 99, Copacabana and *Ponto de Encontro,* Rua Barata Ribeiro 750, Copacabana. All *moderate.*

SWISS

Le Mazot, Rua Paula Freitas 31-A, Copacabana. *Le Chalet Suisse,* Rua Xavier da Silveira 112, Copacabana. *Casa da Suica,* downtown, Rua Cândido Mendes 157 (lunch or dinner, closed Mon.). All *expensive.*

MISCELLANEOUS

Russian food at *New Doubiansky,* Rua Gomes Carneiro 90. Japanese dishes at *Miako,* Rua do Ouvidor 45, downtown, or *Akasaka,* Av. Copacabana 1391; very expensive for what you get.

Danish dishes at *Helsingor,* Rua General San Martin 983. Mexican food at *Lagoa Charlie's,* Rua Maria Quitéria 136. For Spanish food, *Rio Xerez* and *El Faro,* Av. Atlântica 3808. All *moderate.*

OTHER RESTAURANTS

While you are downtown, you might try *Mesbla Department Store, inexpensive,* (Rua do Passeio 42), which also has an economy-priced cafeteria on the first floor; *Aviz,* Av. Antonio Carlos 58 for French food, and *Mosteiro, moderate,* 13 Rua Sao Bento, for classic Portuguese and Brazilian cuisine. The elegant new restaurant on the ground floor of the recently refurbished Municipal Theatre is worth a visit (entrance on Rio Branco). But don't confuse it with the Assyrius nightclub down the avenue, which took the name and furniture from the Teatro Municipal when that building was closed for reconstruction several years ago.

Another unusual spot is the *Rio Restaurant,* opened in 1979 in bay-front Flamengo city park with a splendid view of Sugar Loaf. The building's architecture is the work of Marcos Kondor, creator of Brazil's World War II memorial not far away, and the surrounding gardens are the work of Roberto Burle Marx. Type of food and prices vary according to section you choose—whether outdoors, on a terrace, or behind plate glass with air conditioning. From *inexpensive* to *expensive.*

For the economy minded, *Bucsky,* a popular Hungarian specialty restaurant, Rua Rosario 133; *German Ernesto,* Rua Buenos Aires 100; *Casa Westfalia,* Rua Assembleia 37 and 73 (all for lunch only). *Confeteria Colombo,* 36 Gonçalves Dias, in the heart of the shopping district; good lunch, reasonable, art nouveau decor. All *inexpensive.*

In Botafogo, stop at the *Sol-e-Mar, moderate,* Av. Nestor Moreira 11, a seafood restaurant open for dinner and a bar and terrace open for lunch, where you can enjoy a magnificent view of Guanabara Bay. Sightseeing launches leave from here several times a day.

Rio's beaches are dotted with snack bars and walk-in sandwich stands. Among them are *Castelinho* in Ipanema and *Bob's and Gordon's,* two ever-growing chains of American-style hamburger stands, which serve good snacks and ice cream. But if you want a real American hamburger, get a Big Mac at *McDonald's* at Rua Hilário de Gouveia 74 in mid-Copacabana. This was the first of the "Golden Arches" in South America, opening in 1979. Since then, other air-conditioned locations have opened downtown, in Ipanema, and at the Carrefour supermarket-shopping complex way out in the Barra da Tijuca beach area.

NIGHT LIFE. The legend of Rio nightlife is very exaggerated but there are a number of small little *boîtes* where the customer can buy a drink and listen to a jazz combo or a bossa nova singer. Most shows start after midnight. For excellent Brazilian folklore shows, try the *Hotel Nacional* or the newly opened *Scala* nightclub in Leblon, home of Rio's most elaborate nightclub show. *Regine,* the top society meeting place, now has branches at both Rio's and Bahia's Hotels Meridien.

Remember when ordering drinks that all imported alcohol in Brazil, especially Scotch, wines and liquors, is quite expensive, running two to three times the price in the United States.

For the prettiest Samba dancers you'll ever see the *Oba Oba* at Rua Visconde de Pirajá 499 is hard to beat. For more of the same type, try the *Sambao,* above the Sinha restaurant in Copacabana, or the *Katakombe* in the Galeria Alaska at Av. Copacabana 1241 and Plataforma 1, Rua Adelberto Ferreira 32 (Leblon).

The cavernous *Canecao* features top Brazilian and international artists, and alternating orchestras for dancing. It seats 2,500 persons. Check to see what's on and, unless the show is predominantly Portuguese dialogue, put it on your "must" list for one evening's entertainment. The cover charge is usually around $5, and you can nurse a few beers or have a full meal.

The *Bierklause,* Rua Ronald de Carvalho 55, has a Samba show and Brazilian and German music and food. You can mix Samba and churrasco at *Las Brasas,* Humaitá 110.

Smaller night spots, some with shows, mostly in Ipanema and Leblon, are *Number One,* Rua Maria Quiteria 19; *706,* Av. Ataulfo de Paiva 706; *Special,* Rua Prudente de Morais 129, a jet-set favorite and outrageously expensive; the *Horse's Neck Bar* at the Rio Palace Hotel; and the *Jakui* in the Inter-Continental.

Most of Rio's discos are still going strong, though a few have started converting to traditional live-music clubs. Biggest is still the *Papagaio* (parrot), Av. Borges de Medeiros 1426. Other high-decibel, strobe-lighted spots popular with the young and young-at-heart are *New York,* Rua Visconde de Pirajá 22; *Mikonos,* Av. Bartolomeu Mitre 366; *Papillon* in the Inter-Continental Hotel; *Le Privè;* Rua Jangadeiro 28; *Le Bateau,* Praça Serzedelo Correa 15; *New Jirau,* Rua Siqueira Campos 12 and the *Hippopotamus,* 354 Barao de Torre.

Live dance music is found in the cozy *Saravá* of the Rio-Sheraton Hotel, and at the *Carinhoso,* Rua Visconde de Pirajá 22 in Ipanema.

For a different kind of entertainment, visit the *Assyrius,* downtown at Av. Rio Branco 277—an elegant, sophisticated nightclub with exotic shows. In Copacabana: the *Erotika,* Av. Prado Junior 63; *Holliday,* Av. Atlântica 1424; *Barmen's Club,* Lido Square; *Pussycat,* Rua Belfort Roxo 88-B; *Bolero,* Av. Atlântica 1910; or any number of small boîtes around Rodolfo Dantas and Duvivier streets.

Good singles bars include the *Crazy Rabbit, Lucy's Bar* and *Frank's,* all on Rua Princesa Isabel.

Gay bars are *Zig Zag,* Av. Bartolomeu Mitre 662, *Sotao,* Av. Copacabana 1241; and *The Club,* trav. Cristiano Lacarte 54.

For drinks, snacks, and people-watching in Ipanema: *Lagoa,* Av. Epitacio Pessoa 685 (quiet, with a view over the Lagoa); and *Varanda,* Praça N. Senhora da Paz (a restaurant for Bohemians). *Charlie's Beach,* Rua Anibal de Mendonça 36 (Mexican); and *Jangadeiro,* Rua Teixeira de Melo 20.

PRACTICAL INFORMATION FOR THE ENVIRONS OF RIO

HOTELS. There are still no big hotels on the Barra da Tijuca or Recreio dos Bandeirantes, but there are plenty of small motels and clubs, used principally on weekends.

PETRÓPOLIS

Landmark is *Quitandinha,* built as a super gambling casino with dozens of richly appointed rooms. There are an excellent restaurant and bar, ice rink, indoor and outdoor pools, tennis and squash courts, roller rink, billiard rooms, stables and riding facilities. Landscaped garden has a pretty lake where you can scoot around in a pedallo boat. The hotel supposedly is for members who have purchased shares. Your travel agent may be able to get you in. Room with meals runs from $45 to $80.

Other good hotels with restaurants: *Riverside Parque,* Rua Hermogeneo Silva 522; *Margarida's,* Rua Monsenhor Bacelar 274; *Auto-Tour,* on the highway coming in from Rio; *Casablanca Center,* Rua General Osório 28. Prices average $25 a night without meals and $35 with.

TERESÓPOLIS

No deluxe hotels. You won't go wrong staying at the *Pinheiros,* in Quebra-Frascos suburb; the *Sao Moritz* way out on the newly paved road to Nova Friburgo; *Caxangá,* Rua Caxangá 68; or the *Hotel Alpina* on the highway to Petropolis, all in the range of $30 a night except for the Säo Moritz which charges $50 to $70 including meals. Also recommended: the *Phillip* on Jardim Europa; *Vila Nova do Paquequer,* near the Guarani cascade; or *Higino* at Av. Oliveira Botelho 328. These hotels average $20 a night.

NOVA FRIBURGO

It's a toss up as to whether the *Park* (Sao Clemente 140) or *Bucsky* (Ponto da Saudade) is the best. The latter has a definite European atmosphere and beautifully tended grounds. Other good hotels: *Mury Garden,* on the road to Niteroi; the *Fazenda,* back in the hills out of Säo João (charming); *Floresta,* next to Olifas; *Repouso,* Ladeira Rebaday 6; *Vale do Luar,* on the road to Niteroi; *Chateau das Azaléas,* Rua Itaji in the park; *Garlipp,* in Mury on the highway; *Sans-Souci* (Jardim Sans-Souci); and *Olifas* (Parque Olifas). Most of these hotels include all meals in the room price which ranges from $20 for the less expensive to $45 for the top hotels.

CABO FRIO

Best stopping places in this colonial beach town are: *Malibu Palace* on the Praia da Barra; *Cabanas da Ogiva,* the Ogiva suburb; the *Cabo Frio Sol* and

Colonial, Porto Rocha 160. Other new hotels are *Acapulco; La Brise; Portofino; Palace; Cabanas; Shangri-La.* All have good restaurants, meals included in the room price which ranges between $25 and $50.

BÚZIOS (CABO FRIO)

The village of Armaçao dos Búzios, beyond Cabo Frio, is sometimes considered Rio's "Côte D'Azur" and frequented by the international jet set. Best hotels are *Auberge de L'Hermitage; Pousada dos Gravatás; Casas Brancas Pousada;* and *Estalagem do Guerreiro* with prices ranging from $30 to $60 without meals.

ITACURUÇÁ

Three hotels are located on tropical paradise islands in this area about 55 miles west of Rio. Newest is the *Jaguanum,* on its own beach on Jaguanum Island, about 30 minutes by launch from the Itacuruçá pier. Luxurious apartments and bungalows, deep-sea fishing. European management. Book in advance in Rio. *First class,* including meals.

AGUAS LINDAS

In a cove where many of the wealthy have weekend cottages, on the island of Itacuruçá. Thirty-two rooms and bungalows overlooking the beach. On another side of the island is the *Hotel de Pierre* with several air-conditioned apartments. *First class,* including meals.

ANGRA DOS REIS

Make this your headquarters for visiting some of the 300 islands in the Ilha Grande Bay, staying at the *Hotel do Frade, first class,* on the beach 18 miles from town; at the *Hotel da Praia, moderate,* eight miles out on Ipirapua Beach; or at the *Londres, moderate,* Av. Raul Pompeia 75, in the heart of this village settled in the 16th century.

PARATI

Leading hotels in this colonial city surrounded by beaches, rivers and islands are the small but picturesque *Coxixo, moderate,* Rua Tenente Francisco Antonio 362; *Pousado Pardieiro, first class,* number 74 of the same street; *Pescador, moderate,* Av. Beira Rio or *Pouse Colibri, inexpensive,* Rua Jacome de Melo.

RESENDE

143 kms. from Rio, is an excellent vacation spot in Itatiaia Park. Among its attractions: Agulhas Negras Peak; Funil Dam, a Finnish settlement; Blue Lake waterfalls; Agulhas Negras military academy. Best hotels are the *Simon, first class,* and *Repouso Itatiaia, moderate,* nearby. In Resende itself, the small *Avenida* and *Presidente* are the only choices, both *inexpensive.*

 HOW TO GET AROUND. Regular buses leave from Estaçao Rodoviária every half hour or so for the towns of Petrópolis and Teresópolis; the ride takes slightly more than one hour and costs about $1.00 to the former, $1.50 to the latter. Most of the tourist agencies have special excursions there as well.

Nova Friburgo can be reached either by going there after you've seen Teresópolis or by taking a 3-hour bus trip from the Estaçao Rodoviária. Price is about $2.20.

Cars can be rented in Rio, São Paulo, and Brasilia. There is a new highway to Salvador, capital of the State of Bahia, on which the tourist can drive to the mountain resorts of Nova Friburgo, Teresópolis, and Petrópolis, and many beach resorts can be reached down the Rio-Santos Highway.

Paquetá Island can only be reached by ferry boat, from Praça Quinze, with boats leaving regularly every hour starting from 6 A.M. The last boat to leave the island on the return trip to Rio is at 9 P.M. The trip takes almost two hours and the boats are not too uncomfortable.

WHAT TO SEE? Watch for the strangely shaped rock called the Finger of God on your drive up to the mountain cities. Be sure and visit the Hotel-Club Quitandinha in Petrópolis, if only to just wander among its many salons, and the Imperial Palace, now a museum, with intimate objects that belonged to South America's only royal family. In Teresópolis if you're lucky you may witness a fleecy cloud snuggling right in the middle of the main street. Well beyond Teresópolis is an impressive high-in-the-air Swiss and German colony called Nova Friburgo that contains excellent hotels and offers peace and quiet for those desiring it.

Along the beach northward from Rio is Cabo Frio where there are white painted forts (originally built to chase away French pirates) and deserted beaches. Leaving the city in the other direction are the unspoiled beaches of Barra da Tijuca, now a virtual suburb of Rio, and Recreio dos Bandeirantes. This area is crowded on weekends and holidays, when thousands visit the newly constructed clubs and international restaurants famed for seafood.

If you keep going in this direction, down the new Rio-Santos Highway, you will come to the resort areas of Itacuruçá, Angra dos Reis and Parati, with their hundreds of beaches and islands as well as relics and monuments dating from colonial days.

And way up in Rio's Guanabara Bay lies the island of Paquetá, where automobiles are forbidden and inhabitants ride about in horse-drawn carriages or on bicycles under flamboyantly flowered trees.

RESTAURANTS. In Petrópolis you might try *Chaillot* and *La Belle Meuniere* for very good French cuisine, both *moderate; Willi's, Bauemstube,* and *Buon Giorno* are also recommended, all *moderate.* On Paquetá, the *Netuno, inexpensive,* on Rua José Bonifacio has some very good seafood. At Barra da Tijuca be sure and have either lunch or dinner at the *Bar dos Pescadores.* Reasonable prices, fast service, and the decoration is one of dockside simplicity. Recreio dos Bandeirantes has the *Ancora* restaurant. *Moderate* prices.

In Teresópolis look for *Taberna Alpino, Cremaillere,* and one of Brazil's few good Mexican restaurants, *Los Panchos.* All *moderate.*

In Cabo Frio, try the assorted shrimp specialties or the mullet steaks served at *Dom Bosco, expensive,* on the town square. Also *Toni, Spelunk do Angelo, Picolino,* and *La Taverna,* all *moderate.* In Buzios, *Au Cheval Blanc, La Chimere, expensive, Vip Clube, Maia, Karlitos* and *Frank's, moderate.*

SÃO PAULO AND THE
PROGRESSIVE SOUTH

Industrialized Brazil

No matter how well you've studied Latin America and boned up on Brazil, the city of São Paulo will come as a startling surprise. There is nothing like it in any other South American nation, no other place that can come close or that even hints of coming close. It's the richest area in South America, the fastest growing, and the pride of all the Brazilians.

When you approach the city from the air, it looks like Chicago or Detroit. There are towering skyscrapers—many of them—lining double-lane highways and avenues, where thousand of cars, buses and trucks stream by. More than ten million people call it home. At night the city lights up like a Christmas tree in swirls of neon and fluorescent bulbs, while advertising slogans, weather reports, and the latest news is flashed to the busy Paulistas from the tops of tall buildings. The city boasts the best restaurants in Latin America, the most comfortable movie houses, and some of the best schools. Up higher than Rio and away from the coast, it also has a cooler climate that is conducive to work and study. Here sweaters are the rule rather than the exception.

The state of São Paulo is a fit setting for its active, pulsating, capital city. With some of the richest farmland in Brazil, it supplies almost half the nation's coffee, cotton, fruits, and vegetables. The fertile land is crisscrossed by an excellent system of railways and modern highways, which the industries scattered in the small towns use to their advantage.

Whenever the Paulista needs to get away from the routine of making money, he takes an hour's drive down from his lofty plateau to the equally active, but decidedly tropical seaport city of Santos and the nearby island paradise of Guarujá. Here he goes to the beach, relaxes in nice hotels, and gets his suntan.

The Paulistas say that their area has everything, and they really don't need the rest of Brazil at all . . . except as cash customers.

Gaucho Country

The land of the gauchos is almost fabled. The flat pampas grasslands stretching as far as the eye can see, the spirited proud horses, the women in their skirts and their multicolored petticoats, the thousands of grazing cattle, the lonely nights, the full moon, and the gaucho lament plucked softly on a guitar.

The home of the Brazilian gaucho begins at the border with Uruguay and Argentina and stretches up as far as the state of São Paulo, but the color and the legend, the clothes and the individualism have become centered in Rio Grande do Sul.

Gaucho country has other things to offer as well. There are the old mission cities, now in splendid ruin, built by the Jesuits in the 1600s. There is the rich grape growing area where the best wines in Brazil are produced. And, there is that magnificent wonder of nature, the powerful, unforgettable Iguaçu Falls.

São Paulo

São Paulo is a cosmopolitan city that owes its progress to people from all nations, the richness of the soil and the temperate climate. It is a never ending source of investigation and amazement on the part of sociologists and a richly rewarding experience to those Brazilians who feel their country is capable of becoming an important world power.

From a sleepy little Jesuit colony founded in 1554 it has grown into a metropolis almost three times the size of Paris, with a population increase of 150,000 a year and an industrial district that swallows up mile after mile of surrounding land per annum. There is a violent energy in the air and none of the sentimentality that binds the rest of the nation to the past. For São Paulo there is only the future. The Paulistas like to say that "São Paulo can never stop." And from the way it has weathered every political crisis and change and steered its way through inflation and depression, it looks as if it never is going to stop.

But it is not an inhuman city of robots, concrete, and machines. It is a city of people who have come looking to better themselves from

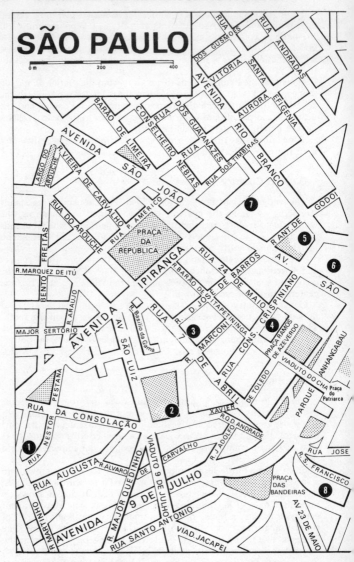

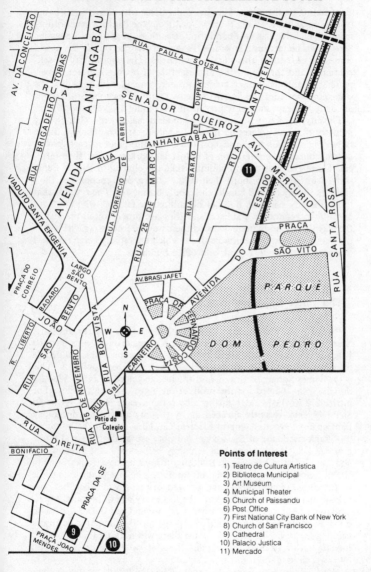

Points of Interest

1) Teatro de Cultura Artística
2) Biblioteca Municipal
3) Art Museum
4) Municipal Theater
5) Church of Paissandu
6) Post Office
7) First National City Bank of New York
8) Church of San Francisco
9) Cathedral
10) Palacio Justica
11) Mercado

every nation on the globe. They are individuals who desire better living conditions and are willing to work for them. The Paulista asks nothing from anyone. He has two hands and uses them to get what he wants. Sometimes his attitude is rather Texan, in that he thinks the world comes to an end at the state's boundaries. His capital city is self-contained and thrives on the manufacture of textiles, clothes, paper, pottery, chemicals, leather, rubber, timber, cement, iron, and steel. His state alone provides one-fourth of the two million new jobs Brazil needs annually to keep unemployment from becoming a severe problem.

The city was first with enough cheap electrical power to handle any industry that was interested in building there. It also offered a direct railway connection to the seaport town of Santos, and its early governors encouraged immigration of industrial workers rather than farmers. Those Europeans who couldn't take the climate of Rio or Bahia thrived in Sao Paulo, built their homes there, and encouraged their children to stay on and handle the family businesses. The result is that today the city counts a number of millionaire families who are third and fourth generation Paulista, and they are proud to tell the visitor the way their grandparents worked their way up from steerage class to the mansions along Avenida Paulista, which are rapidly being replaced today by ultra-modern bank and office buildings.

The Times Square of Brazil

Probably the best place to "feel" the pulse of the city is right in its heart, the bridge over the vast Avenida Anhangabaú. It leads into the Praça do Patriarca. Just stand there and observe the autos and people hurrying below you in what appears to be organized confusion. This is the Times Square of Brazil, and the bridge you're on is the Viaduto do Cha (tea), named for the product once grown in this valley. The intricately worked bridge farther down the avenue is the 65-year-old Santa Ifigênia, recently spruced up by the city and bathed in golden light at night by the General Electric Co. Now look at the buildings that flank each side of the bridge and note especially the squat white granite, solid looking one that is partly below the bridge and partly above it. It is the Matarazzo Building, former headquarters of one of Brazil's most successful immigrant families. The first Matarazzo came to Brazil as an immigrant and arrived dripping wet when his boat overturned going to the shore and he lost every one of his possessions. Undaunted but penniless, he started to buy and sell pork fat door to door. Soon he had a small lard company and this he parlayed into a canning factory. Not long afterward there was nothing that he wasn't manufacturing or operating. Today the Matarazzo businesses are run by his granddaughter and grandsons.

Now walk up Rua Barao de Itapetininga (Paulistas love to give their streets difficult Indian names) across the Praça Ramos de Azevedo along the front of the majestic Teatro Municipal and four blocks to Av.

Ipiranga. Here is the center of the man-in-the-streets haunts, with the huge movie theaters, the elegant and well-kept Praça de Republica and the sidestreets leading off to shops and specialty stores. Most of the tourist and souvenir shops are in this area, as well as the airline company offices and better bookstores.

Edifício Italia, tallest building in South America, is situated at the highest point in São Paulo. Visit one of its rooftop bars or restaurants on a clear day or night. Behind it, on Ipiranga, is the graceful, serpent-shaped apartment and office building designed by famed Brasilia builder Oscar Niemeyer, across the street from the São Paulo Hilton. Turning from Ipiranga and walking down São Luiz, which leads to the Hotel Jaraguá, you'll see new office buildings with shops, theaters, and luxury stores that have sprung up in the past three years. São Paulo is like New York in this respect; wherever you look there is an old building coming down and a new one rising in its place.

In 1888 the state government purchased an old farm house and turned it over to a scientist who had some crazy notion that snake serum could be used to save the life of someone bitten by a snake. His first patients were the horses of the Paulista cavalry, and he had 64 snakes to work with. Today the Instituto Butantan is the largest snake farm in Latin America, counts more than 16,000 live snakes in its collection, as well as thousands of spiders, scorpions, and lizards. It extracts their venom regularly and processes it so it can be flown anywhere in the world when it's needed in a hurry. The institute is open Monday 1 to 5 P.M.; Tuesday to Friday, 8 A.M. to 5 P.M.; Saturday, Sunday, and holidays, 9 A.M. to 5 P.M. Be sure to see them milking the snakes between 10 A.M. and 4 P.M. You can take a bus from Praça da Republica or, of course, a taxi, for it's quite a distance from the downtown area.

Within walking distance of the snake farm is the House of the Flagbearer (Casa do Bandeirante). An old ranch house that goes back to the golden age of the colonials, the building was completely restored in 1954 and decorated with priceless furniture and pottery of the period. Even the outside buildings like the corn crib and the mill are authentic down to the last detail. If you are interested in the antiques of this era, you'll love the place. It's open every day except Monday from 12 to 5:30 P.M. There is a guide there. Entrance is free.

Parks, Museums, and More

Ibirapuera Park is perhaps the biggest one of its kind in the world. It covers two million square meters, is decorated with natural lakes and rolling, well-watered lawns, and contains ten modern exhibition halls where one thing or another is being shown. The entrance to the park is dominated by a statue containing 36 figures of the pioneers, Indians, and horses who braved the unmapped lands and carved out a new empire. The statue, the work of Frenchman Victor Brecheret, is 50 meters long and has been given the rather affectionate if irreverent name of "Don't push." Inside the park you'll be able to visit the Japanese Pavilion, which is an exact reproduction of the Katura Palace in Japan and is kept up by donations of the Japanese colony. There is also a windowless dome of cement called the History Pavilion. Here are the museums of Science, Aeronautics, and Technical Arts. In the Pavilion Pereira, the world-famed Bienal art exhibits are held. The greatest display of contemporary art in Latin America, the show attracts painters from all over the globe who compete for top honors in the art world. Don't miss the beautiful Museu dos Presépios, a year-round display of nativity scenes. The Planetarium is also in this park and is rated the best in South America. Complete, absorbing shows are given each Saturday, Sunday, and holiday at 4, 6 and 8 P.M., and Tuesday and Thursday at 8 P.M. Tickets at the door cost about 90 cents. There is also a radio-telescope (the only one in Brazil) that lets you "listen" to the stars, as well as an interesting corner where telescopes are assembled. Take any bus marked Ibirapuera.

Along the banks of the Anhembi River, at the entrance to the São Paulo-Rio Highway, is Anhembi Park, whose exposition hall is the world's largest aluminum structure. The roof is supported by 25 light columns and the hall is illuminated by 200 aluminum globes. Right beside it is a modernistic convention hall seating 5,000 persons. A 453-room hotel is also under construction nearby.

The Zoological Park is located on Avenida Miguel Estafeno. The largest in the world, it displays over 400 animals and 600 birds. There are few fences or cages and Paulistas dot the lawns on Sunday afternoons with their tablecloths and picnic baskets. It is open daily from 9 A.M. to 6 P.M., and adult admission is about $1.

Near the zoo, on the same avenue, is the orchid farm where there are over 35,000 species. The force of so much beauty is overpowering at times. You may visit the orchids and the zoo by taking a number 546 bus from Praça da Liberdade or Anhangabaú.

Just behind the zoo, but requiring a closed car in which to visit it, is the Simba Safari where lions, camels, monkeys, and cheetahs roam free in their own wilderness, and only the visitors are caged.

If you are interested in collecting stamps or coins, then a must on your itinerary is a visit to the center of downtown Praça da Republica on a Sunday morning. There collectors and dealers traditionally gather to talk, swap, and sell. But today they are outnumbered by "hippies" selling their handicraft—leather goods, furniture, paintings, and trinkets made of glass, straw, and metal.

Three museums should be on your list of musts. The first is the Museum de Arte de São Paulo, on Avenida Paulista. Open free of charge from 1 to 5 P.M. daily except Monday, it is the only collection in South America that shows a panorama of Western art from the Gothic Age to the present. Here hangs Raphael's famed "Resurrection," painted when he was just 17 years old. There is a Rembrandt self-portrait, three Frans Hals, 13 works by Renoir, 10 by Toulouse-Lautrec, and many others. There is a section of 19th-century and contemporary Brazilian painters, a selection of Gobelin tapestries, and a collection of early Italian majolica. The basement houses special exhibits, frequently changed, of art, antiques, glass collections, and other treasures.

The second important museum is the Museu de Arte Contemporánea located in the Pereira Pavillion in Ibirapuera Park. There are over 1,650 works by such modern masters as Kandinsky, Leger, Carrá, Portinari, and various cubists of the pre-World War I era. Open every day but Monday from 2 to 6 P.M. Admission is roughly 65 cents.

Third is the Museum of Brazilian Art on Rua Alagoas 903. Here are copies of all the monuments and statues in the parks and buildings of Brazil, including copies of the famed Prophets of Aleijadinho. Free admission Tuesday through Friday from 2 to 10 P.M.

The Environs of São Paulo

If one cannot understand the "Paulistas" contented "I want to be isolated" attitude from studying their capital city, then it will certainly become apparent when the rest of their domain is seen. The area has everything from sandy beaches to lofty mountain plateaus, from colonial splendor to ultramodern health resorts. To see all of it you need time, much more time than most tourists have to devote to an area. That is one of the problems of visiting Brazil. There is so much to see that it's absolutely impossible to crowd it all in one visit.

The State of São Paulo itself is about the size of Great Britain and Northern Ireland put together, covering 95,800 square miles. Slow to take root (the first colonies founded by the Jesuit fathers were complete failures), São Paulo didn't really start to grow until the coffee plant was introduced in the early 1800s. The product found a ready market, and when in 1847 a landowner near Limeira brought over a colony of Germans to work his fields, the area was on its way at last. The demand for coffee grew and more and more immigrants came from Europe to try their hand with the new plant. From Italy alone came a million people. Portugal sent half a million and Spaniards and Japanese many hundreds of thousands. From the sale of coffee came money enough to start factories, install electrical power, build railways, and clear rich forest land.

Santos is another pride of the Paulistas, for aside from having the biggest dock area in Latin America, it also has a tropical climate and some beautiful beaches. Apart from the basilica of Santo Andre, which faces the beach and the row after row of modern apartment buildings, the city has little to offer the tourist except her beaches. They are different from the ones in Rio, the sand being darker and harder.

The nearby island of Guarujá is lush, green, and lined with towering palm trees—and, increasingly, with high-rises along the ocean. Today, to reach more unspoiled areas you must go north by bus or car, crossing the ferry to Bertioga and beyond (but avoid Sundays and holidays because of long lines). There are some relatively untouched beaches, considering the proximity to Santos and the number of weekend visitors. They offer a pleasant visual and mental change from the hustle of the city. A trip around the island by automobile can be made in an hour, for the roads are paved and in good condition.

The coastal village of Paratí was founded way back in the early 16th century. Its calm, natural little harbor was the perfect jumping off point for adventurers looking for the gold and precious stones in Minas Gerais. For decades the town flourished while it catered to the needs of the miners and helped them spend their money. But the boom calmed down, Santos rose in importance because of its superb harbor, and over the years Paratí was forgotten. Then just a few years ago, the Paulistas rediscovered this colonial village (actually located in Rio de Janeiro state), and the government declared it a national monument whose architectural style must be preserved. Today it is important as a tourist center. With the Rio-Santo Highway passing close by, traffic jams became so great that cars are now banned from most city streets. Those who have taken the time to visit it come back with glowing tales of baroque churches, charming squares, and an unspoiled old-world charm. Many houses have been restored by private parties and the tendency is to preserve as much of the original flavor as possible.

The various spas and hot spring resorts radiate northward into the higher country, away from the capital city. Most of them have a large German or Swiss population and will remind the traveler more of Europe than South America. High in the air and richly gifted with mineral waters, the villages of Aguas da Prata and Caxambú offer the tired tourist rest and health. Every hotel has its own doctor, and some people actually find it fun to get up around six A.M. for a walk to the spring for their first glass of water that day. Brazilians, like the French, blame every ailment on the liver and they constantly bathe this organ in mineral waters, either bottled or *au naturel*. Many of the waters are radioactive.

The hot springs attract an equal number of visitors, who go there to sit in the warm, swirling (at times rather smelly) water, rather than drink it. Campos do Jordao, Poços de Caldas, and Serra Negra all have dry climates and their waters are famous for treating such diverse ailments as rheumatism, skin diseases, and fatigue. Clean and nicely landscaped, these villages are as pleasant to the eye as they are to the skin.

The Land of Gauchos

Porto Alegre will surprise you. One of the most up-to-date and fastest growing cities south of São Paulo, it has modern buildings, amiable people, and well-stocked shops. Lying as it does at the junction of five rivers, it has become an important shipping port, and much of the state's leather, canned beef, and rice are shipped from here to destinations as far away as Africa and Japan. The Lagoa dos Patos on which the city nestles is the largest fresh-water lagoon in South America.

The old residential part of the city is on high ground with delightful views all around. It is dominated by the Governor's Palace (where soldiers crouched with machine guns both when "Jango" Goulart came back as President in 1961 and when he left in disgrace in 1964). Nearby there are an imposing stone cathedral and two high white towers of an old church called the Lady in Pain. The streets of the city wind in and around and up and down, and one of the best ways to enjoy Porto Alegre is to get out and walk; head toward the prisons and the electrical energy plant on General Salustiano. The huge, green-grassed park of Farroupilha is the site of a zoo and botanical gardens and on weekends and holidays is also a setting for folk dancers.

The best Brazilian wine is produced in the area round Caxias do Sul, home of Italian immigrants who transported the art from their native land. Today 28 different companies work at growing, selecting, and bottling the juices from thousands of tons of grapes grown in this region. In March the entire city stops work to celebrate the "Festival of the Grapes."

Farmers arrive to show off their products, visitors come from all over Brazil as well as France and Italy, and regional folk dances are held. There is also more beef eaten than can be imagined and more wine drunk than should be. The owners of *Michelon* (Avenida Michelon 136) welcome visitors to their bottling plant from 7:30 to 11:00 A.M. and from 1:30 to 5 P.M.

In the first years of the 1600s, the Portuguese domination of Brazil didn't go farther south than Laguna in the State of Santa Catarina. Below this was Spanish territory, and it was here that the Jesuits came from Spain to build a series of missions. They managed to win the confidence of the Indians and soon had them making and laying bricks. The Indians stayed near the missions for protection. Then the Portuguese "flagbearers" from São Paulo came rushing south. Enemies of the Spanish, they killed the priests, enslaved the Indians, and destroyed the mission cities. What is left today—towering walls, delicately curved arches, carved angles and cornices—stands in mute testament to the grandeur that the Jesuits tried to implant on Brazilian soil. The Cathedral of São Miguel, roofless and overgrown with grass, is probably the most impressive ruin. There is a museum beside it with some of the wooden images and iron bells that were salvaged from the Cathedral. Other ruins, all reachable in one day, are at São João Velho, São Lourenço das Missoes, and São Nicolau. At this last ruin the legend still holds that the Jesuits buried a treasure chest before the Portuguese arrived.

All through this area and especially near São Borja, the home of both Presidents Getulio Vargas and João Goulart, you'll see the gauchos and their horses. They still wear the bright-colored shirts and neckerchiefs, the balloon pleated trousers, the creased leather boots, and the flat chin strap hat. They will stop and talk to you and may even offer a taste of their chimarrao, the traditional gourd of hot mate tea.

Another unforgettable day will be spent at Iguaçú Falls. Eleanor Roosevelt remarked that: "Iguaçú Falls make Niagara look like a kitchen faucet." The water comes from some 30 rivers and streams from the interior of Paraná, and as it rushes toward the 200-foot precipice, it foams and carries huge trees it has uprooted. The volume of roaring, earth-shaking water has been estimated at 62,000 cubic feet per second. During the flood months of May to July the water plunges over at 450,000 cubic feet per second.

Brazilians and Argentines have both made national parks on their side of the falls and views from both countries are spectacular and different. Your hotel will take care of transportation to the Argentine side and all the necessary customs paperwork. You will be impressed by the Devil's Throat Falls, which must be seen by taking a highly adventurous (not for the weak-hearted and elderly) outboard trip across the rapid currents to a trembling but secure little island. Don't wear your good clothes. The spray of this breathtaking portion of the falls is thrust 500 feet into the air.

Curitiba is a busy city of one million inhabitants standing some 3,000 feet above sea level on the plateau of Serra do Mar. For over a century, its bracing climate and picturesque location have attracted immigrants of Slav, German and Italian origin, who have imparted a few European characteristics to its buildings and surroundings. Formerly best known as the center of the *hervamate* industry, it has now acquired much greater importance as the capital of a flourishing and progressive state that derives its economic prosperity from extensive coffee plantations in the north and vast timber forests in the southwest, as well as fertile areas that produce abundant crops of cereals and other foodstuffs. In addition to being the capital of the State of Paraná, it is the headquarters of the Fifth Military Region and therefore the residence of many officers and their families, and there are barracks for infantry and artillery regiments. There is also a modern and well-equipped military air base. The University of Paraná attracts thousands of students from all over the states of Paraná and Santa Catarina as well as from more distant states of the union.

Places of interest include: the Coronel David Carneiro Museum, with a unique collection of objects of historical interest; the Graciosa Country Club; and others. Also noteworthy are the modern buildings, especially the Civic Center, which houses in one homogenous group the Governor's Palace, State Secretariats, House of Assembly, Treasury, Law Courts, etc. There are two modern theaters (one for plays and revues, one for concerts and ballet) and a library in the center of the town. By bus along a paved road to Sao Paulo (250 miles) takes eight hours; the daily train takes 24 hours.

PRACTICAL INFORMATION FOR SÃO PAULO

WHEN TO GO. The weather information for Rio is also good for São Paulo, except that when it is cool in Rio, it is twice as chilly here. Since the city sits 820 meters (2,665 ft.) above sea level, it is prey to the variable winds that come northward from cold Argentina as well as those breezes coming from muggy Mato Grosso jungles. It is a stimulating climate, one that does not sap the energy of the visitor. There are no big events taking place in the city but rather a continuing series of interesting things like museum openings, art exhibits, industrial fairs, and sports programs. There is always something going on, and the visitor will not have to worry about killing time, in spite of the lack of sandy beaches.

HOW TO GET THERE. Most people visit here after they have been in Rio. The easiest and most comfortable way to come is via the ultramodern, ultraefficient *Ponte Aérea* (Air Bridge), which consists of the constant arrival and departure of airplanes between Rio's Santos-Dumont airport and São Paulo's Congonhas field. They leave every half-hour from 6 A.M. till 10:30 P.M. Reservations aren't needed, unless you want a certain plane. You just show up and take the next plane. It is a good idea to book in advance for a weekend flight, especially Friday evening. Tickets: about $40 one way.

Most international flights land at the Viracopos international airport in Campinas, a two-hour bus or taxi ride from São Paulo. Try to avoid it. *PanAm* and *Varig,* however, have shuttle flights on 727s to Congonhas connecting with most of their international flights to Rio.

The city can also be reached by first-class buses which leave Estaçao Rodoviária every half hour and make the 253-mile trip in six-and-one-half hours on an excellent highway with one rest stop. Either *Expresso Brasileiro* or *Viaçao Cometa* will give you more than satisfactory service. The late-night sleeper buses run about $14 and are extremely comfortable and modern.

Low-cost trains leave Rio's Central do Brasil railroad station. The sleeper leaves at 11:10 P.M., arriving in São Paulo about 8:00 A.M. Not fancy, but clean and comfortable, with a dining car. Sleeper seats and Pullman compartments range from $10 to $40.

 HOTELS. Booming São Paulo is a city of international businessmen and their customers; so it is only natural that the city is prepared to take care of them. There are hundreds of good hotels in town, and rates are about what they are for similar accommodations in Rio. *Deluxe:* single $75–$120, double $80–$130; *first class:* single $30–$50, double $35–$55; *moderate:* single $15–$30, double $20–$35; *inexpensive:* single $7–$15, double $10–$20.

Deluxe

Caesar Park. Rua Augusta 1508; tel. 285–6622. On the fashionable shopping street and a few blocks from the U.S. Trade Center and Avenida Paulista business center, offers European personal service—the staff knows you by name. Restaurants, a coffee shop, bars, banquet and small convention facilities, outdoor swimming pool on the roof, and beauty shop. Conservative, for discriminating people. $90 single; $100 double.

Grand Hotel Ca D'Oro. Rua Augusta 129; tel. 256–8011. "Home away from home." Many American families stay here in suites until their household goods arrive. The owner Fabrizio Guzzoni and his two sons, Eugenior and Aurelio, are always available. Recently remodeled, this 400-room hotel offers the most to a family with children: tennis court, outdoor swimming pool and children's pool and play equipment. Banquet and convention facilities and one of the best formal Italian dining rooms. The only luxury hotel with kennel. $75 single; $85 double.

Maksoud Plaza. São Paulo's newest hotel, located one block from the Paulista business district at Alameda Campinas 150; tel. 251–2233, is acknoweldged as Brazil's finest hotel, some say the best in Latin America. It is deluxe in every sense. Electronic temperature controls in all 420 rooms, room service, TV, and other amenities. Panoramic indoor elevators permit an excellent view of the atrium lobby as they glide to the two squash courts on the top (22nd) floor. American billiards, indoor swimming pool, sauna, VIP Club, convention facilities, as well as shops. Restaurants are *La Cuisine du Soleil* with superb French food, the *Vikings' Scandinavian* smorgasbord, and *Belavista,* the latter open 24 hours a day. $110 single; $120 double.

São Paulo Hilton. Popular hotel for conventions and business people. Located downtown on Avenida Ipiranga 165, its 34 stories command a sweeping view of the world's fastest-growing city; four restaurants, five bars, including the *London Tavern* pub-disco restaurant and large convention center and theater. Outdoor pool, sauna, medical facilities, barber and beauty shop. Jewelry stores, bookshop, Varig and gift shops are located in the building. $100 single; $110 double; tel. 256–0033.

First Class

Augusta Boulevard. Rua Augusta 243; tel. 257–7844. Another modern hotel on this famous shopping street.

Brasilton São Paulo, Rua Martins Fontes 330; tel. 258–5811. Part of the Hilton group, in the center of shopping and downtown, convenient to most everything. A popular hotel for business lunches, international stars; where the action is. Two restaurants, bars, banquet and convention facilities.

Eldorado Boulevard. Av. Sao Luiz 234; tel. 257–0222. Small, but elegant 157 rooms. In the popular downtown three-block hotel district. Terrace coffee shop with view of the busy avenue, fashionable. Pool, nightclub, meeting rooms, international cuisine. Loew's reservation service. $60 single; $66 double.

Eldorado Higienopolis. Rua Marquês de Itú 836; tel. 222–3422. Restaurant, bar and coffee shop. Residential neighborhood. Outdoor swimming pool. Ten-minute walk to downtown commercial area. Sister to the Eldorado Boulevard.

Hotel Delphin. Across the street from the Brasilton, Rua Martins Fontes, 277; tel. 258–0011. Very convenient to the center and to the business district on Av. Paulista. Taxis are easy to get here.

Jaraguá. Rua Major Quedinho 44; tel. 256–6633. At one time a luxury hotel (now 27 years old), 240 rooms ranging from suites to pleasant bedrooms. Centrally located; not recommended for light sleepers without earplugs.

Novotel. Rua Ministro Nelson Hungria 450 in the suburb of Morumbi; tel. 542–1244. Good for executives visiting factories on the Marginal. Outdoor swimming pool and a view of the city. Not convenient to downtown or the shopping area.

Othon Palace Hotel. Strategically located in the center of the financial district, Rua Libero Badaró 196, Praça Patriarca; tel. 239–3277. Part of Brazilian chain of Othon hotels, contains the *VIP Bar, The Four Seasons Restaurant,* and the *Swiss Chalet.* Three large rooms for meetings, cocktail parties, and other social occasions. All air conditioned.

São Paulo Center. Largo Santa Ifigenia 40; tel. 228–6033. Recently redecorated in modern style, adjacent to the heart of the old city. Ifigenia Bridge immediately to the left and within walking distance of the Colegio Patio, founding site of São Paulo. 111 air-conditioned rooms. Very popular executive lunch.

Moderate

Comodoro, on Av. Duque de Caxias; tel. 220–1211, is close to the bus station, and though in a not-too-desirable location is popular with theater and sports groups.

Samambaia. 7 de Abril at Praça da República; tel. 231–1333. Right in the downtown area. Small but excellent service and cuisine.

Others are the *Excelsior Hotel,* Av. Ipiranga 770; tel. 222–7377; *Cambridge,* Av. 9 de Julho 210; tel. 239–0399; *Alvear,* Av. Gaspar Libero 65; tel. 228–8433; *Normandie,* Av. Ipiranga 1187; tel. 228–5766; and the *Ca D'Oro* Rua Basilio da Gama, 95; tel. 259–8177.

Most Paulista hotels serve continental breakfast free of charge.

As in Rio, Apartment Hotels are also available, the top ones being: Trianon Residence, tel. 283–0066, Al. Casa Branca 363; Augusta Park Residence, tel. 255–5722, Rua Augusta 922; and Flat Service Morumby, tel. 531–2121, Rua Minister Nelson Hungria 600.

OUTSIDE SÃO PAULO

There are *Holiday Inns* throughout the State of São Paulo. The latest to open was in the town of Americana, a short distance from Campinas and the Viracopos International Airport (90 kilometers from São Paulo). The city of Americana was founded by southerners who left the United States following the Civil War. For visitors to the coast, there is a Holiday Inn in Santos Av. Ana Costa 555; tel. (0132) 34–7211; with pool and nightclub. Other locations are Marília, tel. (0144) 335–944 and Ribeirao Preto, tel. (0166) 250–186, which may be reserved in São Paulo at 222–0519. A new Inn is scheduled to open in the city of São Paulo in 1983.

Also there is an Inn in the São Paulo suburb of São Bernardo do Campo, tel. 448–3555, Av. Nacoes Unidos 1501. All the Inns are *moderate* except for those in Santos and Ribeirao Preto which are *first class.*

HOW TO GET AROUND. At Congonhas city airport, there are no regular taxis. The red and white airport taxis outside the domestic wing will cost about $4 to your downtown hotel. Air-conditioned "luxury" taxis outside the international wing cost about $9. To take a regular metered cab (many are VW beetles), walk down the few steps to the street and flag one down. Cost: about $2.50 to city center. You may contract with a driver at the airport or alongside Hotel Hilton for a day (around $40) to tour the city in comfort. Avis, Hertz, L'Auto, and National rental cars are available, but São Paulo is a difficult city for the nonresident to get around in. Most cab drivers don't know many streets. City buses are cheap, about 10 cents for most fares, but lines are long at rush hours. A new subway crosses the city from north to south for 20 cents. Ask your hotel porter for information. Tours can be arranged by a local travel agent.

USEFUL ADDRESSES. *American Consulate General,* Rua Padre João Manoel 933; *U.S. Trade Center,* Av. Paulista 2439, 1st floor. *British Consulate,* Avenida Paulista 1938. *Canadian Consulate,* Av. Paulista 854, 5° ANDAR. São Paulo offices of the *Latin America Daily Post* across from the Folha de São Paulo building, Almirante Barão de Limeira 458, 6th floor. *American Society* and *American Chamber of Commerce,* Rua Formosa 367. *Avis,* Rua Consolaçao 204. *Metropolitan Transport,* Av. Luis Antonio 54. *Anglo-American Home and Art Agency,* Rua 7 de Abril 277.

MEDICAL SERVICES. There are English-speaking doctors and nurses at the *Hospital Samaritano* at Rua Conselheiro Brotero 1486, tel. 51–2154. Also, the English-speaking house doctor at the Hilton can probably suggest a doctor for you.

WHAT TO SEE? The hustle and bustle of busy São Paulo itself, anywhere in the downtown area. Viaduto do Chá (Tea Viaduct) over Anhangabaú "valley." Praça da República (hippie fair Sunday mornings). Avenida Paulista, the history and future of the city in a nutshell, where old coffee barons' mansions mingle with modern skyscrapers. São Paulo Museum of Modern Art (Av. Paulista). Ibirapuera Park (Av. 23 de Maio between downtown and the city airport), on whose spacious grounds are the Museum of Contemporary Art (2 to 6:30 P.M. Tues.-Sun.) and the Museum of Modern Art (2 to 6 P.M. Tues.-Sun.). Butantan Institute, snake farm and museum. Nearby the 400-year-old House of the Flagbearer (Casa do Bandeirante) at Praça Monteiro Lobato (noon to 5:30 P.M. Tues.-Sun.). Campus of the University of São Paulo, Brazil's largest. Anhembi Park, exposition hall and convention center.

 SHOPPING. The best shops for both men's and women's clothes are in São Paulo. Here quality and not quantity are stressed. The elegant Rua Augusta is lined with dozens of interesting establishments and many clerks speak English, French, Spanish, and Italian, as well as their own Portuguese. This same street also has some of the finest antique shops in Brazil. Among the internationally known shops here are *Karitas Antiguidades* (Augusta 2725, also in the Hilton Arcade) for antiques, crystal, and fine semiprecious stones. *Cristais Prado* (Augusta 2487) for crystal and pottery, which is also found at *Marcob* (Augusta 2284). At *Majo* you can find watch specialties (Alam. Jau, 1529 at the corner of Augusta). For fashions: *Rue de la Paix* (Augusta 2607) and *Mayflower* (Augusta 891). Leatherwares: *Supercouros* (Augusta 2032) and *Germonts* (Augusta 2566).

São Paulo's big shopping centers, Iguatemi on Av. Faria Lima, and the Ibirapuera on Av. Ibirapuera, offer a wide selection of shops from boutiques to big department stores. There is also the newly opened *El Dorado* shopping center near the Jockey Club.

For fine jewelry and precious and semiprecious stones, *H. Stern* has branches at Praça da República 242 and Rua Augusta 234. Also at São Paulo Hilton, Shopping Center Ibirapuera and, in Santos, at the Parque Balneário Center, with the largest selection in town, multilingual salesgirls and air-conditioned comfort; own office in New York, besides world-wide service. Emerald specialists are *Sauer Jewelers* at Praça Republica 36 and Av. Sao Luis 101; *Amsterdam Gems,* Praça Republica 64; *Santos Stones,* Rua Xavier de Toledo 114, Suite 502, brings stones directly from their mines to their own workshop. Other shops are: *Simon* (Praça Republica 146), *Charles* (Praça Franklin Roosevelt 128), *Casa Indra* (Rua J. Nascimento 391), *Birskawa* (Rua Barao de Itapetininga 167), *Mimosa* (R. J. Nabuco 304), good for souvenirs, as are *Dourado Souvenirs,* Rua Braulio Gomes 115, across from the Eldorado Hotel, and *Roval,* Av. Sao Luiz 153, shop 43, in the Galeria Metrópole. The *Casa do Folklore* at Praça Republica 242 has the best collection of Brazilian handicrafts, reasonable prices; also for folklore is the *Tenda da Bahia* on Rua Barao de Itapetininga 255.

 RESTAURANTS. Prepare yourselves for some of the finest international eating delights on the continent. It is difficult to choose the best when every one is so good. Your dining should not be confined to the following list, as it is merely the *crème de la crème* of the Paulista restaurants. Look around and experiment. The finest restaurants in São Paulo is generally conceded to be the *Ca D'Oro.* Prices are the same as for Rio: *Deluxe,* over $20; *expensive,* $10–$20; *moderate,* $5–$10; *inexpensive,* less than $5.

CHURRASCOS

For good Brazilian meat, don't ignore *Rodeio, moderate,* on Rua Haddock Lobo 1498, where you can enjoy the best steaks in town in a typical Gaucho ranch-style atmosphere. Other recommended churrascos are: *Baby-Beef Ru-*

baiyat, moderate, restaurant chain with unvarying quality and locations at Av. Dr. Vieira de Carvalho 134 downtown, Av. Brigadeiro Faria Lima 533 in Jardim Paulista, and Alameda Santos 86 in the Paraiso district; *Dinho's Place, moderate,* Largo do Arouche 246 downtown, and another at Alameda Santos 45, featuring Santa Gertrudis beef; *Ao Franciscano, inexpensive,* Rua da Consolaçao 257; *Chave de Ouro, inexpensive,* Alameda Santos 2393; *O Profeta, inexpensive,* Rua Alameda dos Aicás 40, and a new branch at Av. Cidade Jardim 377, with typical dishes from Minas Gerais, heavy on pork.

CHINESE

For Chinese cooking try the *Palácio Imperial,* Rua Capitás Antonio Rosa, near Av. Rebouças 2552; the *Genghis Khan,* Av. Rebouças 3241; or the *Sino Brasileiro,* São Paulo's oldest Chinese restaurant, Rua Dr. Alberto Torres 39.

Dishes from Peking and Shanghai are available also at the *Restaurant Peking,* Rua Alvaro Rodrigues 143, in the Brooklin district.

The *Ancoradoura do Queijos,* Rua Princesa Isabel 121, in Santo Amaro, boasts of its delicious cheese soufflés and other good cheese dishes. All of these restaurants are *inexpensive.*

FRENCH

The French are well represented with the Maksoud Plaza's fabulous *La Cuisine du Soleil, deluxe,* the finest French restaurant in São Paulo and a special treat for all food lovers. The traditional *La Cassarole, moderate,* Largo do Arouche, is another fine French restaurant.

Marcel, moderate, Rua Epitacio Pessoa 98, is an unpretentious little restaurant rated among the best in São Paulo.

Noubar, moderate, Rua General Deodoro 236, Santo Amaro, offers Swiss and French cuisine with fondue a house specialty, while *Maison Suisse, moderate,* Rua Caio Prado 183, has the finest selection of Swiss and French cheeses in the city.

Other French and international deluxe restaurants include *Clark's, moderate,* Av. Cidade Jardim 389; *Le Panache, expensive,* Rua Jorge Coelho/Av. Faria Lima; *Estufa, expensive,* Av. 9 de Julho 5872; *Bistro, moderate,* Av. Sao Luiz 258, mezzanine; *Chamonix, expensive,* Rua Pamplona 1446; *La Cocagne, moderate,* Rua Jerônimo da Veiga 358; *La Toque Blanche, moderate,* Av. Lorena 2019-Cerqueira César; *Le Flambeau, moderate,* Rua Pamplona 1704, Jardim América; *Paddock, moderate,* Av. São Luiz 258, mezzanine and now with a larger branch at Av. Faria Lima 1541. *The Four Seasons, moderate,* in the *Othon Palace Hotel.*

GERMAN

If you're in the mood for *Rippchen mit Sauerkraut* and other German dishes, try the *Kitzbuel,* Rua Frei Gaspar in Campo Belo; *Bar Köbes* ("Juca Alemao"), Rua Conselheiro Saraiva 68 in Brooklin); and the casual *Windhuk* on Av. Ibirapuera 3178 in front of the shopping center. All *inexpensive.*

INTERNATIONAL

For an evening of family dining, the *Don Fabrizio,* on Alameda Santos 65, is highly recommended for Italian and international cuisine. The *Terraco Italia,* on top of the Edificio Italia, has a fabulous view of the city and also serves international food. Both are *moderate.*

ITALIAN

There are many excellent Italian restaurants here. Best is the *Ca d'Oro,* *expensive,* on Rua Augusta 129. Some of their specialties are huge raviolis *(casoncelli)* filled with meat and dried grapes, *amaretti* (fluffed-up dough with peanuts), chicken in the pot with *polenta,* and even pheasant. Their wines, cheeses, and smoked sausage come right from the old country. Open every day for lunch from 11:30 to 2:30 and dinner from 6:30 to 10:30. Other good Italian restaurants are: *Trastevere,* Alameda Santos, 1444; *Via Veneto,* Alameda Barros, 909; *Circolo Italiano,* Av. Sao Luiz 50; and *Gigeto,* Rua Avanhandava 63. All *inexpensive.*

JAPANESE

There are many fine Japanese restaurants in São Paulo, and if you are looking for good food as well as company then pay a visit to the *Honmaru, moderate,* at Rua Visconde de Ouro Preto 127; or the *Akasaka, moderate,* on Rua 13 de Maio 1639. Run by Senhora Yuki, who was a geisha in Japan for ten years, she will help you to select a variety of dishes including *tempura* (with shrimp), *sukiyaki* (made right at your table), or *yakitori* (chicken). For dessert try *yokan* (made from beans). More economical is *Eno Moto, inexpensive,* Rua Galvao Bueno 54.

Restaurants also abound in the Japanese sector of Libertade (first Metro stop north of Praça de Sá). On Sunday afternoons there is, in addition, a street fair and special Japanese food.

Another favorite is *Restaurant Suntory, deluxe,* which serves the finest in meats and seafoods. Located on Alameida Campinas 600, the place offers diners a view of a Japanese garden.

PORTUGUESE

Portuguese food is served best at *Abril em Portugal, moderate,* Rua Caio Prado 47. Inside this restaurant waiters serve mouthwatering *bacalhau Maria Rita* (dried cod fish with a special sauce) and *pescada a moda de Vigo* (a Portuguese version of bouillabaisse). Start your meal with a bowl of *caldo verde* (green broth) and finish it with a dessert called *neves de serra.*

Try also the *Alfama dos Marinheiros, moderate,* at Rua Pamplona 1285, where you can enjoy a typical Portuguese cuisine in an atmosphere of candlelight and live *fado* music.

SPANISH

Feel like going Spanish? Then have dinner at *Sancho Panza, moderate,* (Rua 7 de Abril 425) where the *paella, langosta real* (lobster royale), and *pulpos* (octopus) *al salpicon* are just plain fabulous. Also to be recommended is *Don Curro, moderate,* on Rua Alves Guimaraes 230.

OTHER CUISINES

Bahian specialists: *Maria Fulo, expensive,* Rua São José 563, out in the Santo Amaro suburb.

New, elegant, but expensive, is the *Sea Snack* for seafood, Al. Lorena 1884.

The national dish *feijoada* (black bean stew) is served at many restaurants as the traditional Wednesday and Saturday lunch. You might also try it at *Bolinha, inexpensive,* Av. Cidade Jardim 54, very popular with the young society set;

London Tavern at the São Paulo Hilton, and roof restaurant of the Caesar Park Hotel, both *moderate.*

Massimo, moderate, Alameda-Santos 1826, features an American Bar, restaurant and barbecue. *A Tocha,* Av. Santo Amaro 2554, serves international cuisine, plus a typical Brazilian "feijoada" every Wednesday and Saturday.

Both the *Hungaria,* Al. Joaquim Eugenio de Lima 766, and the *Kakuk,* Al. Glete 1023, offer good menus, their own ensembles. Both *moderate.*

Also good: *The Vikings,* for Scandinavian food at the Maksoud Plaza Hotel. Al. Campinas 150. *Moderate.*

 NIGHT LIFE. Surprisingly enough, there are better clubs and bars in São Paulo than you'll find in Rio. The Paulista enjoys going out after a day in the office and seems to have more money to spend on nighttime playing. There are few of the big shows that other metropolitan centers offer however, for the Brazilian prefers to listen to a slow Samba or a *bossa nova.*

The young in heart make their way to the *Beco* on Rua Bela Cintra 308 for the nightly floor show—one of the best in Brazil—and international cuisine.

The *London Tavern* in the basement of the São Paulo Hilton is a real English pub, open for tea and cocktails in the afternoon, and dinner and discotheque dancing until 4 A.M. Friday and Saturday. Very popular with Brazilians and foreign residents.

For hot Samba and bossa nova try the *Telecoteco na Paroquia,* Rua Santo Antonio 1015; *Catedral do Samba,* Rua Barbosa 333; *Sambao do Shalako,* Rua Joaquim Floriano 82; *Kurtisso Negro,* Rua Almirante Marques Leao 500; *Fina Flor do Samba,* Rua Major Sertorio 763.

Other top night spots include: *Clark's,* Av. Cidade Jardim 389; *Charade,* Rua Pamplona 1057; *Sachas,* Rua Augusta 161; *Skorpios,* Rua Nestor Pestana 251; and *Opus* 2004, Rua da Consolacao 2004.

The *Oba Oba* has brought its fame from Rio with bar, restaurant, and samba dancers at Av. Paulista 412. The newest and hottest nightclub in São Paulo is the *Palace* at Av. dos Jamaris 213, with top shows and singers.

Some of the same discotheques are also located here. Among the best are *Papagaio Disco Club,* Av. Brigadeiro Faria Lima 1565; *New York City,* Rua Nestor Pestana 115; *Ta Matete,* Av. 9 de Julho 5725; *Hippopotamus,* Av. 9 de Julho 5872; *London Tavern,* basement of the Hilton Hotel.

Other small *boîtes* called locally *inferninhos* are *Urso Branco, Playboy,* and *Tao Bar. Club de Paris* has nightly shows. Innumerable other clubs of this type can be found on Major Sertorio and Bento Freitas streets behind the Hotel Hilton. Many have shows and dancers on stage. Interspersed among them are gay bars and spots with transvestite shows, so have a good look before you sit down.

PRACTICAL INFORMATION FOR COASTAL SÃO PAULO

 WHEN TO GO. It depends on where you are going. Because of the varying altitude of the region, which ranges from sea level to 9,000 feet above, it can be hot in some places and cold in others at the same time. If you want the seashore, then the months of December to March are the best, espe-

100 SÃO PAULO AND THE PROGRESSIVE SOUTH

cially for the beach towns of Santos and Paratí and the island of Guarujá. Those same months can be chilly in the mineral water spas and hot spring resorts. If it's coffee you are interested in, then the picking and drying season from June to August is the best time for a visit.

 HOTELS. The spas and hot spring hotels are open all year-round and are usually crowded during the months of December to March. It's best to have a travel agent make reservations for you. The seaside hotels are also crowded at this time, and during Carnival almost impossible to get into without advance reservation.

AGUAS DA PRATA

Probably the best at this mineral water spa is the *Panorama,* Rua Hernani Correa 45. Moderate with all meals included in your room rate. *Ideal,* Rua Gabriel Rabelo de Andrade 79, also moderate with meals included.

AGUAS DE LINDOIA

Tamoio at Rua Sao Paulo 622 and *Hotel das Fontes* on Rua Rio de Janeiro 267 are considered the most comfortable hotels here. Both moderate with meals included.

ARAXA

Famous mineral spa in Minas Gerais. Best hotel is *Grande Hotel de Araxa, moderate.* Suggested side trips to springs at Barbeiro, Osario, Cascatinha Gruta de Monje, and Historic Museum of Dona Beja.

CAMPOS DO JORDAO

This picturesque mountain village has become one of the area's top tourist attractions, offering Swiss-style hotels and chalets amidst a setting of pines, mountains, and streams. In the month of June it hosts one of South America's finest classical music festivals and throughout the year there are activities for the guests at the many hotels. Tops amongst these is the *Orotour Garden Hotel, first class* with meals included, a gem perched on a hilltop overlooking lake and mountains. Other fine hotels are the *Toriba* and the *Vila Inglesa,* both *first class* with meals included in your room rate.

CAXAMBU

Very popular mineral water resort across the border in Minas Gerais. Recommended: *Gloria,* Camilo Soares, 590; *Grande,* Rua Dr. Viotti 438; *Palace,* Rua Dr. Viotti 567. All *moderate* with meals included.

Recommended side trips to Parque das Aguias, Colina de Santa Isabel, Chacara Rosalan, Chacara das Ucas, São Tomé das Letras, Corcovado Morro do Caxambu.

GUARUJÁ

Among the many fine hotels is *Jequitimar, first class,* on Pernambuco Beach. Make reservations at Lojas Cristais Prado, Rua Augusta 2487, São Paulo. *The Delphin, first class,* Av. Miguel Estefno 1295, is luxurious, air conditioned. Pool. Convention facilities. *Casa Grande, deluxe,* Av. Miguel Estento 999; *Guarujá*

Inn, moderate, Av. da Saudade 170, *Gavea Palace, moderate,* Rua Marechal Floriano Peixoto 311; *Ancora Praia, moderate,* Jardim Virginia.

LAMBARI (MINAS GERAIS)

Parque, moderate, Rua Americo Werneck 48; *Itaici,* Rua Dr. José dos Santos 320.

POCOS DE CALDAS

Also in the nearby state of Minas Gerais, this hot springs is probably the best one in Latin America. It boasts of 37 hotels but try to get into the sumptuous *Palace, first class* with meals, on Praça Pedro Sanches. Built by the state government, it has up-to-date facilities for treatment of rheumatic, skin, and intestinal diseases. *Minas Gerais,* on Rua Pernambuco 615, *moderate* with meals.

Suggested side trips are to Cascata das Antas, Veu da Noiva, Fonte dos Amores, Morro de Sao Domingos.

SÃO LOURENÇO (MINAS GERAIS)

Primus, moderate with meals, on Rua Coronel Jose Justino 681; *Brasil, moderate,* Praça João Laje; *Negreiros,* Rua Veneceslau Bras 242.

SANTOS

Hotels and boarding houses on every corner. Best: The old *Parque Balneário,* which has been rebuilt and recently re-opened as a *Holiday Inn, first class,* still the city's biggest and best, located on the beach at Av. Ana Costa 559; *Indaia, inexpensive,* Av. Ana Costa 431-Gonzaga; *Ritz, inexpensive,* Rua Marechal Deodoro 24-Gonzaga; *Praiano, moderate,* Av. Barao de Penedo 39; *Maracana Santos* (beach), *inexpensive,* Av. Pres. Wilson 172.

SERRA NEGRA

Best hotel: *Grande Hotel Pavani, first class* with meals, on Bairro das Palmerias. All others are definitely second-class in comparison.

HOW TO GET AROUND. From Rio to Santos, it's best to go via São Paulo, unless you rent a car and drive up the scenic new Rio-Santos highway. This has been described in the section "Exploring São Paulo." From Santos to Guarujá, there is a new highway link, or you can take the ferry boat (30 cents) at the end of Avenida Almirante Saldanha da Gama, which is the final stop along the beachfront. The boats leave every fifteen minutes or so on a first-come, first-serve basis. They handle cars as well as people and the trip takes 15 minutes. On the other side there are buses waiting to transport passengers to the various beaches. A word of warning: the ferry boats to Guarujá and back on the weekends are very busy, and the highways up the mountain to São Paulo from Santos frequently have bumper-to-bumper traffic on Sunday evenings.

WHAT TO SEE? The beaches of Santos, Guarujá, Ubatuba, and Paratí. The docks in Santos that make this city the most important harbor in South America and the leading coffee port in the world. In Paratí almost everything in this old colonial city is worth seeing, especially the churches and the brightly tiled commercial buildings. At the spas and hot springs you just relax.

RESTAURANTS. In the spas and hot springs, you'll dine at your hotel, because you'll probably be on some special diet and won't want to experiment outside (providing there is some place to experiment, that is).

In Santos you have a choice of a number of fine eating places. On the beach are: *Jangadeiro* (seafood), Av. Almirante Saldanha da Gama 88; *Fifty-Fifty*, Av. Bartolomeu de Gusmao 119; *Adega Transmontana* (barbecue), Rua Marechal Floriano 202; *zi Tereza* (Italian), Av. Bartolomeu de Gusmao 39; *Brumar*, Av. Pres. Wilson 100; *Vista ao Mar*, Av. Bartolomeu de Gusmao 68. All *moderate*.

PRACTICAL INFORMATION FOR THE GAUCHO COUNTRY

WHEN TO GO. Try not to come in the winter months from June to August; cold winds from the south whip across the pampas. Almost any other time is good, and the spring (October-December) is especially enchanting with the fresh green grass, the new wildflowers, and the young calves and lambs.

HOTELS. There are many fine accommodations in the Gaucho Country.

CAXIAS DO SUL

This is the capital of the wine country. Good hotels are: *Alfred Palace*, *moderate*, Rua Sinimbu 2302, and the older *Alfred*, *moderate*, next door at 2266; *Samuara*, *moderate*, 12 miles from downtown on the Parque do Lago; *Volpiano*, *moderate*, Rua Ernesto Alves 1462; *Cosmos*, *moderate*, Rua 20 de Setembro 1563; *Itália*, *inexpensive*, Av. Julio de Castilhos 3076.

CURITIBA

Numerous fine hotels here include the *Iguaçu*, *moderate*, Rua Cândido Lopes 102; *Del Rey*, *moderate*, Rua Ermelino de Leao 18; *Iguaçu Campestre*, *first class*, on the BR-116 highway; *Mabu*, *moderate*, Praça Santos Andrade 830; *Caravelle Palace*, *moderate*, Rua Cruz Machado 282. Also the *Novotel*, *moderate*, Rua AT5, 2401; *Deville Colonial*, *moderate*, Rua Com. Araujo 99 (downtown); *Araucaria Palace*, *moderate*, Rua Amintas de Barros (downtown); *Guaira Palace*, *moderate*, Praça Rui Barbosa 537, *Ouro Verde*, *moderate*, Rua Dr. Murici 419; *Tibagi*, *moderate*, Rua Cândido Lopes 318; *Tourist Universo*, *moderate*, Praça Osório 63; and the new *San Martin*, *moderate*, Rua João Negrao near Rua XV de Novembro.

FLORIANOPOLIS

Florianopolis Palace, *first class*, Rua dos Ilheus 26 (Sta. Catarina); *Querência*, *moderate*, Rua Jeronimo Coelho; *Faial Palace*, *moderate*, Rua Felipe Schmidt 89 (downtown).

FOZ DO IGUAÇÚ

The city of the falls. Absolutely tops, even from the international tourists' point of view is the Varig Airlines-owned *Hotel das Cataratas, first class.* The food is good and they've guides with automobiles to take you to the falls. It's best to make a reservation with a Rio travel agent or wire ahead for rooms. Other good hotels are the *Salvati,* Rua Rio Branco 951 in town, and out of town on the Cataratas Highway headed towards the falls, the *Bourbon, Carima, San Martin,* and *Panorama.* All *moderate.*

PORTO ALEGRE

The best in town are: *Plaza Sao Rafael* on Av. Alberto Bins 514, with its 218 rooms, air conditioning, bar, nightclub, and central location making it the ideal spot while in the Gaucho capital; the *Porto Alegre City* on Rua José Montauri 20; the *Plaza* on Rua Senhor dos Passos 154; the *Everest Palace* on Rua Duque de Caxias 1357; *Alfred Executivo,* Av. Otávio Rocha 270; *Lido,* Rua Andrade Neves 150; *Umbu,* Av. Farrapos 292; *Embaixador,* Rua Jerönimo Coelho 354. More modest and with no restaurants are the *Hermon,* Av. Vigário José Inácio 541; *Metrópole,* Rua Andrade Neves 59; and *Presidente,* Ave. Salgado Filho 140.

SANTO ANGELO

Known as the mission stopoff. Best in town are the *Maerkli,* Av. Brasil 1000, and the *Avenida II,* Av. Venancio Aires 1671.

HOW TO GET AROUND. There are regular plane connections from all large cities to Porto Alegre, which should be your starting point. You can take buses all over the area. Since the land is flat, the highways run smoothly and buses stick to a tight schedule that is bound to please. Automobiles can also be rented in Porto Alegre, and Varig airlines has regular service from Porto Alegre to many small towns in the interior that can be explored on foot.

RESTAURANTS. It's an iron-clad, proven rule that you can't go wrong anywhere in the Gaucho country if you eat in the local *churrascarias.* Here you can be sure —and in any town—that the meat is fresh, the rice fluffy and delicious.

CURITIBA

You will find good food in the dining rooms of the better hotels and the following: For churrasco—*Pinheirao Campestre,* Rua Vítor do Amaral 1010. German foods—*Schwartze Katz,* Rua Franco Torres 18; French and international dishes—*Frau Leo,* Rua Visconde Guarapuava 4069, and *Ile de France,* Praça 19 de Dezembro 538; Italian—*Bologna,* Rua C. Carvalho 150, and *Palazzo,* Rua XV de Novembro 3119. Also numerous fine Italian restaurants in the Santa Felicidade area, such as *Madalosso, Veneza, Pinheirao Colônia.* All *moderate* with the exception of the churrasco and Italian restaurants, *inexpensive.*

PORTO ALEGRE

Probably the best beef in all Brazil is served in this town. In most churras-carias, you slice your own steak off the sizzling skewer, and eat it with a salad of lettuce, tomatoes, and hearts of palm—washing it all down with an inexpensive pitcher (caneca) of *vinho verde*. Start with a *salsichao grosso* (grilled sausage), then move on to filet, *picanha,* or *lombo de porco* (pork loin). There are just too many good spots with this mouth-watering specialty grilling over smouldering charcoal to list all, but start with the *Mosqueteiro* near the Olímpico Stadium; *Quero-Quero,* Praça Otávio Rocha 47; *La Cabanha,* Praça Maurício Cardoso corner of Félix da Cunha; and the *Capitao Rodrigo* in the Plaza Sao Rafael Hotel. All *moderate.*

In the unlikely event you tire of the succulent beef, try Italian food at *Don Nicola,* Av. Getúlio Vargas 577, or *Viareggio,* Rua Barao de Santo Angelo 189, both *inexpensive;* French and international at the panoramic *Everest Roof, expensive,* Duque de Caxias 1357, or *Le Bon Gourmet, expensive,* Rua Alberto Bins 514; German at the *Ratskeller, moderate,* Rua Cristóvao Colombo 1564, or *Franz, moderate,* Rua Protásio Alves 3250 in Petrópolis.

CENTRAL AND NORTHEAST
BRAZIL

Brasilia, the Mining Region, and Salvador
(Bahia)

To visit Brasilia, Brazil's capital, is more than a step into the future, it's a headlong leap into the 21st century. Rising amidst the scrawny jungle of the high red earth plateau, stands one of the most unusual, most strikingly different, most beautiful cities in the world.

There is nothing outdated about Brasilia. In fact, everything there, architecturally, is far in advance of its time. Like something out of Buck Rogers, the city's administrative buildings spread out along the ground, coil around, then leap up in a shaft of white marble to capture the rays of the sun.

It was a city "they" said couldn't be done, but others, more dedicated and more determined, went ahead and did it. With a rare thrust of Brazilian energy, a city rose in just three years, in the very spot where once the jaguar roared.

No trip to this magnificent and confusing country is complete without a visit to this city. It's not quite the same as visiting Italy and not seeing Rome—but almost.

Yet all around this spanking new wonderland of modernity nestles the old Brazil—the land of coffee beans and beef cattle, of palm trees and sluggish rivers, of shoeless peasants and Indians.

While it would be unfair to say that the area neighboring the new capital hasn't progressed with the city, it is a gross exaggeration to say that it has greatly changed. Belo Horizonte, the most important interior city after São Paulo, has taken advantage of the geographical fact that almost everyone and everything traveling by highway to the new capital passes through it. But it was a bustling and prosperous town before Brasilia, as its steel mills and hundreds of factories attest. Goiania, a vibrating little town that has sprung up in the past half century, was doing all right before Brasilia was even thought of. But it, too, has managed to cash in on the boom.

One city, in the Brasilia area but far enough away from any national progress not to be tarnished, is Ouro Preto. The sleepy, colonial prize still rings with the sound of hooves on its cobblestone streets, the sound of Latin chants coming from its thick walled churches, and the sad plaintive notes of a lover's guitar being strummed beneath a balcony. The city at one time (the 1700s) was a bustling capital state with gold, silver, diamonds, and slaves. But hemmed in by tall, almost impassable mountains, it slowly strangled in the commercial competition of the 20th century. In 1897, it lost its status as capital city of Minas Gerais, and Belo Horizonte came into prominence instead. Preserved by the National Patrimony, it stands as a proud reminder of the glory that was once Imperial Brazil. Here, too, are many works by Brazil's greatest artist, the sculptor Aleijadinho.

Building Brasilia

Brazil has had three capitals—Salvador, Rio de Janeiro, and, since 1960, the new city of Brasilia. The reason for the move from Salvador to Rio was that the Portuguese court wanted to be near the center of all the mining and exporting activity. The reason for the move from Rio to Brasilia was that the nation had stagnated for too long along the coast and officials wanted to waken the center of this sleeping giant.

It was not a new idea. As far back as 1808 newspapers were clamoring that Rio was not an adequate place for a capital and were proposing the construction of a city in the interior, where communications could be made with the rest of the country: "Our present capital is in a corner of Brazil and contacts between it and Pará or other far removed states is extremely difficult. Besides, Rio subjects the government to enemy invasion by any maritime power." In 1892, Congress authorized a special expedition to go into the backlands and study the terrain in the center of the nation where "a city could be constructed next to headwaters of big rivers and where roads could be opened to all seaports." After a three-month overland trip, the expedition leaders decided on the planalto area of Goias. They turned in their report and nothing was done with it.

It took a sharp politician named Juscelino Kubitschek to bring the idea into reality. He needed a campaign platform when he was running for President, and one night at a rally someone shouted to him about building a new capital. Immediately he took up the idea as his own and, as soon as he was installed as President, he set the wheels in motion.

It was a monumental undertaking, one without equal in the modern world. What had to be done was to build a totally new city that would become the center of government for the biggest nation in the Western Hemisphere—with all the conveniences of light, power, telephones, sewage, housing, streets, police protection, fire protection, schools, hospitals, banks, industry, commerce, ministries, churches, theaters, as well as all the necessary buildings needed by the Congress, Supreme Court, and the President to govern the country. Brazil was in debt to everyone. Her exports were woefully out of balance with her imports. Her people needed a thousand and one reforms in health, nutrition, and education; nevertheless plans were rushed through and the new capital became a reality.

In the very beginning there was nothing there but scrub trees, red dust, and wild jaguars. President Kubitschek flew there, had Mass said, stayed the night, and set up a long list of work committees. The chief of one of these was Oscar Niemeyer, who was ordered to design every building needed; the chief of another was Lucio Costa, who was to lay out a plan for the city; and another committee chief was Israel Pinneiro, who was to get the city built. Money came from all over the world in the form of loans and government grants. The Brazilians pushed the button on their printing presses and turned out billions of cruzeiros that inflated their economy (from which they still suffer) as never before.

Very few of the raw materials needed for such a grandiose enterprise could be obtained in Brasilia and had to be contracted from outsiders. In the months of September to November 1958 alone, over $14 million in steel tubing, wire, power equipment, telephone trunk lines, and dam construction materials were ordered. Airplanes flew in continually from Rio and São Paulo, loaded with steel bars and bags of cement. The roads to the new capital were still under construction, so all this heavy equipment had to be brought in by air.

Literally thousands of unskilled, uneducated workers, who needed money and were willing to face any hardship to get it, came from the northeast of the nation. They learned fast and worked hard. Living in wooden shacks and working as much as 15 hours a day, they built Kubitschek's dream city. For months on end the noise of hammering could be heard 24 hours a day as swing-shift crews worked on. At night, what visitors thought to be fireflies were really red hot rivets being tossed through the darkness from man to man. Holes were dug quickly, foundations laid in record time, and entire buildings seemed to grow from the soil. Workers would have to wait until the draftsmen gave them the designs of the next floor. And overseeing it all was President Kubitschek, who would arrive suddenly from Rio, hop into a jeep, and climb over girders to see that progress was being made. He was a true "man of the people," and the unschooled workers loved him. He would sit down with them at meal time, open his own lunchbucket, and talk to them about their families and their jobs. Wherever he went he left a trail of friends, and after one of his visits the men worked twice as hard.

Back in Rio, opposition to the new capital was loud and heated. Debates in the senate turned into fistfights, and investigating committees were formed to see where all the money was going. Very few people wanted to move to Brasilia and they complained bitterly about the "lack of everything" there. They said their children would not have the proper schools, that they would be unable to pay the high prices that the artificial city was commanding, and that they would be separated from their families and friends. Actually, most of the big politicians were unhappy about being away from the beach and afraid that their investments in Rio apartment buildings and commercial shops would suffer once the city ceased to be the nation's capital. Kubitschek's government countered this with special inducements to civil servants of a 100 percent increase in salary for working in Brasilia, special tax considerations, and an earlier retirement age. He also promised free transportation of government workers and their household effects, commissioned furniture factories to manufacture modern styles to be sold to workers at wholesale costs, and put rentals on new houses and apartments at ridiculously low rates.

Those who came in the first few waves were either very brave or else went back to Rio fast. There was not a blade of grass or a tree anywhere to stop the monstrous billowing clouds of red dust that rose from the bulldozers and moving trucks. Businessmen had to change their white shirts at least three times a day, and the dining room of the completed and swank Brasilia Palace Hotel was filled with men in rough, mud-caked boots and dust-stained workclothes.

A Bit of Wild West

"Freetown," where most of the construction workers lived, had grown into a city of over 100,000. It was a rough, sprawling, dirty, vice-ridden place, where anything went as long as there was money to buy it. It was straight out of Hollywood. There were wooden store facades with false second stories. Instead of horses, men parked their jeeps in front of the 101 bars. Two movie houses did a roaring business.

Kubitschek had set the date for the inauguration of the city for April 21, 1960, and in spite of all odds it was ready. The inauguration itself was a memorable day that began with a Mass in the uncompleted cathedral and ended with a fireworks display, during which the name Juscelino Kubitschek burned in letters 15 feet tall. Guests came from all over the world, as did newspaper reporters and television men. There were few accommodations available to them, and many slept on the floors of unfinished apartment buildings or slung hammocks in the nearby woods. One man made a fortune selling straw-stuffed mattresses for $15 apiece (they sold for $2 in Rio), then going back after the festivities and collecting them all.

For all of the troubles and haste that Brasilia generated, it is today a modern, comfortable, functioning capital city. It offers many things of interest to the visitor (see the following section on Brasilia) aside from its architecture and feeling of unreality. It has already started to do what those journalists of 1808 wanted. The area around the capital is being opened and a new era of pioneering and colonization has started. There are roads (the Brazilians call them highways) that stretch outward from the new capital to far off Acre, and upward to the coastal city of Belém, and others under construction will go to Fortaleza and Salvador, Bahia. All along these roads, families are coming in, clearing the land, and raising their children. Little communities are forming, and the poor of the big cities are finding out how much nicer life can be in the country than in a cramped favela slum. It will be a long time before the city really "works" or the interior of the country is really settled—maybe another hundred years—but there is no doubt that Brasilia has kicked off the much-needed social improvement.

Brasilia

Brasilia, in spite of its world fame and the fact that it is the capital of South America's largest nation, is still a moderate-sized city, with a population of one million. Tourists can see it all in one day, if pressed for time, or two days if they are interested in the various architectural wonders or in studying more closely the mode of life of a group of people who have been recently uprooted from their original environment.

Most visitors to Brasilia take an early plane from Rio—there are flights from 6:30 A.M. onward—land in Brasilia before noon, take a sightseeing tour around the main buildings, and have lunch at one of the two good hotels; in the afternoon they continue their tour, this time visiting the old "free city," and are delivered to the airport in time to catch a flight back to Rio and dinner.

There is one treat that the linger-awhile type of tourist gets that the one-dayer doesn't. That is to see the city illuminated at night. There is probably no lovelier urban sight in all Brazil than the federal buildings, all white marble with reflecting glass windows, shimmering under dozens of huge, superbly placed spotlights, while the stars shine brightly out of a jungle sky of black velvet. As one old peasant woman told her daughter after she made the trip to the new capital in the back of an open truck: "It looked like I always expected Heaven to look at night. It was difficult to tell where the building lights ended and the stars began. They seemed to be put there to show off the other."

Another thing you'll notice about Brasilia is the sky. It is bluer than the sky in Rio and turns purple. There are always fleecy cloud formations decorating it. Another noticeable item is the red earth of the city. Not unlike the red soil of Georgia, it has stained the bases of the buildings, has tinted the carefully planted grass, and, in a sudden gust of wind, is just as liable to coat your face and clothes with a fine red powder. The earth is very poor in minerals; artistically, it looks as if it had been placed there on purpose for contrast.

Those with only one day to spend should be able to cover the most important points of the city by using this itinerary.

Leaving the airport, take a taxi (if you prefer to drive yourself, there are rental cars available at the airport, too) and watch for the white arrow-shaped signs saying "cidade" (city). If you turn right, take a dip curve, and come up again to where the sign says "Eixo Rodoviario,"

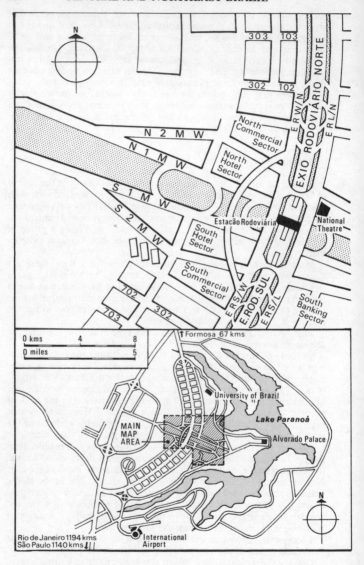

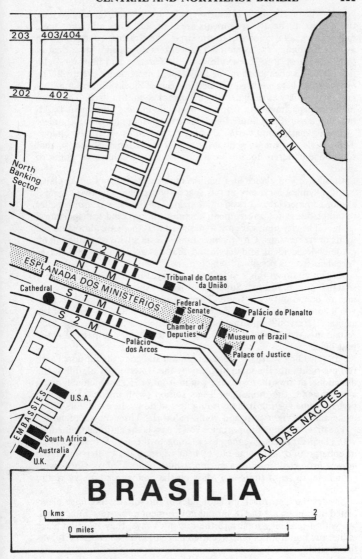

BRASILIA

you will be on the main avenue of the south wing of the city. Along this avenue the luxury apartments are built, and since all rooms have huge plate glass windows onto the street, the Brazilians refer to them as "the Candango's television." The workers do spend a great deal of time looking up into the windows of the senators and ministers who live there. It's cheaper than the movies and much more eventful! The area through here has been planned into Super Blocks (Super Quadras) and each block was designed to be a complete unit in itself. There are high-class apartments in front, then middle-income apartment buildings in the rear. Each Super Block has its own shopping area, complete with supermarket and barber shops, etc., as well as a Catholic chapel. There is also a primary school for almost every Super Block, so that school-age children do not have to cross streets coming or going to class.

Brasilia, if you glance at a map, is built in the form of an airplane, a fitting symbol for a city in this space-minded age. The two "wings" are for commercial and residential areas. The fuselage, from propeller to tail blades, is for government, communications, and transportation centers. The city highways are so designed that there are almost no red lights or traffic signs. City planner Lucio Costa's wife was killed in an automobile accident and he vowed that he would make Brasilia as "accident free as possible," which it is.

As you go down this residential highway, turn off beneath another sign that directs you to a Super Quadra and explore the internal workings of community life there. Then, heading in the same direction, you'll come out onto Avenida W3, the commercial main street of the capital. Here you'll find the shops, both chic and mundane, the good restaurants, a movie house, the banks, the telephone company, and the post office.

After heading south on W3, turn around and go to the far north and, turning right onto the main highway by the Hotel Imperial, follow the directional arrows that will take you in front of Hotel Nacional, down a ramp under the monumental bus station (with music, shops, and perhaps some visiting Indians riding up and down the escalators), then make another right turn and you'll be on the Three Powers Square.

The first building of importance you'll pass is the national Cathedral, with clasped fingers of concrete reaching to the sky. Worshippers go in underground and come out to hear Mass in the center under the fingers, protected from the elements by huge panes of glass. Check with your hotel to see if there is a Mass on the Sunday or holiday you're visiting.

Besides the Cathedral, on both sides of the square, like huge glass-plated dominoes, are the 18 various government ministries. Functional, but with a tendency to absorb the hot sun's rays, they take the place of literally hundreds of offices scattered around Rio when that city was the capital.

Beyond the last building on the right is what many people claim to be the most beautiful building in Brasilia, if not in all Brazil—the Ministry of Foreign Relations (Palácio dos Arcos on the map, "Itamaraty" to all residents), with its water garden and soaring concrete arches. Despite its extravagance—those arches support nothing but themselves—it's a must for the amateur photographer.

Congress in Two Orange Halves

Across the way, almost floating on air and the shallow reflection pools, is the magnificent Congress building with its twin, 28-story towers where senators and deputies have their offices. The two orange halves, sitting on each side of the towers, are the Senate Chamber and the House of Deputies. The Senate is the smaller, inverted one. It is completely air conditioned and perfectly illuminated within. The building can be visited but permission must be obtained from the blue-uniformed guard at the desk just across the ramp on the upper level. If either of the houses are in session, the Brazilian flag is flying from either of their flagpoles.

Continuing down the plane's nose, you'll see the small but perfectly balanced Supreme Court on your right with a modern statue of Blind Justice in front. Further along, you'll come to a plump, oblong cement box, with a huge head of Juscelino Kubitschek in its courtyard: it is the Brasilia Museum.

Directly facing the Supreme Court is probably one of the most beautiful of all the buildings, the Planalto Palace, where the president has his offices. Guided tours can be arranged. Be sure to see the luxurious Hall of Mirrors, where state receptions are held, the severe but lovely room to the right where the President holds open conferences, and the sun-illuminated interior corridors on the second and third floors, where tropical plants grow in profusion.

Head east now, toward the lake, past what seems to be miles of modern lamp posts, until you come to the exclusive Alvorada Palace, official president's residence, at the "propeller" of the airplane. This was the first administrative building ready and the most expensive. Every inch of cement, all the steel girders, the pipes, the glass, tiles, everything had to be flown in, because there was no way to reach Brasilia by land. Beside this jewellike palace is a small circular chapel, where the presidential family attends Mass. Because President Figueiredo prefers to live at his country "Granja do Torto" home he occupied as chief of the National Intelligence Service, the Alvorada now occasionally serves as guest house for visiting heads of state.

The long, low, burned-out building nearby is the Brasilia Palace Hotel, gutted in a fire in 1979.

After lunch, you will still have some three hours to see the other less important things or to go back for a closer look at what you saw that morning. You could visit the handsome national theater, a pyramid of weathered concrete near the bus station, head off in the same direction for the Yacht Club (where you get an interesting side view of the Three Powers Square), or continue way out on the as yet almost deserted North wing and arrive at the other side of the lake, where many expensive homes have been built or are going up.

For a sharp contrast of a "satellite city" to modern Brasilia—from the "architecture" of a dust town to the year 2,000—take a 20-minute drive beyond city limits to one of the communities settled by the Brazilian builders. You may want to hire one of a group of American guides, right opposite the Hotel Nacional.

If you will have an hour or so before your plane, take a quick look at the wild-west, clapboard satellite town called Free City. Though the bulk of Brasilia's working class now lives far out in the satellite towns of Gama or Taguatinga, the *Cidade Livre* (Free Town) still stands as a monument to those hardy northeasterners who built the 21st-century capital city.

The Mining Region

Belo Horizonte is the leading city in the Brasilia region because of its 1,100 factories, skyscrapers, good climate, and friendly people. It gained international attention a few years ago when a group of atomic scientists called it one of the safest spots in the world in case of an atom bomb war between Russia and the United States. Apparently it lies at just the right longitude and latitude and is caressed by certain winds that would carry the barest minimum of radiation down upon the people.

Belo Horizonte is a very young city. In fact, it only celebrated its 75th birthday in 1972, but already it has a population approaching 2 million and is one of the fastest-growing metropolises in Latin America. There are many things for the tourist to do. One of them is to stroll along the shady downtown streets and watch the new buildings going up all around. Another is to visit the municipal park located in the heart of the business area. Town fathers planned well, for should you become tired of cement and commerce, you can cross over into the well-kept park, with its tree-lined walks, its small lakes, its rustic bridges, and red flowered bushes. There is something going on there almost all the time, and it is a favorite spot for lovers, nursemaids and photographers.

Another interesting place is the Minas Tennis Club, one of the biggest sports arenas in the state. Extremely modern in design, the gymnasium can hold 10,000 people. Its swimming pool is Olympic size and its separate courts for volleyball, basketball, and tennis have caused favorable comment from many international sportsminded figures.

Just as modern, but much more controversial, is the oddly shaped church at Pampulha, just outside the city. Designed by famed Brasilia builder Oscar Niemeyer, the church, once constructed, was refused consecration by Catholic authorities because both Niemeyer and Portinari (whose frescoes adorn it) were known Communist sympathizers. The battle raged for a number of years until the people of Minas put pressures to bear on the Bishop and the church was blessed.

The Tassini Museum has a collection of maps, crystal, lamps, work tools, photographs, and general miscellanea collected over a 30-year span by one Raul Tassini and donated to the city. It is devoted strictly to objects that figure in the history of Belo Horizonte and the early diamond mining days. Well worth a visit, it is open every day except Monday.

Ouro Prêto (Black Gold), for its type, is definitely one of the most interesting cities in Brazil. Little known outside of the country, it is revered by Brazilians the way Italians revere Venice or the Americans, Williamsburg. Founded in 1711 with the name Vila Rica (Rich Village), it soon became the center of the gold, diamond, and semiprecious stone trading in the colonial era. So much gold came from the hills around Ouro Prêto that the area was named simply "minas gerais" or "general mines."

It became *the* place to live in those days, and the rich built fine houses and palaces, donated gold to construct churches, and hired the very best artists to decorate them. One of the most famous names to come out of this period was a crippled mulatto sculptor called Aleijadinho. The man could do no wrong when he was working with wood or stone, but his inherited, diseased blood and his sexual escapades turned him into a monster. His facial features became so deformed by disease that he put a sack over his head so that no one could be frightened by his ugliness. His legs refused to coordinate and his fingers and hands became so contorted that his assistants used to tie his hammer and chisel to his wrists with leather thongs so he could work. What he did with the beauty inside him is in evidence in Ouro Prêto and the surrounding area and is part of the rich Brazilian cultural heritage.

The Glorious Churches of Ouro Prêto

The best place to see Aleijadinho's artistry is the Church of São Francisco, located just down the hill to the left from the Praça Tiradentes. Note the twin towers in an almost salt-and-pepper-shaker form. Be sure and inspect the huge soapstone medallion high up over the front door, as well as the intricately carved doorway. Inside, the main altar with cherubic faces, garlands of tropical fruits, and allegorical characters is still fresh with the original paint. Also note the twin soapstone side altars. Just doing one of them is enough for a man to be hailed as a genius, and he did two for this church alone.

His work can also be seen in the impressive Monte do Carmo Church, in whose tall towers hang two bells that weigh 7,000 pounds. The altar dominating the church of São José was also done by Aleijadinho.

There are 11 churches in this one town in the Brazilian hills. If any were in Europe, they would be international "musts" on any tourist itinerary, but hidden away as they are here, they have preserved their charm and offer a new delight to the tourist with spirit enough to come this far to see them.

While in Ouro Prêto, don't fail to take a slow tour of the Museum of Inconfidência. Housed in an impressive baroque building that was started in 1748 and finished in 1846, it was at one time the home of the Municipal Congress. It was here that the first Brazilian rebellion against the Portuguese was started and here that the first rebel, a white-bearded martyr nicknamed "Tiradentes" (tooth puller), was captured, then taken to Rio and brutally executed. The museum is full of clothes, children's toys, slaves' manacles, firearms, books, and gravestones of the turbulent era. The director, who speaks English very well and is proud of his Brazilian past, will be delighted to show you around personally. Admission is free.

Many people stay two days in Ouro Prêto, savoring the winding old streets and the colonial buildings and dodging the donkeys and horses and carts that still move among the automobiles. Ever since 1933, when the entire city became National Patrimony, not a thing has been changed, and it is to the Brazilians' credit that many things have been restored and cleaned up. The second day, you might hire a taxi and travel a few miles to the sleepy village of Congonhas. The main attraction there is the Church of Bom Jesus de Matosinhos, where Aleijadinho sculpted 12 life-sized statues of the Prophets and placed them outside at the front entrance.

These works, breathtaking in their exact details and expressive faces, have been called "a genial mixture of Quasimodo, Beethoven and Michelangelo." Aside from a number of statues inside the church, he did the Stations of the Cross in life-size, using 66 different figures that are housed in six separate buildings. Rarely visited by the Brazilians themselves, these figures are "finds" for the really discriminating tourist.

Aleijadinho, deformed and crippled though he was, got around. His works can be seen in the churches of the nearby town of Mariana and São João Del-Rei. Baroque lovers should also visit the churches of Sabará.

Diamantina took its name from the diamonds that were extracted in great quantities from its soil in the 1700s, and even today the mines still supply gold, iron ore, and rock crystal. It was here also that the famous Chica da Silva, the mulatto slave who captured the heart of the wealthy Portuguese mine owner, lived. He showered her with gold and precious stones, built her a palace with hanging gardens and even transported a sailing yacht overland for her pleasure. Then he turned around and dug her a lake to sail it in.

The city looks very much like it did in the days of Chica. Be sure to note the covered overhanging roofs with their elaborate brackets.

Bahia, the Coast and the Interior

If you have only time to visit two Brazilian cities, make them Rio and Salvador. The latter is usually referred to as Bahia, the name of the state of which it is capital. Salvador has all the ingredients of a South American town. There are red-tile roofs tacked atop white plaster walls. There are palm trees, baroque architecture, an abundance of churches, and happy carefree people. These are the expectable things. Then there are the thousands of black faces, with bodies swathed in cloth of neo-African styles. There are dishes of hot strange foods prepared nowhere else in the world. There is a strange drum beating voodoo ritual that mingles the best of the African and Christian ideals into a powerful, frighteningly personal religion. There is a fight dance called *capoeira* that originated in Bahia and is only practiced here. There are modern automobiles vying with plodding donkeys. There are sumptuous mansions vying for a place in the sun with mud-thatched shanties.

If you stay there for awhile, you'll find Salvador is not just a city but an entire way of life, where the arts and the human personality are more important than money or political ambitions. The city has been called the "Renaissance of Latin America," because of its attitudes towards beauty and self-expression and the number of artists from all over the nation (and the world) who have gone there for inspiration. But this does not mean that Bahia is all siestas in the sun. Far from it. One glance at the dozens of new office buildings and the hundreds of modern apartment houses will dispel that idea. It is simply that the Bahianos have found a way to live with the best of both worlds, and, like their hybrid religion, their city has become a surprising, fascinating experience.

Bird's-eye View of the Northeast

The area the Brazilians call the Northeast is that part of their nation that bulges out into the Atlantic Ocean up north. It is composed of ten states: Sergipe, Alagôas, Pernambuco, Paraiba, Rio Grande do Norte, Ceará, Piauí, Maranhao, Bahia, and part of Minas Gerais. All of them are underdeveloped and plagued by innumerable ills. They are as different from the south of the country as Paris is from Algiers. The same language is spoken and the allegiance to the same flag is taken, but otherwise one would hardly believe he is in the same country.

When the Northeast is not parched and dying from droughts (that come about every three years), it is inundated by rains and flash floods. The land along the coast is fertile in places. Inside the country there is less water than there is in Israel. Educationally and politically the area has been neglected by the rest of Brazil. Those trying to improve their lot have gone south and few return.

For the tourist, this offers some of the most picturesque sights in the country. There are the jangada fishing boats along the coast, the forts and churches, the women weaving fine lace, the leather-clad cowboys and clay sculptors. While you should be prepared to rough it away from the state capitals, the area's unspoiled nature makes it worth a visit before tourism becomes a large-scale industry here—as it soon will if government plans are carried out.

Salvador (Bahia)

Salvador was the first city the Portuguese built up when they colonized Brazil. That was in 1549. Today this city spreads around the bay of Todos os Santos (All Saints), which is so wide (1,052 square kilometers) it could supposedly hold all the ships in the world. Salvador was built by the early settlers to keep the Spanish, French, and Dutch away from the new colony belonging to King Dom João III. The administration buildings and residences were built on the hills, the forts, docks, and warehouses on the beaches. To this day, it is still divided into upper and lower cities. From 1500 to 1815, Salvador enjoyed being the nation's busiest port. The sugar from the northeast and the gold and diamonds from the mines in the south all passed through this town. It was a golden age for Salvador when magnificent homes and richly decorated churches were built. Its churches have few rivals anywhere in the world. Thanks to a federal commission called The National Historic and Artistic Patrimony Service, created in 1941, many of the city's old churches are the same today as they were the day they were built. Entire squares, such as Largo do Pelourinho, hundreds of private homes and even the hand-chipped street paving bricks have been preserved. Salvador counts 97,000 buildings and about 20,000 of them are over 250 years old. Yet there are brand new buildings going up everywhere to meet the living requirements of the progressive citizens of today.

Salvador may be seen, if necessary, in three days. Save time for some shopping and maybe an extra day to go back for a closer look at some of the things seen in passing.

The first day. Start out on foot from the Tourist Department at Praça da Sé. They have English-speaking guides if you want one. The formality of previous years has disappeared in Salvador and the city is nearly as relaxed as Rio, with all manners of dress accepted. It gets hot here so be comfortable. To the left of the Tourist office is the Archbishop's Palace, built in the 18th century and today used as the Catholic Law School. On the other side of the Tourist office is the 18th-century Holy House of Mary church. Walking up Guedes de Brito Street, you'll see Saldanha Palace with its impressive gateway. The School of Arts and Crafts is there now. As you walk up Bispo Street you'll pass São Damaso Seminary, built in 1700, and will come to a little square and the Church of São Francisco Convent. It is one of Brazil's most famous and undoubtedly one of the most beautiful in the world. Hand carved in every nook and cranny and then covered with shining gold, it is so impressive that many tourists stay around all day just watching the play of light on the walls. It is especially beautiful during a High Mass. The image of St. Peter of Alcantara on the lateral altar on the right is so well done that church authorities had a battle with Emperor Dom Pedro II, because he wanted it for his private chapel. Only the men may visit the blue-tiled cloisters of the monastery; women must be content to peer through the grillwork. There are Franciscan fathers there who will show you around. When you leave drop some money into the poor box, for the church does an impressive job three times a day supplying warm meals for the poor. Right next door is the church of the Third Order of São Francisco. Inside there is a room that is worth seeing full of life-size statues. The intricate façade was carved in 1703 but hidden for many years by a thick coat of plaster. It was a major art find when it was uncovered recently. Now to the square of Terreiro de Jesus with the 16th century Basilica Cathedral, the church of the Third Order of São Domingos (1731), and the church of St. Peter of the Clerics. From here, up Alfredo de Brito Street you come to the architectural spectacle of the Largo do Pelourinho. It was here that thousands of slaves were chained together, then sold on that platform on the right side of the street. Note the typical old balconies, the tiles and the people who look as if they've stepped from a Debret engraving. Walk slowly down to Taboão Square where five streets cross and then up the Ladeira do Carmo. Now take a quaint flight of steps that leads to the Church of the Passo and continue to the top of the street. Here the Carmo Convent and the Church of the Third Order of Carmo stand side by side. The church is famed for its image of the crucified Christ. To enter the convent, you have to know the way. Beside the biggest door in the room hangs a cord. Pull it and from somewhere inside a smiling guard appears to escort you about. Be sure and tip him when you leave. Going up the Ladeira do Carmo, there is a corner of blue-tiled houses.

Tell the driver to take you to Baixa do Sapateiro, a street filled with shops and private homes that time has somehow forgotten. Afterward look at the Convent of the Desterro (1678), where the sisters have a well-deserved reputation as candy makers. It is Brazil's oldest and most beautiful convent. Go up Avenida Joana Angelica to the Tororó steps. Below them lies the Dique, an artificial lake made in the 17th century as part of the city's defense system. You can go for a ride in one of the boats if you wish.

Coconuts and the Great Outdoors

The second day should be devoted to beaches and outdoor scenery. Rent a car and driver for the day and tell the driver to go *slowly* towards the Lagoa do Abaeté. The first impressive building you will pass is the white columned University Rectory. If you wish you may go in to see the blue tiles and the reconstructed auditorium. On Avenida Oceânica you'll go for about 20 miles past fishermen's houses, beaches, palm trees, and little boys selling fresh coconuts. If you stop for one, watch how deftly a boy can nick off the top with his knife. The milk is warm and sweet. Ask him to split open the coconut and then go on and eat the soft white meat with your fingers. You will pass famed Itapoa Beach with its tall coconut trees and finally reach the lagoon. Brazilian composers have written dozens of songs about this strange inland lake with its contrast of white, white sand and black, black waters. Native women wash their clothes here, and there are some good restaurants in the area for lunch or a cooling drink. Take your bathing suit too, for you might like to sample one of the beaches on the way going or coming.

Arriving back in the city, you'll pass the Barra lighthouse and the fort, built in 1598. Drive along Avenida Sete (7) de Setembro and stop to look at the fort of Santa Maria, built in 1650. A little farther on is the fort of Sao Diogo. It was on this spot that Tomé de Sousa landed in 1549 to found the city. The avenue then passes the church of Santo Antonio de Barro and the church of Victoria built in the 16th century and restored in 1809. Now let's take Rua da Graça and visit the Igreja da Graça, the first church built in Bahia. It was constructed by Catarina Paraguaçu, the Indian wife of the first white man to settle there. If there is not a *capoeira* exhibition at the Tourist Office that evening, go back to your hotel, have a fast bite, and try to see a *condomblé* (voodoo religious ceremony) that evening. Remember not to take photos unless the permission of the Mae do Santo (priestess) is given. Be prepared to be separated from your friends once you arrive there. They will tell you where to sit and its always men on one side and women on the other. There is nothing to be frightened of either, but don't be surprised to see the Brazilian beside you suddenly become "possessed" by spirits, fall onto the ground, roll his eyes, and then dance in a contorted, uncomfortable position. When you leave (sometime after midnight) show your appreciation by placing some money at the feet of the chief drummer.

The third day. Now you'll visit the other end of the city on the Itapagipe peninsula. If you leave about 9 A.M. from the Tourist Office, the car will go down commercially busy Rua Chile to Castro Alves Praça, then down the Ladeira da Montanha (where many accidents have happened when the brakes didn't hold) and reach the lower city. That big column of white cement rising to the upper city is the Lacerda elevator and is used to join the two levels of Salvador. Imagine if you had to walk up and down those steep hills every time! Taking Avenida Frederico Pontes, you'll pass the attractive Fort of Lagartixa and the Noble House of Jequitaia built in the 18th century and now used as an army officers' school.

Ask your driver to go to the Bonfim church, and on the way you'll pass the 18th-century Archbishop's summer palace, which is connected to the Penha church by a very interesting passageway. Now at Bonfim church, you are really in Bahia, for this church is the city's main sanctuary. It is not ornate or covered with gold, just a simple building with years of tradition among the faithful. It is said that the Lord of Bonfim never fails anyone and the room of miracles looks as if that might be so. Here you'll see wooden, silver, and plaster reproductions of parts of the human body hanging on the walls. These are there in gratitude for cures worked through prayers to the Lord of Bonfim. Almost always the cures are said to be miracles, as the many inscriptions indicate. It is here, on the Thursday before the third Sunday in January, that thousands of black women dressed in their colorful regional dress and carrying pottery jugs with flowers and water come to symbolically wash down the church steps. It is one of the most time-honored fiestas in Bahia. Spectacular view from atop this hill.

Back in the car, go to the Fort of Mont Serrat, named for the great shrine of the Black Virgin in Spain at Montserrat, near Barcelona. Its white walls rising from the seacoast, this 16th-century building looks like a giant ready for flight. There is the Mont Serrat Church nearby with its renowned carving of the Repentant St. Peter. If the church is closed, call the guard who lives at the back, and even though he grumbles, he'll show you the tiny jewellike interior. A tip calms him down amazingly. Now you can go to the Cacao Institute, where pictures and graphs tell the story of the chocolate industry from the planted seed to the finished foil-wrapped bar. More than $100,000,000 of cocoa is exported annually from Bahia's ports. Unfortunately one of the traditional sights of Salvador, the Modelo market with its row after row of handicrafts, was destroyed by a fire in 1983. Plans existed at press time to reconstruct the market at the same location. Now take a boat at the Cairu docks for a quick look at the Fort of São Marcelo right in front of the market in the bay. It was built in 1650 and kept invaders away. Then it was used as a prison and now serves more for curiosity than anything else. Back in your car, go to the lovely Museum of Sacred Art on Ladeira de Sodré. You'll be impressed with the tiles and the silver altar. It is unquestionably the most beautiful museum in all Brazil. Then, if there is still time, visit the Museum of Modern Art in the Castro Alves theatre.

The Northeast

Recife has been called the "Venice of Brazil" because it is a city built on three rivers and connected by many bridges. It is the third largest city in the nation, with an estimated metropolitan population of over two million. The city got its name from the reefs that line the coast and make the beach of Boa Viagem an unusual place. Those who come here as tourists are always impressed with the beach. In the morning, when the tide is in, the waves come up almost to the road, then as the tide recedes, the rocks of the reefs slowly appear. Depending on the time of the day, individual swimming pools are formed, fish flap around the bathers, and the hidden rock formations dry into odd colors in the afternoon sun.

Another sight to see along this beach is the departure (about 6 A.M.) or the return (about 2 P.M.) of the *jangadas,* those crude, log rafts with the beautiful sails that local fishermen take out onto the high seas. Many stories and legends have been written about them, and they are as dangerous as they look. Only an expert navigator and swimmer should try one. It looks easy for the sunburnt men of Recife, but they have been working on them all their lives.

There are many old churches in this town. Most impressive are the São Pedro dos Clerigos (for its beautiful sculptured front, 1782), Conceiçao dos Militares (with its unusually fine ceiling, 1708), Madre de Deus (altar and sacristy, 1707) and the Convento de São Francisco (its interesting Portuguese tiles, 1606).

Olinda is a small colonial city, five miles to the north of Recife, that can be reached by a bus, which leaves from the front of the Governor's Palace. Go to the end of the line and walk across the street and up the hillside. Here you will see old houses, monasteries, and the mayor's office, which was once the home of the Viceroys. The city was built by the Dutch who controlled Recife in the late 1600s. Many of the houses still have the original latticed balconies, heavy doors, and pink stucco walls.

You will notice small clay statuettes in the shops for sale. Almost all of these are made in the interior town of Caruaru. Reached by daily bus or special taxis on Wednesdays and Saturdays, the days of the fair, the trip is well worth it. Not only will you be able to see a very colorful interior market place, but you'll be able to rub elbows with the leather-clad cowboys of the harsh, dry region, see the way the people live on the parched soil, and be entertained by strolling musicians and dancers. Allow one full day for this.

In Fortaleza, the beach is the main attraction, but the old lace makers are in close second. Aracati is the town that contains most of the artisans. There you will see little girls of three years learning to thread a needle and unravel snarled thread, as well as old grandmothers almost blind from the years of close, delicate labor.

A new highway (BR-010), cut through the jungle between Belém and Brasilia, connects 32 new cities and villages. Daily motorcoach in both directions is available. The trip lasts 3 days and is well worth the cost of $50 (approx.) if you are the adventurous type.

PRACTICAL INFORMATION FOR BRASILIA

 WHEN TO GO. The best time is probably the summer, from November to around the middle of April. It gets chilly in Brasilia. Because the city is on a high plateau, some 3,500 feet above sea level, and in the direct path of winds from the moist warm jungles as well as those from the colder south, its climate is variable and invigorating. Sweaters at night during the winter months are almost a necessity, and no matter what the season, you'll probably want to sleep under a blanket.

 WHAT TO SEE? Everything. The two presidential palaces (the Alvorada where the man in power lives and the Planalto where he works), the twin-towered Congress building at the Praca dos Tres Poderes, the domino-placed Ministry buildings in the same area, the crown-shaped cathedral at the Eixo Monumental, the national theater also at the Eixo Monumental, the modern spacious apartments, and the bustling—almost small town—atmosphere of the business district. A visit should be paid to the yacht club and the area known as Embassy Row. A visit to the shrine of Dom Bosco is also in order, not just to pay him homage, but to get an over-all, complete view of the city. There are no museums as yet of any importance, nor any special collections. The exteriors of the buildings are more interesting than the interiors (with a few exceptions mentioned already), and don't forget to take note of the way the highways and by-passes have been laid out. Also study the faces of the "candangos," the dusty but courteous immigrant workers who built the city with almost nothing but bare hands and determination.

 HOW TO GET AROUND. Take a taxi. Many people prefer to have a guided tour by one of the registered agencies. If you only have time for a once-around-lightly view of the city, then *Ciclone-Hinterland Turismo* at the Seitor Commercial Sul, or *Trips, Toscano, Excelsior,* or *Presmic,* all located in the arcade of the Hotel Nacional, will give you the best service. They have their own cars, usually Brazilian-made Volkswagen "Kombi" station wagons, and their drivers speak English as well as half a dozen other languages. Prices are moderate but a little higher than in Rio for the same service, about $15.

You might, just for the fun of it, get on any of the buses that leave from the street level platform at the centrally located Highway Terminal ("Estaçao Rodoviaria") and stay on it till it takes you back to the terminal again. No matter which line you take, you'll get odd and interesting angles of the city that other tourists don't catch from the guided tour. But it's best to do this after you've seen Brasilia the regular way, so you can appreciate what you are seeing even more. Bus fares are about 10 cents.

SPORTS. In Brasilia, there used to be such an exodus of governmental workers, especially such important types as congressmen and ministry directors, that weekend activities were limited. But the city is now developing a social life of its own, even on weekends. The one favorite focal point is the *yacht club,* on the artificially created Lake Pinheiro. Although open only to members, your travel agent or almost any Brazilian citizen can get you in. There is a nice big pool, a small but more than adequate restaurant, and if you look sad and wistful, some friendly Brazilian is bound to ask you if you'd like to take a ride on the lake in his "yacht." There are about ten other good social clubs that have also sprouted up—all normally crowded and lively on sunny weekends.

People do go fishing, some as far away as on Bananal Island. Check with your tourist agent in Brasilia about this and see if they can arrange a two-day trip to the Carajá Indians, who will act as your guides. There is a hotel there; it was called the *Juscelino Kubitschek* until the latter's political disgrace, whereupon it became *John Kennedy* (same initials!). Don't go there without a reservation. *Andre Safari & Tours,* in the Torre Palace Hotel, specializes in this trip.

HOTELS. A number of new hotels are in various stages of study, planning, or construction, by such chains as *Inter-Continental, Holiday Inns, Sheraton,* and *Hilton,* among others. Still one of the most popular is the *Nacional, first class,* (phone 226–8180), situated in the heart of the city with an incomparable view of the Congress, Ministries, and the banking section. Ten floors of comfortable apartments each with bath and telephone. Off the spacious lobby is an excellent restaurant where one of the daily specialties is a long smorgasbord table with 100 different dishes to choose from. The wine cellar is excellent and the European-trained chefs add a Continental touch. There is a small bar done in beautiful jacaranda wood paneling, and a pool outside open to guests of the hotel. The basement is equipped with a modern Finnish-style sauna as well as steam baths and massage parlors. For evening entertainment, one of the best nightclubs in town is on the ground floor, alongside a patio *churrascaria.* There is also a *H. Stern* store.

Another good hotel is the *Eron Brasilia, first class,* (226–2125) 200 rooms with refrigerators, TV, and FM music in each. Central air-conditioning, panoramic-view elevators up the side of the building, a small pool, bar, and nightclub. Also the *Carlton, first class,* (226–7320) with pool.

Other hotels that can be recommended are the *Alvorada Hotel,* 223–3050; *Torre Palace,* 225–3360; *Bristol,* 225–6170; *Das Nacoes* (225–8050), *Diplomat* (225–2010), *Itamarati Parque* (225–6050), *Planalto* (225–6860), *Brasilia Imperial* (225–7050), *Americas* (223–4490), *Aracoara* (225–1650) and *Casa Blanca* (226–0255). All *moderate.*

RESTAURANTS. Brasilia does have some good restaurants. For good solid Brazilian beef, done "churrasco gaucho" style, pay a visit to the *Churrascaria do Lago,* (223–9266) on the banks of the lake, in walking distance of the Hotel Brasilia. Their specialty is a "mixto," which is a little bit of everything, both beef and pork, served with rice, manioc flour, and a special barbecue sauce of raw onions, tomatoes, and vinegar. *Moderately* priced.

Another good *churrascaria* is the *Tordilho,* (223–4688) *moderate,* with music and a fine view of the lake. The Centro Commercial Gilberto Salomao has a number of spots. This same commercial center, where bureaucrats and diplomats of all levels gather nightly, also is home to the *Gaf* (248–1754), *moderate,* for international cuisine; the *Bier Fass* and *Berlim* (273–2890), both *moderate,* for German food and beer: the *Amarelinho,* (248–0987) *moderate,* for Italian dancing.

PRACTICAL INFORMATION FOR MINING REGION

Like the rest of the country, this area is no exception when it comes to distances. Belo Horizonte is 453 miles from Brasilia, but that doesn't stop people from Brasilia going there to do their shopping. Ouro Prêto, the living museum city, is a full 75 miles away from Belo, but the people in the state capital consider it "a suburb." And Diamantina (another colonial jewel in the Minas hills), is 180 miles away, but citizens in Belo will calmly tell visitors who have nothing to do for the day, "Why don't you run over and see Diamantina?"

Fortunately, there is regular train service between Belo Horizonte and Diamantina, and a new paved road from Belo to Ouro Prêto. Taxis will drive you there and back for $25 or so, and a regular bus line charges about a dollar for the same service.

HOTELS. The Mining Region offers a range of hotels but most are quaint inns and pensions.

BELO HORIZONTE

Othon Palace. Av. Afonso Pena, corner Tupis e Bahia. Newest, biggest, and most luxurious in the city, with 317 air-conditioned rooms, rooftop pool and bar, international restaurant, coffee shop, sauna, conference facilities for 800 persons. Overlooking trees and lakes of Municipal Park. *First class.* 226–7844.

Brasilton Contagem. Contagem industrial district on a hilltop near Belo Horizonte. First Hilton Hotel in Brazil outside São Paulo, the Brasilton Contagem opened early in 1978. Rooms are built around central courtyard with pool and tropical gardens, and all have air conditioning, heat, color TV, well-stocked mini-bars. *Moderate.* 351–0900.

Hotel Del Rey. Pça Afonso Arinos 60. One of the best traditional hotels downtown; 270 non-air-conditioned rooms, private baths, 24-hour room service. *Moderate.* 222–2211.

Normandy. On Rua Tamoios 212. Service is very good; the rooms large and airy; modern restaurant and bar are fine. Located in the center of the city's business district, it is one of the most popular meeting places. Insist on an outside room. *Moderate.* 201–6166.

The Amazonas. On Avenida Amazonas 120, is new and small but service is very good. Excellent restaurant on the 11th floor. *Moderate.* 201–4644.

Other hotels include the *Excelsior* (250 rooms), *Serrana Palace, Financial,* Rua Caetes 753, 207–2600; Rua Goitacases 450, 201–9955; Av. Alfonso Pena 571, 201–7044. All *moderate.*

OURO PRÊTO

Grande Hotel on Rua Rocha Lagoa. Built by Brasilia designer Oscar Niemeyer, the hotel is comfortable and modern, even if its style is in shocking contrast to the rest of the city. Good restaurant. *Moderate.* (551–1488).

Pouso do Chico Rei. An old restored home that is one of the most charming and "typical" hotels in the entire town. Located on Rua Brigadeiro Musqueira 90, it has very few rooms so service becomes a personal thing. Telephone 333 for reservations in advance. *Inexpensive.* (551–1223).

Hotel Estrada Real. On the highway leading to Belo Horizonte. Like all of the city's accommodations, small, with 12 bungalows. *Moderate.* (551–2122).

Other hotels, all *inexpensive,* are the Pousada Ouro Preto, (551–2244), Rua Alfredo Baeta 16 (run by Luxor in tastefully-restored colonial mansion; gourmet restaurant); *Pilao,* (551–2057) Praça Tiradentes 57; *Colonial,* (551–1552) Travessa Camilo Veloso 26; *Toffolo,* (551–1385), Rua Sao José 76.

CONGONHAS DO CAMPO

Cova de Daniel. Small but quaint combination of inn, restaurant, and antique shop flanking the church of Our Lord of Matosinhos, which features great masterworks by South America's Michelangelo, a crippled mulatto who lived in the 17th century, known as "Aleijadinho." *Inexpensive.*

DIAMANTINA

Tijuco. Located on Rua Macau do Meio 211, this is the best hotel in this old-world village. It adheres faithfully to the historical atmosphere demanded by the visitor. *Inexpensive.* (931–1022).

 RESTAURANTS. While you are in this area be sure to try some *carne desfiado com tutu,* which is dried jerked beef torn to shreds, fried with onions, and served with mashed black beans. This dish is also referred to as *roupa velha* (old clothes).

Belo Horizonte has the best places to eat in the area. In the other towns stick with the food served in the recommended hotels. If you are very brave and adventurous, you might eat at some small, not too clean places you'll discover on a side street. It can lead to all sorts of gastric disturbances, but can also be fun.

BELO HORIZONTE

Fanciest spot in town is called the stock exchange—*Clube Bolsa de Valores,* expensive, high on the 14th floor at Rua dos Carijós, downtown. Coming down, in height and price, two among the city's many *churrascarias* stand out for their thick, juicy steaks: *Mangueiras,* Praça São Francisco da Pampulha 30 in Pampulha suburb; and *La Alhambra,* both *moderate,* Av. do Contorno 8835 in the Gutierrez district. Meat places downtown are *Farroupilha,* Rua Aimorés 1451-A; *Favela,* Rua Pouso Alto 720; *Minuano,* Rua Prof. Morais 635, all *moderate.*

For international cuisine, try *Vila Romana, moderate,* Rua da Bahia 1271, downtown; *Casa do Baile, inexpensive,* Av. Otacilio Negrao de Lima in Pampulha; or the *Nacional Clube, moderate,* Rua Josafá Belo 100 in Cidade Jardim.

Best Italian food is at *Dona Derna,* Rua Tomé de Souza 1380, or the *Terrazzo Ângelo,* on Rua Marte in Contagem. *Inexpensive.*

A touch of old Germany is the *Alpino* on Rua Tupinambas 173, with its ice-cold draft beer, its homemade black bread, and such items as *Hasenpfeffer* and *Konigsberger Klops.* But check beforehand, as sometimes they are out of their specialties. Prices are *moderate.*

Most popular night spots, which also serve meals or specialty dishes, are *Chorare,* Rua da Bahia 1450, with good music; *O Papa Papatutti,* Av. Getúlio

Vargas 823, for good pizza and beer. Other nightclubs are *Cafe Society, Le Bateau Blanc, Le Chat Noir, People, Samantha,* and *Tenda.*

PRACTICAL INFORMATION FOR SALVADOR

(BAHIA)

WHEN TO GO. Because of its consistently warm climate, almost any time of the year is a good time to visit Salvador. But there are certain events that will make this attractive city even more interesting if you plan your trip to coincide with them.

January 1 has the celebration of Our Lord the Good Jesus of the Navigators. Hundreds of boats float offshore, decorated with flags and streamers. Later, there are exhibitions of drum beating and capoeira fighting. January 1, Festa de Nosso Senhor dos Navigantes takes place at Monte Serrat. On January 6, Festa dos Reis is celebrated in all parts of the city.

February 2 is devoted to Iemanjá, the goddess of the sea, who is also the Virgin Mary. In Rio Vermelho and Itapoan, celebrants make offerings all along the shores, and boats are gaily decorated. Festa de Rio Vermelho, in honor of Saint Anne, is held two Sundays before Carnival. Carnival itself is celebrated as in Rio and all business stops for four days. Must be experienced to be believed.

May 10 has the procession of St. Francis Xavier, a feast day in honor of the city's patron saint, held since 1686.

In *June,* twelve days after Holy Ghost, there is a Christian procession. At the same time candomblé worshippers hold services to Oxosse, the African God of the Hunt. Festa de Santo Antonio, a religious feast, takes place in June, while the 24th has the Festa de São João, a popular festival with local dances, entertainment and fireworks. On *June* 29 a twelve day and night voodoo celebration honors all the gods.

July 2 is devoted to the heroes of Brazil's fight for independence. Aside from parades, there are folklore dances and candomblé ceremonies.

On the second Sunday in *September* is held an impressive procession to the sea of Our Lady of Monte Serrat, while on the 27th the twin gods Cosme and Damião are honored with banquet tables loaded with rich regional cooking.

October, all month long, is devoted to the African gods Exú, Iabás, Ogum, Omulu, and Oxum.

December 4 is the Festa de Santa Barbara. Three days of festivities at Saint Barbara's Market, Daiza dos Sepateiros. *December* 8 has the celebration of Conceiçao de Praia, held in front of Our Lady of Conceição Church and includes candomblé, capoeira and folksingers. *December* 13: Festa de Santa Lucia, in front of the Pilar church.

HOW TO GET THERE. Salvador's 2 *de Julho* airport was classified as one of Brazil's international fields in 1975 and anticipates increased international travel in the near future. But today, unless you come in on *Varig's* weekly flight from Lisbon, you'll probably be coming from Rio on one of several, daily 90-minute flights (round trip costs about $250). There are also frequent flights from Brasilia and, of course, cities in the Northeast. Alternatives are driving or taking a 27-hour bus trip ($30 one way, or $45 on a "deluxe sleeper")

up the new highway from Rio, or calling on one of the cruise or cargo ships that stops here.

HOTELS. Outside Rio, Brazil's biggest spurt in construction of tourist-type hotels has taken place in Bahia. The latest addition is the **Quatro Rodas Salvador,** an excellent *luxury* hotel located near the beach on Rua Pasargada. Other top hotels are the *Meridien* and *Othon Palace,* which opened in 1976 and 1975. Alternate choices are the charming little (70 rooms) *Pousada do Convento do Carmo* downtown or the 164-room beachfront *Salvador Praia,* both also opened in 1975. Nearby Itaparica Island offers two top quality resort hotels, the **Club Mediterranee,** in an exotic, secluded setting with nonstop activities and the **Grande Hotel de Itaparica.** Both *First Class.*

Bahia Othon Palace. *Deluxe.* 247–1044. Av. Presidente Vargas 2456 on Ondina Beach. Built in a "Y" shape, with all 301 rooms facing the ocean. Swimming pool, nightclub, convention hall, sauna, and everything you'd expect in a modern new hotel. Pride of the Othon chain and one of Brazil's best.

Grande Hotel da Barra. *Moderate.* 247–6011. Av. 7 de Setembro 3564. Beachfront at harbor entrance. Calm waters for swimming. Air conditioned.

Luxor Convento do Carmo. *Moderate.* 242–3111. Largo do Carmo, in the heart of the old section of Salvador. A restored former convent whose cells have been made into hotel rooms with wooden floors and ceilings lighted by rustic lanterns. Small swimming pool in inner courtyard. Chapel and art gallery in same building. Lots of atmosphere.

Meridien Bahia. *Deluxe.* 248–8011. Rua Fonte de Bahia 216. Overlooking the ocean, 30 minutes from the airport, 15 minutes from downtown Salvador, deluxe class, 502 rooms including 2 deluxe suites, 77 suites, and 27 cabanas. Conference and banquet facilities. Congress hall equipped with audio-visual aids and for simultaneous translation; 5 meeting rooms. Panoramic restaurants and bars at the top. Discothèque, beauty parlor, sauna, solarium, sea- and freshwater swimming pools, tennis, marina, boutiques.

Ondina Praia. *Moderate.* 247–1033. Av. Presidente Vargas across from Ondina Beach. Modern, with pool, bar and restaurant.

Quatro Rodas Salvador. *Deluxe.* 249–9611. Farol de Itapua, on Itapua Beach. The newest of Salvador's top hotels, it features all-weather tennis with both indoor and outdoor courts plus a permanent Tennis Clinic. There are four restaurants, an ocean-view rooftop nightclub, beach, pool, and a bar on the banks of a lagoon.

Salvador Praia. *Moderate.* 245–5033. Av. Presidente Vargas 2238 (Ondina Beach). Pool, bar, restaurant, convention rooms. Mural by famous Brazilian painter Caribé and sculpture by Mario Cravo dominate the lobby.

Vela Branca. *Moderate.* 248–7022. Av. Antonio Carlos Magalhaes on Pituba Beach. Modern, motel-type accommodations with bar, restaurant, pool.

Other hotels include *Baia do Sol, moderate,* 7 de Setembro 2009; *Armaçao, moderate,* Av. Otavio Mangabeira, Piata Beach; *Itapaa Praia, moderate,* Rua Dias Gomes 4; *Marazul, moderate,* Av. 7 de Setembro 3937; *Praiamar, moderate,* Av. 7 de Setembro 3577; *Do Farol, moderate,* Av. Pres. Vargas 68; *Paulus, moderate,* Av. Otavio Mangabeira; *Villa Romana Hotel, inexpensive,* Rua Lemos Brito 14, Barra.

Pensions: *Pensao Anglo-Americana,* Av. Sete de Setembro 329; and *Pousada da Praça,* Rua Rui Barbosa 5. Both *inexpensive.*

USEFUL ADDRESSES. *U.S. Consulate,* Av. Presidente Vargas 1892, first floor, tel. 245–6691. In addition to the consulate there is a *U.S. Information Service Office* in the Edificio Casa Blanca, Av. Sete de Setembro 333. *The American Society of Bahia,* tel: 8–0073. *Police;* Radio Patrol: Dial 190. *Medical facilities:* Pronto Socorr, tel: 5–0000.

Bahiatursa (Bahia State Tourist Board) has several information booths and its main offices are at Rua Mariscal Floriano 1, Canela. Telephone 247–4793 or 245–8433 (Salvador). For general information call 241–4333.

HOW TO GET AROUND. Buses are overcrowded, dirty, and never on schedule. Taxis are plentiful and cheap, but bargain first if you're going to use one by the day. You should be able to make a deal for around $15 to $20. There are tourist agencies with cars for hire at $20 to $30 for the day, and your hotel can usually supply you with a limousine and an English-speaking driver. But the best way to see most of the city is just to get out and walk around the old streets. Nothing will happen to you. You're a lot safer in the back streets of Bahia than you are in New York or London. You can charter a native schooner for a day's cruise of the bay for $150 to $250, from either *L.R. Turismo* at Av. Sete de Setembro 540 or *Panorama Turismo,* Rua Marquês de Caravelas 110.

WHAT TO SEE? Spread out over the length and breadth of this intriguing city are dozens of things that belong on your itinerary. The most important are: Agua de Meninos market, steep streets of Pelourinho and Baixa dos Sapateiros, the Praça Terreiro de Jesus artisans market Sundays, the Lacerda elevator between the city's upper and lower levels, the harbor filled with multicolored sail fishing boats, the lighthouses and the old forts, the churches with special emphasis on São Francisco and Bonfim, the museums of Modern Art and Sacred Art, the beaches with the fishermen and their nets, the lagoon of Abaeté, the artists at work, a capoeira fight, and most definitely a candomblé ceremony.

Candomblé is the term adopted in Bahia for the religious ceremony of African origin, which are called in Rio de Janeiro "Macumba," and "Xango" in Recife. In Salvador, these cults have been preserved in almost original form and are a vital part of the culture. Ceremonies honoring the various divinities, called "orixas," are held in temples called "terreiros." These consist of a large room for public ceremonies, with various smaller rooms or huts for other ceremonial purposes. Visitors may attend the public ceremonies, which are usually held on Sun. nights around 8:30 P.M. Some of the most important "candomblé" terreiros are: *Engenho Velho, Voo Afonja, Menininha do Gantois, Olga do Alekato.*

Folklore shows are very worth while for the visitor because they include examples of several dances typical of Bahia, such as "samba-in-a-circle," the "maculele" (rhythmic jousting with sticks and knives), which originated in the interior of Bahia, the "dance of the fishermen" pulling in the net, "capoeira," and scenes or dances from the "candomblé" ceremonies. These shows are presented daily at 9 P.M. at the *Centro Folklorico da Bahia* at the Praça Castro Alves. During the tourist season (June, July, Jan., Feb.) additional shows are given at the *Teatro Castro Alves.*

ART GALLERIES. *Atelier Renot,* Av. Sete de Setembro 437, Barra. Tapestries. *Galeria Canizares,* Av. Araujo Pinho 15, Canela. Works by students and other artists. *Kennedy Galeria de Arte,* Av. Sete de Setembro 283. Tapestries and paintings. *Sue Galeria de Arte,* Av. Sete de Setembro 30. Works of touristic subjects.

Many artists in Bahia maintain exhibits at their studios. Before visiting these artists, please phone for an appointment. A number of them speak English. *Carybe,* Rua Medeiros Neto 9, Brotas. Drawings and paintings. *Fernando Coelho,* Parque Florestal, Brotas, Rua Waldemar Falcao. Paintings. *Floriano Teixeira,* Rua Ilheus 33, Rio Vermelho. Paintings. *Hansen-Bahia,* Jardim Jaguaripe, Piata. Woodcut engravings. *Jenner Augusto,* Rua Bartolomeu de Gusmao 7, Rio Vermelho. Paintings. *Mario Cravo Jr.,* Rua Caetano Moura 39, Federacao. Sculptures in metal and plastic. *Mirabeau Sampaio,* Rua Ary Barroso 12. Sculptures and drawings. *Walter Sa Nenezes,* Av. Tiradentes, Roma. Paintings.

MUSEUMS. *Museu de Arte da Bahia.* Located in a restored mansion at Avenida Joana Angelica 198, Nazare. Ceramics, chinaware, ornamental tiles, antique furniture. *Museu de Arte Sacra.* Rua do Sodre. An outstanding collection of figures of saints and other religious art. *Museu Carlos Costa Pinto,* Av. Sete de Setembro 2490. Antique furniture, Baccarat crystal, jewelry, china, silverware, and paintings. Also collection of "balangadas" (silver charms). *Museu de Arte Moderna,* at the Solar Unhao. Expositions of paintings only when announced—no permanent collection. *Museu do Carmo.* Located in the Convento do Carmo. Vestments and other religious art objects. *Museu do Reconcavo Wanderley Pinto.* About an hour's drive from the city, not far from the port of the Industrial Center of Aracatu. Engravings, old maps, historical notes. *Musea da Cidade,* Pelourinho 3, has an interesting collection of figures of Orixás or deities venerated in the *Candomblé* rites with their costumes and weapons; also the world's largest collection of ceremonial women's headgear of African origin.

SPORTS. Salvador has miles of beautiful beaches. The cleanest and most attractive tend also to be the most distant, located beyond the district of Pituba. Because it is ideal for children, "Pla-K-For" is a favorite of Americans. This beach, like others, by bus. With luck you many see fishermen pulling in their big nets at beaches named "Praia Chega Nego," across the Aero Clube, "Piata" and "Itapoa."

Capoeira, originally an African way of fighting with the feet, was developed in the days when slaves were forbidden to use their fists or to carry weapons. Now it is preserved in a very acrobatic form of dance, accompanied by the typical instrument known as the "berimbau," tamborines, drums and other percussion instruments. Shows are given by the following "schools" under the direction of the Master, whose name the school bears: *Mestre Bimba* (located in the Nordeste de Amarlina) on Tues., Thurs. and Sat. at 8 p.m. *Mestre Gatto* (located at "Bogun," Rua Apolinario Santana 154) on Mon., Wed. and Fri. at 9 p.m. and Sun. at 3 and 5 p.m.

SHOPPING. The most typical souvenirs of Bahia are the "balangandoes" (singular "balangandao"), a macumba cluster of gourdes, fruit, and a *figa* in silver or alloyed with tin. Also typical of the many items carved from "jacaranda," the Brazilian rosewood. For these try: *Gerson Artesanato de Prata Ltda.,* ground floor of the Convento do Carmo. *Penitenciaria do Estado,* Lemos Britto (State Prison), located in Mata Escura do Retiro, accessible by car or taxi only. All prices are clearly labeled at the *Instituto Maua,* Av. Sete de Setembro 261, while bargaining is widely practiced at other places. For antiques, wooden figures of saints, furniture, etc., walk along Rua Ruy Barbosa off Avenida Sete de Setembro, near the Cinema Guarani and the "A Tarde" building. Especially reliable are: *Casa Moreira,* Rua Visconde do Rio Branco 1, behind the City Hall, *Jose Pedreira,* Alameda Antunes 7, Barra Avenida, or any number of shops along Rua Ruy Barbosa, roughly between numbers 30 and 65. The modern *Shopping Center Iguatemi,* with all types of shops and restaurants, is well worth a visit. It is located at Largo da Mariquita 3 in the Rio Vermelho district.

RESTAURANTS. If you want to sample local dishes ask for: *Acaraje,* dumplings with bean mash; *vatapa,* a fish stew; *caruru,* a type of shrimp creole; *ximxim de galinha,* chicken cooked with peanuts and coconut; *muqueca de peixe,* fish creole; *camaroes a baiano,* shrimp creole; *frigadeira de camarao,* spicy shrimp omlette; *efo,* stew with beef tongue and shrimp, traditionally served during candomble (voodoo) services; *sarapatel,* a stew of pork intestines, tripe, brains, kidney cooked in a pig's blood—not for the weak of stomach; *cocada,* a desert made of coconut; *quindins,* an egg and coconut dessert. Remember all Bahian dishes are spicy and the chile peppers and sauces are extremely hot. The leading alcoholic drink is called "a batida."

Salvador has a wide variety of restaurants. The following seem to appeal most to American tourists:

For regional food, among the best restaurants are: *Panelinha,* Rua Helio Machado 6; *Tenda dos Milagres,* Av. Amaralina 553; *Casa do Tempo,* Rua Orlando Moscoso 4; and *Byblos,* Rua Barao de Sergy 156. All *moderate.*

SENAC, inexpensive, the national commercial training school on the Ladeira do Pelourinho, offers one of the best bargains in the city; self-service restaurant with over 40 typical dishes, folkloric shows in open-air bar-arena, air-conditioned theater featuring plays by Bahian playwrights, museums, exhibits and an artisan shop.

Don't fail to try a *muqueca mixta* (mixed seafood dish) at the **Lampiao**, *expensive,* at the Bahia Othon Palace, or almost any dish at the **Forno e Fog ao**, *moderate,* at the Pousada do Carmo. **Solar do Unhao**, on the shoreline off Av. do Contorno and expensive, was originally a slaves' quarters in the 18th century, and is worth a visit.

Others: **Casa da Gamboa,** *moderate,* Gamboa de Cima 51, is excellent. Dinner only. **Chez Bernard,** *expensive,* Rua Newton Prado 11. One of the oldest and best. French cuisine; dinner only. Also **Le Saint Honore,** *expensive,* at the Bahia Meridien Hotel. **A Moenda,** *moderate,* on the shore road beyond Pituba, in Armacao. Rustic atmosphere, Samba show. Lunch and dinner are served at **Solar do Unhao,** on the beach at Av. do Contorno; **Teresa Batista,** *inexpensive,* at the corner of Av. da Franca and Rua da Belgica; **Perez,** *inexpensive,* in the "Passeo Publico" behind the Governor's Mansion on Av. 7 de Setembro; **Tiffany's,** *moderate,* Rua Barao de Sergy 37; and **Bella Napoli,** *inexpensive,* Rua Nova de Sao Bento 43 for Italian food.

Also try *Churrascaria Alex, moderate,* at the Boco do Rio, for outdoor barbecue specialties.

PRACTICAL INFORMATION FOR THE NORTHEAST

HOW TO GET THERE. By plane from almost any city in the country. Each capital has its own airport, and most of them are equipped for jet traffic now. *British Caledonian* has several weekly flights that stop on their way from London to Rio, São Paulo, Buenos Aires, and Santiago. There are buses that run from state to state in the northeast; some of them comfortable.

HOTELS. Accommodations range from large hotels in the larger cities to quiet inns in the less populated areas.

RECIFE. If you are mainly interested in the delightful beaches, where the reefs form warm pools of still water at low tide, then you'll want to stop at one of the hotels on Boa Viagem Beach. They are about a half-hour from the downtown area, but the cool breeze and pleasant atmosphere make it well worth the ride.

Miramar, first class, 326–7422. Rua dos Navegantes 363, newest and most modern, has 120 air-conditioned rooms, swimming pool, bar, restaurant, nightclub; *Mar,* first class, 341–5433, Rua Barao de Sousa Leao 451, also has its own pool; *Boa Viagem,* first class, 341–4144, Av. Boa Viagem 5000, oldest hotel on the beach (ask for a front room with balcony); *Internacional Othon Palace,* first class, 326–7225, Av. Boa Viagem 3772; *Savaroni,* Av. Boa Viagem 3772; *Casa Grande e Senzala,* moderate, 341–0366, Av. Conselheiro Aguiar 5000; *Jangadeiro,* moderate, 326–6777 Av. Boa Viagem 3114; *Vila Rica,* moderate, 326–5111, Av. Boa Viagem 4308; *Sea View,* inexpensive, 326–7238, Rua dos Navegantes 101; *Cote d'Azur,* inexpensive, 326–6444, Av. Boa Viagem 3402.; and *200 Milhas,* inexpensive, 326–5292, Av. Boa Viagem 864.

If in Recife on business your best bets are:

Grande, moderate, 224–9366, Av. Martins de Barros 593, comfortable, old-world charm with good restaurant and air conditioning; *Sao Domingos,* moderate, 231–1404, Praça Maciel Pinheiro 66; *Guararapes,* moderate, 224–7844, Rua da Palma 57; *Quatro de Outubro,* moderate, 224–4477 Rua Floriano Peixoto 141; or *Central,* inexpensive, 222–1824, Av. Manoel Borba 209. The nearby historic city of Olinda has a new *Quatro Rodas Hotel,* deluxe, top hotel in the area, 431–2955, on the beach.

FORTALEZA. Most comfortable for the tourist are *Esplanada Praia,* first class, 224–8555, the *Imperial Palace,* first class, 224–7777, and the *Beira Mar,* first class, 224–4744, on Av. Pres. Kennedy in the Meireles district, or the *Colonial Praia,* moderate, 226–7644, on Rua Barao de Aracati in the same area. Closer to town is the *Iracema Plaza,* moderate, 231–0066, Av. Pres. Kennedy 746. Downtown the best is the 12-story *Savanah,* moderate, 231–1077, Rua Major Facundo 411 at Praça do Ferreira. Others nearby are the *San Pedro,* moderate, 231–0666 Rua Castro e Silva 81; *Premier,* moderate, 231–1166, Rua Barao do Rio Branco 829; *Excelsior,* inexpensive, 231–1533, Rua Guilherme Rocha 172; and *Lord,* inexpensive, 231–6188, Rua 24 de Maio 642.

MACEIO (Alagoas state). The top hotels, both new and on the beach, are the *Jatiuca*, first class, 231–2555, Lagoa da Anta 220, 95 rooms with tennis and pool, and the *Luxor*, moderate, 223–7075, Av. Duque de Caxias 2076, with 112 rooms, all facing the front. Acceptable older hotels in the city are the *Pajucara Praia Hotel*, moderate, 231–2200, Rua Jangadieros Alagoanas 1292; *Beira Mar*, moderate, 223–8022, Av. Duque de Caxias 1994, and *Ponta Verde Praia*, moderate, 231–2200, Av. Alvaro Octacilio 2933.

JOÃO PESSOA (Paraiba state). Best here is the *Tambaú*, first class, 226–3660, 110-room circular hotel built into the sea at Av. Almirante Tamandaré 229. Two others with swimming pools are the *Tropicana Cabral*, moderate, 221–8445, on Rua Alice de Azevedo, and—on Cabo Branco (White Cape) 10 kilometers from town—the *Casa de Repouso O Nazareno*, inexpensive, 226–1183. More modest are the *Aurora*, inexpensive, 221–2238, Praça João Pressoa 51.

NATAL. Here you'll want to stop at the *Reis Magos*, moderate, 222–2055, half a mile from downtown on Av. Café Filho, on Praia (beach) do Meio. Pool, nightclub, good restaurant. Acceptable downtown hotels are the *Ducal Palace*, moderate, 222–4612, Av. Rio Branco 634; the *Samburá*, inexpensive, 222–0041, Rua Professor Zuza 263, and the *Tirol*, inexpensive, 231–4223, Av. Alexandrino de Alencar 1330. There is a 16-room *guest house* on Ponta Negra Beach, nine miles from town.

TERESINA (Piaui state). The *Luxor Hotel do Piauí*, first class, 222–4911, Praça Marechal Deodoro 310. It now has swimming pool, bar, restaurant, and air conditioning. Other downtown hotels include *Teresina Palace*, inexpensive, 222–2770, Rua Paiçandu 1219; *Sambaiba*, moderate, 222–6711, Rua Elizeu Martins 1570, and *Sao Jose*, moderate, 223–2176, Rua João Cabral 340.

SÃO LUIS (Maranhao state). Probably best hotel for the tourist is the *Quatro Rodas*, deluxe, 227–0244, on Calhau beach, with 112 air-conditioned rooms, pool, tennis courts, bars and restaurants. Closer in (2 kilometers from town) is the *Grande Hotel Sao Francisco*, moderate, 227–1155, also on the beach. The traditional downtown hotel is the *Central*, moderate, 222–5644, Av. Dom Pedro II 258. For more economy, *Lord*, inexpensive, 222–5544, Rua Joaquim Távora 258.

VITORIA (Espirito Santo state). Top hotel in this port city is the recently completed *Senac Ilha do Boi*, first class, 227–3222, on the beach at Ilha do Boi R–7. Also good are the *Novotel*, moderate, 227–9422, Av. Adalberto Simao Nader 133, and the *Vitoria Palace*, moderate, 227–8833, Rua Jose Teixeira 323. Recommended downtown are the *Cannes Palace*, moderate, 222–1522, Av. Jerônimo Monteiro 111; *Sao José*, moderate, 223–7222, Av. Princesa Isabel 300; *Helal*, moderate, 222–2955, Av. Jerônimo Monteiro 935; and *Estoril*, inexpensive, 223–5155, Praça Presidente Roosevelt.

GUARAPARI (Espirito Santo state). In this city famous for its magnificent beaches, best hotels are the *Hostess*, moderate, 261–0222, Rua Joaquim Silva Lima 701, and the newer *Porto do Sol*, first class, 261–0011, on Muquiçaba beach. Others recommended are the *Coronado*, moderate, 261–1709, Av. Desembargador Lourival de Almeida 312; *Thorium*, inexpensive, 261–0444,

Praça Floriano Piexoto downtown; *Novo Hotel Vieira,* moderate, 261–1122, Rua Joaquim Silva Lima 310; *Miramar,* inexpensive, 261–1330, Ladeira São Luís; *Radium,* inexpensive, 261–1014, Rua Ciríaco Ramalhete 52; and *Atlâtico,* inexpensive, 261–0386, Av. Edésio Cirne 332.

 RESTAURANTS. There is a lack of good restaurants all through the northeast. Most recommended hotels have average restaurants. Try the lobsters and shrimp, filet of white fish, and fresh coconuts.

RECIFE. Most interesting from the local color point of view is the *Buraco de Otilia,* moderate, on Rua Aurora 1231. It is run by a fat mulatto woman named Otilia, who has moved from her shanty where her cooking made her famous and taken up residence in an old house in the center of town. While you sample her lobster in coconut milk or her chicken in blood sauce, she will be staring either at you or the blaring T.V. set. Prices are reasonable, food is very good.

Adega da Mouraria, moderate, Rua Ulhoa Cintra 40; *Leite,* moderate, Praça Joaquim Nabuco 147 on the river; *Costa Brava,* moderate, Rua Barao de Sousa Leao 698; all have good international food. *Costa do Sol,* expensive, Av. Bernardo Vieira de Melo, and *Lobster,* moderate, Av. Boa Viagem, 2612, for sea food. Brazilian specialties at *Senzala,* moderate, Av. conselheiro Aguiar 5000, and *Baluca,* moderate, Av. Boa Viagem 4750.

FORTALEZA. One of the best in town is at the *Ideal Club,* moderate, on the beach. Old-world charm, with white columns and dark carved wooden balcony overlooking a grove of palm trees. The restaurant is part of the ultra chic Ideal Country Club. Another private club with a good restaurant is the marble *Nautico Beach Club,* moderate, Av. Aboliçao 2727.

The *Lido Restaurant,* moderate, on the beach and across the street from the Iracema Hotel. Rain comes in through the roof and strolling vendors sell everything from hammocks to ship models, but the food is quite good. Lobster here is a specialty, as is fried chicken.

Other good international restaurants: *Sandra's,* Av. Perimetral; *Panela* at the Iracema Plaza hotel; the *Iate* (Yacht) *Clube,* Av. Matias Beck 4813 in Mucuripe. For seafood, try the following, all on Av. Pres. Kennedy along the beach: *Trasteveri* at 2666; *Bem,* 4492; *Alfredo,* 4606; *Tocantins,* 4294; *Expedito,* 4320; *Martin's; Peixada do Ceará,* 4632; *Copacabana; Anísio,* 3990; *Snoopy's,* all moderate with the exception of *Sandra's* and the *Iate Clube, expensive.* For a little variety, Italian restaurants *Il Fornello* and *La Perla* are located along the same avenue, both inexpensive.

 SHOPPING. In Fortaleza, be sure and buy some of the intricate lace work made by women in the interior of the state. Best place to shop first is the public market near the Praça de Sá. There you have a complete collection of hammocks, lace blouses, tablecloths, embroidered skirts, and other items at such unbelievably low prices that you'll end up buying articles for every person on your list. There is also a shop for regional articles owned by *Joe Ney,* at 376 Rua 24 de Maio. Also see what *Casa Humberto* on Rua Liberato Barroso 222 has to offer in the line of off-beat souvenirs. In Recife, don't miss the Artene store run by the government. You will be surprised by both the high quality and the low prices of the regional goods sold there. Good native handicraft in ceramics and leather can be found around the Patio de Sao Pedro and also Boa Viagem beach.

THE AMAZON

Most Romantic of Destinations

The Amazon region has figured so prominently in novels and films that few people who come to see it don't have some preconceived notion of what they will find. Most often they expect an impenetrable jungle, herds of animals, flocks of swooping birds, and unfriendly Indians. In reality, there is little groundcover vegetation, the trees range from 50 to 150 feet in height, little animal life can be spotted, and the birds nest in the tops of the high trees.

Francisco de Orellana, a Spanish Conquistador, sighted the river in 1541 and was so taken by the size that he called it Rio Mar, the River Sea. Exploration was slow and arduous, and as explorers forged their way through unknown territory, they encountered and fought what they thought was a race of women warriors, whom they called Amazons. Whether they actually believed they were face to face with something out of pagan mythology is not known; but it is easy to imagine that they felt the name "Amazon" and its implications were pointedly appropriate to this hostile land, and this name came to refer to the entire region.

Most of the Amazon basin has been explored and charted. The river itself is 3,900 miles long, the second longest river in the world, and has 17 tributaries each over 1,000 miles long plus over 50,000 miles of navigable trunk rivers. Ocean-going vessels can travel 2,700 miles upriver to Iquitos, which is still about 600 miles from the origin of the river.

About one-third the world's oxygen is produced by the vegetation, and one-fifth the fresh water in the world is provided by the Amazon. Although there are over 18,000 plant species in the basin, the extremely heavy rainfall leaches the soil of its nutrients and makes organized cultivation extremely impractical. Although poor in agricultural possibilities, the Amazon is rich in among other products, gold, diamonds, lumber, rubber, oil, and jute.

American travel firms began to make it more accessible in 1956. The region is now becoming increasingly open to tourism. Such cities as Belem, Manaus, Santarem, Porto Velho, Leticia, and Iquitos are easily reached by air and offer fine hotels, good food, excellent services, and fascinating sightseeing.

The Jungle

The main attraction in the Amazon is the jungle. It extends into nine countries of South America—French Guiana, Suriname, Guyana, Venezuela, Ecuador, Peru, Bolivia, Colombia, and Brazil. Most of these countries have developed tourism facilities—most of them new— enabling the visitor to explore the basin in reasonable safety and comfort. However, as it is a primitive area, many tourist facilities call for "roughing it."

Brazil

The city of Belem is the gateway to the Amazon, 90 miles from the open sea. Ultra-modern highrises dot the horizon, mingling with older red-tile-roofed buildings.

While here, walk to the Praça da Republica, faced by the Municipal Theater, to see the Victorian marble statues. Stop in the Goeldi Museum; in addition to an extensive collection of Indian artifacts and excellent photographs, there is a zoo with many local animals in their natural surroundings. In the Jungle Park, a large area of virgin forest has been preserved and traversed by trails, which lead to reflection pools with huge water lillies. Also worthwhile is the Agricultural Institute, where rubber and Brazil nut trees are cultivated. Or, delve into history with a visit to an old rubber plantation.

The port of Belem itself is best seen by boat; arrangements are available through local travel agencies or your hotel desk. It's best to see the Ver o Peso Market and dock from 5–10 A.M. You can also arrange a boat trip to Jaguar Island, with its luxuriant vegetation and array of birdlife. A small river dissects the island; a short boatride provides interesting insight into the lifestyle of the islanders.

Another nearby island is Marajó, which is bigger than Denmark. Travel there by boat or plane to see its two distinct zones of vegetation, forest, and grassy plains. Lumber is one of the major industries of the region, with cattle—crossbreeds of Portuguese and Indian cattle— herded by Brazilian cowboys.

Beyond Marajó is Macapá, a town of 38,000 people lying directly on the Equator, where herds of water buffalo are raised.

The Trans-Amazon Highway has given access to more remote towns: Paragominas with its modern hotel, Imperatriz, now with 75,-000 inhabitants; and Porto Franco and President Kennedy villages—all with good, clean accommodations.

Between Belem and Manaus lies Santarem, now enjoying an unprecedented boom due to the discovery of gold. Originally settled by American Civil War Confederate soldiers, the town boasts names like Higgins and MacDonald. The *Tropical Hotel Santarem* offers superior accommodations and arranges local boat trips on the Amazon and its tributaries.

The Brazilian shipping company, Enasa, is now operating two catamaran-style vessels between Belem and Manaus with a stop at Santarem. They boast 53 double and 8 quadruple air-conditioned cabins with private baths plus a small pool, bar, dining room and discotheque. The twice-monthly sailings are usually on Wednesdays from Belem arriving in Manaus the following Monday. Departures from Manaus are on Thursday arriving in Belem on Monday.

Manaus, Brazil

A sprawling city of nearly one million, built in the densest part of the jungle, Manaus has re-established its role as the key city of the Amazon basin after years of dormancy (the long-hoped-for expansion of the Amazon basin did not attain the desired results despite the inauguration of seasonal road connections with Belem and Brasilia). Vestiges of Manaus' opulent rubber boom days still remain; the famous Opera House, completed in 1910, where Jenny Lind once sang and the Ballet Russe once danced, has recently been restored to its former splendor. The building is adorned with French ironwork and houses works of art and chinawear—seemingly out of place in the jungle. For further insight into the rubber boom period, visit a rubber plantation.

The Custom House and Lighthouse were imported piece by piece from England and reassembled alongside the floating dock, built especially to accommodate the annual 40-foot rise and fall of the river.

Comtemporary Manaus is a combination of modern highrise buildings scattered among lower, older stucco structures. Still, the city has more than its share of hotels, restaurants, and unusual sights. Wander through the City Market Building, where caged animals and parrots are offered for sale alongside exotic fruits and vegetables.

For shopping, try the Credilar Teatro, an imposing edifice of native redstone and glass. Or, taxi to the suburb of Cachoeirinha to see the Little Church of the Poor Devil (Pobre Diablo) built by one poor laborer; it's only 12 feet wide and 15 feet long. While in the suburbs, stop at the Salesian Mission Museum to see a complete documentary of the now vanished "Floating City"; also, visit the Indian Museum operated by the same order.

For natural beauties, plan a trip to Taruma Falls and, of course, a boat ride beginning on the Rio Negro that detours onto a small tributary that is completely covered by a green umbrella of giant trees and vines. Birdlife is abundant in this region and with luck, you might spot a scampering monkey high in the trees. The fascinating end to the voyage cruises is the "Wedding of the Waters," where the coffee-brown Amazon and the inky-black Rio Negro meet and continue for miles toward the Atlantic before intermingling.

Colombia

Colombia's only port on the Amazon is Leticia; it's a small, sleepy town with an appealing charm lending itself to leisurely strolls through the town itself and along the waterfront. Although Leticia is limited in the number of hotels, sightseeing is fascinating and diverse. Boat excursions into the jungle are available in all directions from Leticia; several unusual ones to backwater black lakes boast the Victoria Regia waterlilly. Yaguas and Ticuna Indian villages are close by and Benjamin Constant, Brazil, is only a slow two-hour boatride from Leticia's pier.

A small animal collecting compound, which permits viewing of the difficult-to-see animals of the deep jungle, is maintained at the Parador Ticuna Hotel. Fishing is rewarding, too, with a type of catfish called bagres reaching 300–400 pounds. Fishermen should bring their own gear, as no rentals are available.

The Upper Regions

The upper reaches of the Amazon River are generally more interesting than the lower portions because the upper river is only one-half mile wide and the channel flows close to either shore most of the time. Indian life is far more evident.

Weekly tour/cruise service on the upper Amazon between Iquitos, Peru and Leticia, Colombia resumed in July 1984. Reconstructed especially for cruising on the Amazon, the M/V *Rio Amazonas* sails from its home port of Iquitos each Wednesday and arrives in Leticia Saturday morning; return sailings depart Leticia Saturday afternoons and arrive in Iquitos Tuesday mornings. Sailing times in both parts are coordinated with air service to/from Bogota, Manaus, Iquitos and Lima.

The *Rio Amazonas* carries 55 passengers in 16 air-conditioned twin cabins with private bath and 10 non-air-conditioned twin/triple cabins with community bath facilities at half the cost. All meals, twice-daily shore excursions, lectures and films on the flora, fauna, and Indian life are all included in the cruise cost. Shore excursions are not duplicated on the in-depth roundtrip cruise, six nights from Iquitos back to Iquitos.

Iquitos, Peru

Of all the cities along the Amazon, Iquitos has the most highly developed tourism facilities—in spite of its population of only 250,000 people. New hotels in all categories have opened and a half-dozen jungle lodges operate overnight hostelries for visitors. Boat transportation, nature walks, Indian visits, boat rides, all meals, and a restful atmosphere are included in the rates.

Furtherest afield, 50 miles downriver from Iquitos, is Explorama Lodge, requiring 3 to 4 hours one-way river travel time. Twenty-five miles from Iquitos are the *Amazon Lodge* and *Jungle Amazon Inn;* allow 2½ to 4 hours for one-way boat trips to these places. An hour's boat ride from Iquitos are the *Amazon Camp* and the *Amazon Village.* Special interest trips along the Amazon can be arranged through any jungle lodge or a local travel agency.

For the naturalist and really adventure-minded traveler, the *Explornapo* and *Aventurama Camps* are located deep in the jungle and are accessible only by hydroplane. Accommodations are clean but primitive. Still, this is the best way to really see virgin Amazon jungle. Aero Amazon, located in Iquitos, also provides hydroplane jungle overflights.

The downtown area of Iquitos also warrants some time in any visit to the Amazon. The daily marketplace near the floating village of Belen sells everything from plastic dishpans to exotic fruits, nuts, and fish. The inhabitants of Belen float in their houses on the Itaya River during highwater time, but when low water comes, their colorful houses rest on the muddy banks at amazing angles. Local agencies can provide a riverview boat trip, or you view it on foot from the shore.

Iquitos' small Municipal Museum at the corner of Tawara and Fitzcarrald streets houses animal exhibitions, as well as examples of Amazon Indian handicrafts. The Iron House at Putumayo and Prospero streets is a national monument. This metal, prefabricated building was bought by a Peruvian rubber baron, shipped to Iquitos and reassembled where it stands now. Designed by Eiffel, the prefabrication idea resulted in the construction of Paris' famous Eiffel Tower years later.

While on Putumayo, stroll toward the Amazon River and note the former Palace Hotel, now the Fifth Regional Military Headquarters; built by one of the most powerful rubber companies during the boom, the building's materials were imported from Europe, including the exquisite ceramic tiles and wrought iron work seen on the exterior. The Promonade (Malecon Tarapaca) along the Amazon River impresses most visitors with the busy water traffic; ocean-going freighters vie for the channel with boat-mounted gasoline stations, pharmacies, and water buses destined to remote towns as far away as 600 kms.

Outside of town is the Zoological Park at Quistacocha Lake, where examples of the hard-to-see jungle animals in well-tended gardens make a morning's outing both informative and enjoyable.

For the true adventurer and nature lover, a trip to Puerto Maldonado is a must. Known for its stretches of virgin jungle and filled with Amazon birds and wildlife, Puerto Maldonado is accessbile by air and is one of Peru's best bird- and butterfly-watching areas. There are two jungle lodges open to travelers. The *Cuzco Amazonico* is a one-half hour river ride from Puerto Maldonado on the Madre de Dios River. The *Explorer's Inn* is located in the Tambo Pata Wildlife Reserve 4 hours on the river from Puerto Maldonado; it sits on the Tambo Pata River. Both lodges can provide guide services. For travel information, contact a Lima travel agency or the South American Explorer's Club.

Ecuador and Bolivia

Ecuador features the upper Napo region, which is the Amazon side of the Andean foothills. Three-night (Fri. to Mon.) and four-night (Mon. to Fri.) weekly cruises on the Napo River have operated for several years now on the *M/V Orellana;* airflights to/from Quito, all meals and shore excursions are included in the cruise price. Cabins are with private bath but are not air-conditioned; the option of staying overnight ashore in thatched roofed cottages is available.

Local sightseeing companies in Quito also offer overland packages from three days to ten days duration featuring the Banos/Puyo area or comprehensive extensions into the Napo region with overnights in tents.

PRACTICAL INFORMATION FOR THE AMAZON

WHEN TO GO. Since the Amazon Valley lies close to the Equator, winter and summer in the usual sense do not occur. High humidity is common only in the deep jungle, not in the cities or on the river. Average temperature is 80° F. Nights are always cool. Rainy Season—December to June (high water). Dry Season—July to November (low water). Travel in both seasons is good.

HOW TO GET THERE. From USA: Gateway is Miami, via *Lloyd Boliviano, Varig, Faucett,* and *Suriname Airways, Avianca* and *Aeroperu.*

From S.A. to Manaus: *Varig, Cruzeiro, Vasp, Lloyd Boliviano.* To Belem: *Varig, Suriname Airways, Vasp, and Cruzeiro.* To Leticia: *Avianca* and *Cruzeiro.* To Iquitos: *Faucett, Aero Peru, Cruzeiro.*

WHAT TO TAKE. Light summer clothing. Drip dry shirts and khaki slacks for the men. Cotton dresses for the ladies or skirts and blouses. Pants and pantsuits for women arc also acceptable. All shirts and blouses should be long-sleeved. All colors may be worn with the exception of green. Very comfortable shoes are a must, and sneakers or tennis shoes will come in handy. In addition, for its jungle tours, *Amazon Explorers* (see below under *Useful Addresses*) has the following suggestions and comments: (1) Rubber boots (high) for walk through the jungles. A must. (2) Hat or head cover. Flashlight— Since electricity is limited. (3) Insect repellent (for overnight trips a mosquito net will be supplied). (4) Knife, scissors, first aid kit, toilet paper, sewing kit, sunglasses. (5) Camera and *plenty* of film. Plastic bags to store exposed film. (6) All medications as needed. (7) Walking stick if needed will be supplied. (8) For fishermen: please bring variety of hooks and line. (9) Binoculars—good quality binoculars for bird and animal watching—500 varieties of tropical Amazon birds are constantly around you. (10) As the life on the Amazon is much more relaxed and primitive than anywhere else in the world, you must be prepared for constant changes, delays, or cancellations of flights or steamers according to the moods of the river. Should such changes occur while traveling, your guide will notify you immediately and make new arrangements accordingly.

Note: See *Practical Information for Brazil* for important information on Visas.

 HOTELS. Once a wilderness area as far as hotel accommodations were concerned, the Amazon has now thoroughly acceptable, even luxurious, lodging. Our price categories for this region are as follows: *Deluxe* is $60 and up for single, $85 up double; *First Class,* $45 up single, $60 up double; *Moderate,* $25 up single, $35 up double; and *Inexpensive,* less than above. These rates are based on hotels in Manaus; other hotels are less expensive.

BELEM

First Class

Hilton. Praca da Republica. Finest hotel in town, all rooms with private bath, air-conditioning; 2 bars and 2 restaurants.

Equatorial Palace. Av. Bras Aguiar 612. One of the best in the city, with a bar, pool, and restaurant; the rooms have bath, air conditioning, telephone, TV and refrigerator.

Regente. Av. Governador Jose Malcher 485. Rooms with private bath, air conditioning, and TV.

Selton Belem. Av. Julio Cesar (airport). Rooms have private bath, air conditioning, telephones and TV; bar, restaurant and pool.

Excelsior Grao Para. Av. Presidente Vargas. Rooms have bath, air conditioning and telephone; bar and restaurant.

Novetel. Av. Bernardo Sayao 4804. 121 air conditioned rooms near Rio Guama.

Moderate

Central. Av. Presidente Vargas 290.

Sagres. Av. Gov. Jose Makler. 136 rooms, all air-conditioned, TV, bar, restaurant, and pool.

Vanja. Rua Benjamin Constant 1164. Rooms with private bath, air conditioning and telephone.

IQUITOS

First Class

Acosta II. Ricardo Palma. 35 rooms, air-conditioned. Breakfast room only, no restaurant.

Amazonas Hotel. Km. 2.5 Aviacion Ave. 120 air conditioned rooms. Pool. Disco. 3½ miles from downtown.

Safari. Napo 118. 42 air-conditioned rooms. Downtown. Coffee shop.

Turistas Iquitos. Malecón Tarapaca. 73 rooms; some air conditioned. Downtown overlooking Amazon River.

LETICIA

First Class

Anaconda. Carrera 11, Calle 7a & 8a. This hotel overlooks the river and offers 56 air-conditioned rooms; swimming pool and cabanas; dining room, night club.

Colonial Hotel. Calle 6a. The newest, most modern hotel in Leticia. Same management as the Parador Ticuna. 20 air-conditioned rooms.

La Manigua Residencias. Nice, clean, small hotel. 18 rooms with private bath.

Parador Ticuna. Carrera 11, #6-11. 13 cottages, some with air conditioning. A delightful pool and good restaurant in typical Amazon surroundings.

Residencias Alemenas. Immaculately clean; best buy in Leticia. 12 rooms, 8 with private bath. Run by Germans.

Moderate

Pension Cano. 11 rooms, some with private bath.

MANAUS

Deluxe

Tropical. Built and operated by Tropical Hotels, a subsidiary of Varig, on good beach overlooking the Rio Negro. 341 air-conditioned rooms, swimming pool, excellent restaurant, night club. About 10 minutes from the new airport and 45 minutes from town. Best buy.

First Class

Amazonas. Praça Adalberto Valle. Located in the center of the city, this 10-story building has 214 air-conditioned apartments and two elevators. All rooms have private bath, hot and cold water and telephone. Permanent buffet service. Swimming pool.

Hotel Imperial. Via Getulio Vargas 227. 100 air-conditioned rooms, TV and bar in every room.

Novotel. Av. Mandii, 4. Newest in town. 111 air-conditioned rooms in commercial section.

Central. Rua Dr. Moreira. Centrally located, this 50-room, 3-story hotel has air conditioning, private baths and telephones.

Flamboyant. Av. Eduardo Ribeiro. Mid-town, the 23 rooms all have private bath and telephone. Bar and swimming pool. Near the Opera House.

Lord. Rua Quintino, Bacaiuva 217. In the center of the city, this 6-story hotel has 53 apartments all with private bath, hot and cold water and telephone. Restaurant.

Rio Salomao. Rua Dr. Moreira 119. In the center of the city, these 28 apartments have air conditioning, private bath, and telephone.

Moderate

Lobo D'Almada. Rua Lobo D'Alamada 181-A. Mid-town, with 26 rooms with air conditioning, telephone and private bath.

Monaco. Rua Silva Ramos, 20. 60 air-conditioned rooms with private bath, color TV, and pool. Downtown area.

National. Rua Dr. Moreira 59. Also downtown, this small hotel has 16 rooms with private bath.

In addition to the hotels listed, there are a number of small pensions offering rooms for $15–$25 per day. However these are not recommended.

SANTAREM

Tropical. Av. Mendonca Furtado 114. Offers 120 air-conditioned rooms with refrigerators. First class, one of finest hotels in the region.

Nova Olinda. Av. Adriano Pimental 140. A small hotel with local flavor but no air conditidning. Moderate.

TEFE

Grand. 20 rooms without air conditioning. Moderate.

 HOW TO GET AROUND. There are regular plane services that take you into Belem, the capital of the State of Pará on the mouth of the Amazon River. To get to Manaus, the capital of the state of Amazonas, you must go by plane. *Cruzeiro* flies Manaus/Tabatinga/Iquitos and return twice weekly; Tabatinga is one mile from Leticia by taxi. *Varig* and *Vasp* fly from Rio and Brasilia to Manaus, as well as to Belem and Paramaribo.

Enasa operates two catamaran-style vessels between Belem and Manaus with a stop at Santarem, usually twice a month. Sailings are usually on Wednesdays from Belem, arriving in Manaus the following Monday. Departures from Manaus are on Thursday, arriving on Monday in Belem. Rates per person are $550 for an outside cabin and $460 for an inside double cabin. For reservations, contact Gran Para Tourismo, Ave. Presidente Vargas #679, Belem, Para, Brazil.

 SPORTS. Most popular sports in this area are *hunting* and *fishing*. *Selvatour* provides all services in Manaus. They are experts at arranging jungle expeditions.

 SHOPPING. The streets of Belem have a number of shops that sell jungle items; but remember that live animals or birds may not be imported into the U.S. Skins of protected animals such as alligators or crocodiles, or shoes/handbags or other articles made of these skins, are also not allowed into the U.S. and will be confiscated by the U.S. Customs.

Manaus, a free port, has hundreds of shops, stocked with goods from all over the world. *House of the Hummingbird,* which is owned and operated by Richard Melnyk, features rare and unusual artifacts handcrafted by Indians, Caboclos (half-breeds) and regional artisans. Will ship anywhere without service charge.

 RESTAURANTS. The favorite Brazilian dish is *pato no tucupi,* which is duck in yellow soup with a herb that tingles all the way down the throat and long after it's in the stomach. An average lunch or dinner will cost $7 to $18 per person; there are, however, numerous coffee shops and cafeterias where a meal may be had for as little as $5.

BELEM

For international food try *Augustu's,* Av. Almirante Barroso 439, *Well's,* Av. Gov. Jose Malcher 2388, and *La em Casa,* Av. Governador Jose Malcher 982.

Avenida, on Av. Gen. Deodoro 1294, offers good regional food in comfortable surroundings.

For barbecue, *Garrafao,* Av. Serzedelo Correia 75, *Gaucha,* Av. Governador Jose Malcher 2731, and *Adegao,* Rua 28 de Setembro 284, can all be recommended.

Other specialties: Japanese food at *Miako,* Rua Caetano Rufino 82, and Portuguese food at *Santa Rita Casa Portuguesa,* Rua Manoel Barata 897.

LETICIA

It is best to eat at the hotels, but if you wish to experiment, many local restaurants serve meals from $.20 to $3.50.

MANAUS

For French cooking, sample the menu at *Palhoca*, Estrada da Ponta Negra. *Chapéu de Palha*, Rua Fortaleza 619, and *Peixada Rio Negro*, Emilio Moreira 1233, serve fish, especially the rare, local fresh-water specialties, the *pirarucu* and *tucunaré*. *Kavaco*, Av. Sete de Setembro 987, has pizza.

 NIGHTLIFE. Though they are not abundant, this region does have nightclubs, at least in the larger cities like Manaus. The disco at the Tropical Hotel, *O Uirapuru*, is the hottest spot and the *Catedral* on Rua Saldenha Marinha 609, has a show and dancing.

VOCABULARY

ENGLISH-PORTUGUESE
TOURIST VOCABULARY

TEN-MINUTE PORTUGUESE

The following words are absolutely indispensable if you want to enjoy yourself in Brazil:

eu	I	quarenta	forty
você	you	cinquenta	fifty
êle, ela	he, she	cem	hundred
nós	we	mil	thousand
êles	they		
		meia duzia	six (or half dozen)
um	one	conto	1,000 old cruzeiros
dois	two	kilo	2.2 pounds
três	three	dez	ten
quatro	four	Domingo	Sunday
cinco	five	Segunda-feira	Monday
seis (or meia duzia, or meia)	six	Terça-feira	Tuesday
		Quarta-feira	Wednesday
sete	seven	Quinta-feira	Thursday
oito	eight	Sexta-feira	Friday
nove	nine	Sábado	Saturday
eu vou	I go	kilometer	1,100 yards
você vai	you go	hoje	today
estou com fome	I'm hungry	amanhã	tomorrow
onde está	where is	dia	day
quanto é	how much is	noite	night
		horas	hours
vinte	twenty	ano	year
trinta	thirty	semana	week

ENGLISH	PORTUGUESE	PHONETIC PRONUNCIATION
Good morning (afternoon) (evening), (or good night).	Bom dia (boa tarde), (boa noite).	bone dee'-uh (bo'-uh tar'-dee), (boh'-a noy'-te).

ENGLISH	PORTUGUESE	PHONETIC PRONUNCIATION
I don't speak Portuguese.	Nao falo portugues.	now faw'loo Por'too-gays
I don't understand.	Nao compreendo.	now comb-pree-en'-doo
How are you?	Como está?	comb-oo ess-taw'
Very well, thank you.	Man's answer: Muito bem, obrigado.	Mwee'-too bain, oh-bree-gaw'-doo
	Lady's answer: Muito bem, obrigada.	Moo'-ee-too baying, oh-bree-gah' da.
Where are you going?	Onde vai?	On'-djee vie'?
When are you returning?	Quando volta?	Kwahn'-doo vohl'-ta?
Many thanks.	Muito obrigado. (Lady-Muito obrigada).	Moo'-ee-too oh-bree-gah'-doo. (Lady-Moo'-ee-too oh-bree-gah'-da).
More slowly.	Mais devagar.	My'ees de-va-gahr'
Pardon me.	Desculpe-me.	Dis-kool'pe me.
I don't know.	Nao sei.	Nah'-oong say.
Do you know?	O senhor (a senhora), (a senhorita), (voce) sabe?	Oo se-nyohr (a se-nyor'-a), (a se-nyoh-ree'ta) (Voh-say') sah'-be?
Today.	Hoje.	Oh'-jee
Tomorrow.	Amanha.	Ah-mahn-yah'.
Yesterday.	Ontem.	On'-tain.
This week.	Esta semana.	Es'ta se-mah'-na.
Next week.	A próxima semana.	A pro'-see-ma se-mah'na.
Don't forget.	Nao se esqueca.	Nah'-oong se is-kay'-sa.
All right.	Muito bem.	Moo'-ee-too bayng.
See you later.	Até logo.	A-tay' loh'-goo.
Goodbye.	Adeus.	A-day'-oos.
Come here, please.	Venha ca, por favor.	Vayng'-ya kah, poor fah-vohr'.
It doesn't matter.	Nao tem importancia.	Nah'-oong tayng eem-poor-tahn see-a.
Let's go.	Vamos.	Vah'moos.
Very good. (bad).	Muito bem (mal).	Moo'-ee-too bayng (mah'-l).
Where can I change my money?	Onde posso trocar meu dinheiro?	Ohn-de po'ssoo troo-kahr' may'-oo dee-nyay'-roo?
Monday.	Segunda-feira.	Se-goon'-da fay'-ra.
Tuesday.	Terca-feira.	Tayr'-sa fay'-ra.
Wednesday.	Quarta-feira.	Kwahr'-ta fay'-ra.
Thursday.	Quinta-feira.	Keen'-ta fay'-ra.
Friday.	Sexta-feira.	Ses'-ta fay'-ra.
Saturday.	Sábado.	Sah'ba-doo.
Sunday.	Domingo.	Doh-meeng'-goo.
Black.	Preto, negro.	Pre-too, nay'-groo.
White.	Branco.	Brahng'-koo.
Red.	Vermelho.	V-mel'-yoo.
Green.	Verde.	Vayr'-de.
Blue.	Azul.	A-zool'.
Yellow.	Amarelo.	A-ma-re'-loo.
One.	Um (uma).	Oong (oom-a)
Two.	Dois (Duas).	Doys (Doo'-as)
Three.	Tres.	Trays.
Four.	Quatro.	Kwah'-troo.
Five.	Cinco.	Seeng'-koo.
Six.	Seis.	Say'ees.
Seven.	Sete.	Se'-te.
Eight.	Oito.	Oy'too.
Nine.	Nove.	Noh'-ve.
Ten.	Dez.	Dayz.
Eleven.	Onze.	Ohn'zay.
Twelve.	Doze.	Doh'zay.

INDEX

INDEX

PRACTICAL INFORMATION

GEOGRAPHICAL

(The letters H and R indicate hotel and restaurant listings)

7 Good Reasons
why
FODOR'S
Travel Guides
are
America's Best-Known Travel Guides

- **FODOR'S** guides are revised annually, and not just by changing the date on the cover; an average of sixty percent of a revised guide's pages contain corrections. In addition, each guide is *completely* reworked every four or five years.

- **FODOR'S** has a global team of correspondents who actually live and work in the areas they cover.

- **FODOR'S** gives you the world, covering more countries and areas than any other American-produced travel series.

- **FODOR'S** guides are different from many other travel guides because they give a *balanced* picture of a location—history, geography, and culture, as well as what to see and do, all in one book.

- **FODOR'S** Facts At Your Fingertips provide all the information needed to plan a trip, covering everything from travel documents and travel agents to transportation and health tips.

- **FODOR'S** maps and plans are revised and updated annually.

- **FODOR'S** guides include Practical Information about Accommodations, Restaurants, Entertainment, Night Life, Museums, Places of Interest, Local Transportation, Shopping, Telephones, Sports, Tours, Useful Addresses, and much more.

All Fodor's Guides are available from your local bookstore or write to us for a complete list, with prices:

FODOR'S TRAVEL GUIDES
Sales Department
2 Park Avenue
New York, N.Y. 10016